# WE'LL SUPPORT YOU EVERMORE

MAINSTREAM SPORT

# WE'LL SUPPORT YOU EVERMORE

## THE IMPERTINENT SAGA OF SCOTTISH FITBA'

### EDITED BY IAN ARCHER AND TREVOR ROYLE

MAINSTREAM PUBLISHING

EDINBURGH AND LONDON

First published in 1976 by Souvenir Press Ltd

This edition published in Great Britain in 2000 by
MAINSTREAM PUBLISHING COMPANY (EDINBURGH) LTD
7 Albany Street
Edinburgh EH1 3UG

ISBN 1 84018 313 6

A catalogue record for this book is available from the British Library

Printed and bound in Great Britain by Creative Print Design Wales

# Acknowledgements

acknowledge the permission of the following who have allowed original work to be reprinted in this volume: Akros Publications for 'Fireworks', 'Yon Night' and 'Crack' by Tom Leonard; Tom McGrath for 'There was that time . . .'; Gordon Wright Publishing for 'Tynecastle' by Donald Campbell; John Rafferty for the match report of the 1967 Scotland versus England game; James T R Ritchie for 'The Jagging of Hearts', 'Rangers Coming Out' and 'Easter Road'; William Collins and Sons Ltd. for 'Scotfree' by Patsy Thomson; Barrie and Jenkins for 'Play up, play up and get tore in' by George Macdonald Fraser, the *West Highland Free Press*; the *Glasgow Herald* for the Centenary Scottish Cup Final match report.

The Editors acknowledge the permission of the following who have allowed original photographs and illustrations to be reprinted in this volume: the Press Association, George Outram Ltd, Mrs Stewart, Jim Turnbull for his cartoon which originally appeared in the *Daily Record*.

# Contents

# List of Illustrations

Brissit brawnis and broken banis
Strife discord and waistis wanis
Crookit in eild syne halt withal
Thir are the bewtis of the fute ball

# Introduction

This is a book about football written by a number of writers who love the game. It is also about Scottish football and that makes it very special. There can be very few other countries of similar size who have the passion for football that the Scots have. We even pride ourselves that it is a different ball game altogether north of the border. Born in Glasgow, brought up in the Vale of Leven and nurtured in the cities it produced the great teams: Celtic, Rangers, Hibernian, Motherwell, Partick Thistle, Heart of Midlothian. The players and their style of play were different too. Something of their style you will find in these pages.

Not many people living in Scotland today have been unaffected by football. They either follow a team, love it or curse it, read the back page of a newspaper first or play the game in the myriad pitches of damp corporation parks. Names, too, create their own memories: the Wembley Wizards, Third Lanark, the Terrible Trio, the Famous Five, Jim Baxter – the list is endless. Who can still listen to the Old Comrades March and not feel that the six-fifteen classified results are near at hand on a long and dark winter's Saturday evening?

The writers who have contributed to this book have written about aspects of the game which interest them. They either live and work in Scotland, or in the case of one or two expatriates work within a Scottish way of thinking where their lives have been moulded by Scotland and her past. Some are best known as football journalists and too often their work is forgotten when the next day's edition appears. Which is a pity for what they write is good. The publication of this book should remedy that by giving some permanence to their work.

Above all we hope that readers, whether or not they follow the 'gemme' will get a great deal of pleasure from what we have to offer. Amongst the articles, which were specially commissioned, there is the best of current writing about football in Scotland. If names or memories appear more than once, and if the slant is to the big teams and the great occasions we excuse ourselves by saying that we frail humans only remember the memorable. Everyone has his own great footballing moment.

Finally, we offer our thanks to Ernest Hecht and Tom Wiseman for their valuable interest and advice. We are playing away from home in this book but we are confident that the home team will want to publish the result of our labour throughout the land.

Ian Archer
Trevor Royle
October 1975

# See Scotland?

GORDON WILLIAMS

Upstairs on a corporation bus, don't ask me what corporation. Lady in fur hat turns and sneers with a sniff; 'Your sort is a disgrace to Scotland.'

Away and boil your head, you frosty-faced old ratbag. I said, awa' an' bile yur heid –

Oh look, Missus, don't mind my pal, he's just been celebrating the big win –

Aye, I was there, Missus, Hampden Park in the rain, Scotland two Inglin Nil! Strong men crying, strangers hugging, we'll support ye ever more! Scotlin two Inglin nil, joy joy. Fancy a wee nip, Missus, no everyday your counry smashes the white-shirted might of the master race, is it? Ach well, never mind her, probably a Third Lanark supporter. She looks a bit like Jimmy Harrower.

Let's get off this bus before you get us arrested.

We are arrested already, arrested development. Don't you sneer at me for being a common s-h-i-t-e, Missus, I got my Highers, don't you worry.

'Pity you didn't do more with your education then.'

Droppen Sie dead, Bella. Hey, Ian, there's a pub!

All right but I'm just having a couple of lagers to wash out my mouth mind, I'm not getting involved in another big sesh.

For all I care you can get involved with Jinkie Johnstone in an open boat. What's so great to keep sober about? It's the greatest day of our lives, isn't it? Hey Jimmy, two halfs and two pints a lager. At the gemme wur ye? Oh great, just great. Never thought I'd see the day. Norman Hunter couldnae stand the pace! See that team? They were heroes today. Made ye proud to be Scottish. When the first goal went in I threw a wee fella

next tae me up in the air, he turned out to be English wearing a
tartan rosette for safety reasons! Nice enough wee bloke though.
Aye, it's easier to like people when you're winning. We are the
people! Haven't had much practice at it, have we? See the first
Scotland-England game I got into? Bought a ten-bob ticket offa
bloke from Saltcoats outside Wembley. Big deal – it was the nine-
three game! I was living down in London then, I honestly felt
there was a stain on me for weeks afterwards, know what I mean,
an actual blemish on my face. That's no' just a game of football
played by professionals, that's you on trial for your life. And they
wonder why everybody drinks at these games? I'll tell you why,
your guts are churning so bad you *need* to be half-bevvied or
you'd faint. Please God let us win this year. Please God don't
let the team do anything silly. Please God give Scotland a break.
Are they going to let us down – again? Will England get a jammy
goal after our midgets have missed chances by the score? Remember that time Ramsey walked round the Wembley pitch with
his arm round Bobby Brown's shoulders? Kiss of death in front
of one hundred thousand people. Oh aye, Ramsey liked to beat
Scotland – if ye hate Alf Ramsey clap yer hands. What's that?
No singing allowed? Typical. Greatest day in our history and ye
cannae sing a wee bit. Where's my pal gone? To hell with him,
rushing off to change his shirt for a big date with Joyce, they've
got a joint account in a building society but she doesn't go all
the way, saving herself for the great day! My legs are aching.
Excuse me, Missus, is this the right bus for my house? I'm
saying is this the richt bus fur ma hoose, Mrs McFlannel? Non
comprendey? Come on, ye crabbit auld devil, give us a song and
I'll gie ye a swig. We'll support ye ever more. Aye, ye're right
there, Missus, greatest wee country Goad iver pit breath intae.
They were *heroes*. Davie Hay? Strode about like a veritable
colossus. Wee Jinkie? I'll tell you, if you could marry men I'd
have proposed to him. So all ye Dundee lasses tak this advice frae
me, never let a laddie an inch above yur knee – Jesus Christo,
I'd better get a grip. No want a wee sip, Missus? Ach well, suit
yersel, sanctimonious auld psalm-singer. I know the type, her
man's a haberdasher with a funny handshake, gets half cut once

a year at the Burns Supper and recites the four lines he knows of Tam O' Shanter before he spews up the haggis, then he sits on the bench and gives common bastards thirty days. See if Burns moved into their street? They'd get up a petition. I'm saying, Missus, the only good poet's a dead one. What d'ye mean, drunk? I was just having a few to celebrate the big win. My pal turned all vicious. What really got his psychotic goat was me being able to remember the nineteen-forty-nine wizards – I mean, he thinks he's the Hampden Park patriot, gallus sea-you-en-tea that he is. You remember the forty-nine wizards, Missus? Cowan, Young, Cox; Evans, Woodburn, Aitken; Waddell, Mason, Houliston, Steel and Reilly. England one, Scotland three! I was a wee boy then, listened to it on the radio. Happy days then, eh? Football-daft we were. Just imagine, if we'd put all those hours kicking a ball into playing the piano or swotting our lessons – too late now. Gone alas like our youth too soon. Sausages is the boys. The Firhill lum. Pat Roller in the Record. Nero and Zero? Charlie Tully – he was my hero, I was brought up Protestant but the first time I saw that bowly-legged wee devil my life changed. No joking. I saw him once at Ibrox, put his foot on the ball and pointed to the left wing. Big George Young and Big Woodburn both fell for it – they bumped into each other! Tully's still stand-ing with his foot on the ball. That's all I can remember, football. See in our street? You were middle-class if you wore your dentures in mid-week. Get a grip. Disgrace again. I'll emigrate. How far does this bus go, Missus? Single to Canada, please. Send on my share of the oil money. Did ye emigrate or were you asked to leave? It's raining on my face. Am I dreaming or am I under a hedge? I wish I was a wee boy again and didn't drink. That's why the games stand out in your memory – you were sober enough to see every kick of the ball. I've seen me at Hampden spending half the match with my back to the game arguing about whether Willie McNaught of Raith Rovers should get a public apology for all the Scottish caps he never got. In those days you got a cap if you managed to play two consecutive games for Rangers without actually strangling anybody. Selectors? Shoot the lot of them I would. Waddell, Gillick, Thornton, Duncanson and Caskie. Oh God, I've done it again. Tears me apart, seeing Scotland, the big crowd, the pipes, the yellow flags, the thunder of the shouting and then they run out – oh God, please let Scotland win this time, I'll never drink again if you let them win, God. See me? I only go through the motions of living. In my head it's still a pouring wet Saturday at the Greenock Road end of Love Street, Paisley, Willie Reid has just lashed the leather spheroid past Rangers' helpless custodian Bobby Brown. Saints have beaten the Gers! Conn, Bauld, Wardhaugh. Used to get crowds of forty thousand at Love Street if the Celtic were playing. No lavatories – hey, Jimmy, mind yer back. Does anybody else still imagine it's quarter of a century ago? Big Don Emery of Aberdeen? Jock Govan of Hibs? Alfie Boyd of Dundee? Andy Paton of Motherwell – *there's* a name to send a shiver up your spine. Smith, Johnstone, Reilly, Turnbull and Ormond. I was a failure at sixteen – no scout ever tapped me on the back. All I ever wanted to do in this life was play for St Mirren – or anybody. I can still keep it up forty times. Heiders on the beach at Millport. Christ, when it was really pouring we used to play headers in the living-room! Jimmy Mason of Third Lanark. Long Throw Jackie Husband of Partick Thistle. Mortensen kept blasting them in but Jimmy Cowan made saves at pointblank range. He should have been given a knighthood, Jimmy Cowan. How come Willie McNaught never got the caps anyway? Or Willie Telfer of St Mirren? I wish I could meet these blokes today and just say – Scotland owes you an apology. Be quite old now, I suppose. Charlie Tully's dead – heart attack, quite young man, too. I remember Jock Stein playing centre half for Albion Rovers, big bloke with a left foot. I saw Ronnie Simpson playing for Queen's Park as a teenager. Bobby Flavell? Lil Arthur Milne? Alf Ackerman of Clyde – only bloke I ever saw who wasn't scared of Willie Woodburn, used to knock him down! Knock Woodburn down? You could win El Alamein with two like him. Big Ken Dawson of Falkirk – thunderbolt shooting? Peter Ma Baw McKennan of the Jags? People sneer, I mean those who don't go to Hampden or Wembley and think we're just a lot of drunken hooligans – but I know. That's the only time I love Scotland. I mean, just as the teams are coming out I could die for Scotland. Honest. Tears, the lot. What else is there? See if we get an assembly or a Parliament? Want a bet it'll be the same old gang of bigmouths and windbags and chisellers? You think they'll do as good a job for the country as they did for football? The big sell-out, we're so familiar with it you could almost call it genetical. Greatest talkers of rubbish in the world. Scots? Wee boys looking for fairy-tales. Ach, I'm as bad. I wish I'd put the hours into learning something useful. If a scout had tapped me on the shoulder and I'd had one game, just one, A N Other in the reserves, just one game to be able to say – I mean, it's your whole life at stake when Scotland goes out there, those strips of ours always look so neat, the blue, the badge, oh God please give Scotland a break otherwise what have I been doing with my life? Playing twice on a Saturday, kicking a tennis ball in the street, kicking a marble under the lamp-posts, watching games at Ibrox, Paradise, Cappielow, Dens Park, Firhill, sticking in football photos, swapping cigarette cards, talking about last Saturday's game with everybody in the town till Wednesday then talking about the next Saturday's game, supporting your team but always seeming to be criticizing it, hanging about the back of the stand to see the players, walking about the town imagining you're actually Willie Woodburn. Shaw. Gray, Shaw. Football-daft. Bertie Peacock. Eddie Rutherford. Waddell, Gillick, Thornton, Ducanson and Caskie. Football charging through your whole life, tramping down the flowers in Mrs Train's garden, tramping down everything, kicking and shouting and dummying the left back, Conn, Bauld, Wardhaugh, my mother will kill me when she sees the state I'm in, oh God why didn't you –

## JOHN THOMSON

Hail and Farewell! we say of those
Who come, and pass too soon,
The broken arc, the blasted rose,
The life cut short ere noon.

Hail and Farewell to you, Dear John,
More regal than a king,
More graceful than the fleet-limbed fawn,
Your year ends at its spring.

The athlete rare who typified
All that is best in life,
Your brilliant deeds! the death you died!
Our lovely lad from Fife.

The unerring eye, the master touch
More buoyant than the ball!
The fearless heart, the powerful clutch,
The genius praised by all.

The squirrel's swift leap, the falcon's flight,
The clear quick-thinking brain:
All these were yours, for our delight
Never, alas! again.

We did not need your death to tell
You were the sportsman true.
We bow to Fate, Hail and Farewell!
We shall remember you.

T Smith (of Darvel).

# Come Back, Numbers Eight and Ten, Your Country Needs you

HUGH TAYLOR

The whole trouble with Scottish football today is that we have no Willie Sharps, no Jimmy Williamsons, no Derek Griersons, no Torry Gillicks, no George Hamiltons and if any young whipper-snapper who believes football begins and ends with all-purpose players and faceless robots has the cheek to ask just who these people were, I'll be glad to tell him.

Sharp, Williamson, Grierson, Gillick, Hamilton – and scores of Numbers Eight and Ten like them – were really the men who made our soccer great. They were, indeed, the lifeblood of the game. Alas, not one of them is really entitled to the soubriquet, Great Master of Scottish Football. But they weren't a kick in the shin behind the men who have a place in the Football Hall of Fame (supposing we had one) and the thing about them was: there were plenty of them. And that was why the old-time football was mellow and golden because these great inside forwards laced it with velvet passes, grace, courtliness and magical use of the open space.

Every club in the old days had one – Sharp of Partick Thistle, Williamson of Kilmarnock, Grierson of Falkirk, Gillick of Rangers, Hamilton of Aberdeen, Robertson of Clyde, Gemmell of St Mirren, McMillan of Ayr United, Wardhaugh of Hearts . . . but why go on, I'm only making myself cry.

And if these players were second-raters, merely shadows of the James's, Steels, Walkers, Masons, Whites and McPhails, how I wish we had their likes today; for they would never be out of a Scotland international team. That, in fact, is just what is wrong with modern Scotland international teams: they lack class at inside forward, if such a team is permissible in these days when all is jargon and too much football is also unintelligible.

You will see that I am in love with inside forward play. Of

course I am. I am fascinated by all footballers. My memories, which go back much further than I care to admit, are bejewelled with glittering gems. Sometimes I think nothing can compare with the sparkle of Stanley Matthews in action – the casual shoulder-shrug which left a defender floundering, the exhilarating burst of unexpected speed, the bewildering trickery, the superb ball control. Then I consider the catlike agility and graceful leaping of goalkeeper Jerry Dawson, the steady full back play of Danny Blair, the silky touch of wing half George Brown or Jock McEwan, the deadly scoring prowess of Jimmy McGrory, and I am equally entranced.

In the end, however, I return to the inside forward and I am convinced that the man in the mould of Walker and James is the man who matters most in football, and the absence of gifted artists in that position is the reason the game is losing its lustre.

Of course we don't expect a Bobby Walker or even a Tommy Walker to appear in every decade, but it is worrying to realize that nowadays we are without such talented exponents of the ancient inside forward craft as Sharp, Williamson or Gillick, who brought such pleasure to the fans.

The players I have mentioned were the intellectuals of the game. Some looked fragile. But they made up in brain what they lacked in brawn.

And we need them back. Because the lack of highly-skilled individuals is the reason the crowds are dwindling, even in the age of a super-league.

I have no doubt that too many people today are trying to make the game an exact science, and when football becomes mass-produced, no matter how gleamingly perfect, much of the excitement vanishes. The spirit of adventure departs when the formula becomes all and how formidable, then, the obstacles that confront an aspiring James, Mason, Buchan, Mills, Tolland or Venters. (And if you think there's nothing I like better than rolling these great names off my lips you're right.)

The hopes of an aspiring football genius are quenched, first, by the highly engineered precision play which has become the style nearly all over the world, play in which every man is no more than a unit, though probably much more highly skilled than we old-timers care to admit.

Football has become more violent, reeking of the jungle or the gladiatorial arena of old Rome. Some may like it this hot and say the heroes of yesteryear weren't fit enough or strong enough to be at the top today. I may be old-fashioned (I *am* old-fashioned) but I prefer the artistry of yesterday to the attrition of today.

My fondness for the suavity and grace of the men of arts and parts – which contrasted so bizarrely with their cumbersome equipment of iron-toed boots, laces that would have tied a liner securely to dock, long-john pants, shinguards that turned legs into supports for a snooker-table and jerseys as old-fashioned as grannie's bathing costume – may be laughed to scorn by the 'mod' athletes of today, so arrogantly *soigné* and energetic and 'with-it' in footwear as supple as an Indian's hunting moccasin and a strip as superbly designed for the job as the holster for a Colt pistol.

They would not laugh, though, had they seen the inside forward of real style.

And it is my regret that almost extinct is the type of player who was once symbolic of the artistry of Scottish soccer.

To the Williamsons and Sharps and Hamiltons flair was all. The shrug of the shoulders, the flick of the hip, the dummy, the careful precision pass, the oily swerve – these were the weapons of the true inside man and how well he used them. He was a specialist in altruism. His job was to make goals, not necessarily score them, to hold the ball for the fraction of a second needed for his younger and sometimes more virile colleagues to take up position, then slide the ball to the man most likely to be able to shoot without distraction. He was master of the ball and, like a true craftsman, he wanted time to caress his love. Football to him was pure enjoyment. The method player of today would be anathema to a James.

Don't forget that it was from the great inside forwards that most of Scotland's soccer fame sprung. The true father of the distinctively Scottish type of inside forward play was Bobby Walker, of Heart of Midlothian, who had 29 full international caps for Scotland. He wasn't fast. But no one had quicker mental agility; no one had his power of deluding opponents.

Whether my heroes – yes, Williamson, Grierson, Sharp, etc, etc – were as good I don't know. I never saw Bobby Walker. But, I'm happy to say, I saw Gillick and Sharp and Williamson. And many more.

What was so great about them? The ability to stop and think, to dally with the ball, secure in the knowledge that their educated feet could flick it delicately away from lunging tackles. How many can do that nowadays? Now there is no time for trickery, no time to toy with the ball. Vulgar assault sees to that.

While the style of play has changed, however, there is still something about our football that remains exactly in 1975 as it did in 1925 – the clacking of Scottish tongues. The great Scottish footballers have never been strong, silent men. Most of them were wee wisps with fiery tempers and whiplash tongues and even the aristocratic inside forwards were known to lash out with frightening oaths. Even today Scottish players are great talkers and crowds abroad, unaccustomed to running commentaries on the field of play, grow restive as they are assailed by a Doric cacophony of yelps, bawls, complaints, snarls, advice, encouragement, condemnation and appeal.

And it is as well that foreign players seldom understand what their Scottish opponents are saying to them: otherwise there would be mayhem. For nothing can be crueller than a venomous insult about one's parentage, lack of courage, immoral way of life or looks delivered in a rich Scottish accent. That brings me to Alex James, the greatest of them all.

I didn't see a lot of him. But when I did gaze in awe at the plumpish little man in the baggy breeks – who said the best footballers had to look like athletes? – I knew nightingales were singing over Wembley or Highbury or Starks Park and there was magic abroad in the air.

James was possibly the most entrancing of them all. It is of inside forwards that the Scottish troubadours sing and the heroic tales are told. The supreme inside rights and inside lefts – to hell with midfield men – have always captured the eye and gripped the imagination of the fans to a greater extent than players in any other position, and the reason for this, I believe, lies in the average Scot's respect for craftsmanship. And the inside forward is the engineer of the team. You cannot assert that the Scottish inside forwards emerged from the same conveyor belt, that they all played alike. You could never compare Bobby Walker with Billy Steel, Jimmy Mason with Bob McPhail. Some were more devastating scorers than others. Some played more powerfully. But at the heart of their play was the same beat. They were all masters of design. Even those of baroque genius; even those whose principal asset was a spectacular burst through a bewildered defence, were essentially builders. Like a Clydeside engineer, they pinned their faith in stout construction, a distinctive touch and true Scottish craft. They were painstaking in their efforts to make their teams flow. They knew they were the mainsprings, they knew they were the men whose job was to construct pads from which the missiles flew. They did their task superbly.

But the inside forward most deserving of a stained-glass window was James, a small, bullet-headed chatterbox, with George Robey eyebrows and a centre hair-parting that was the trademark of so many Scottish sporting heroes of the twenties and the thirties, and the buttoned sleeves.

And how he could talk. Unlike some players for whom Yes and No are an excess of conversation, Alex was a wonderful talker, both on and off the field, and one of the most delightful stories told of him was related gleefully by Jimmy McMullan, captain of the Wembley Wizards team.

After that memorable match he was asked by a sportswriter if there had been a plan to beat England. Jimmy grinned and said: 'Aye, we laid down a plan. It was a simple one. I told the boys: "Now, I don't want any unnecessary talking. Get on with the game and don't talk to opponents or referee".'

The awed reporter said: 'That was good. It seemed to work all right.'

McMullan replied: 'Did it hell. Alex James's tongue went like a gramophone from the kick-off.'

The reporter asked: 'Did you tick him off?'

'Don't be daft,' said McMullan. 'How could I? If his tongue went like a gramophone, so did his feet.'

Another well-known talker was Billy Steel, the first of what can be termed the international jet set of players. He had springs for muscles, a choirboy's face that masked a devouring, often ruthless determination to achieve football perfection – and a caustic tongue that frequently angered team-mates more bitterly than opponents, and a style and ability that, in this modern age, would have had the wealthy clubs of Europe bidding frantically for his transfer.

Unlike so many of his predecessors, who were indelibly stamped with the style of their birthplace, Steel was classless. No one watching this chirpy little man in action could have said from which soccer school he graduated. About Bobby Walker, Tommy McInally, Jimmy Mason, Bobby Johnstone there was something essentially Scottish. Steel was different. His touch was Scottish, of course – but later in his career he welded to that eternal grace an iron physique. He belonged to the elite corps of players who came after the Walkers and the James's – the corps that includes Di Stefano, Pele, Puskas, Law, Suarez, Rivera, Kopa, Beckenbauer, Cruyff, Orcwirk, Seeler: the global greats.

His secret was that of Denis Law, to shake the soccer scene much later: an agile brain, a puma's pounce and extraordinary gymnastic ability that put him a move ahead of his colleagues. There was nothing svelte about Steel: he exuded vitality, he had the killer instinct of a boxing champion, he was the type of aggressive attacker who was so keen to win that he would have sworn at his best friend if he felt he hadn't been pulling his weight.

I recall a famous Hibernian player telling me how surprised he had been when Steel suddenly turned to him in a match in which Dundee were chasing the Scottish First Division championship and snarled: 'How would you like to play with a bunch of mugs like that every Saturday?'

That was Steel. He had been playing his heart out, as usual, and his blood was up and he couldn't stop his tongue wagging. And there was an occasion in an international match when, coming off the field at half-time, he snapped at a colleague: 'You'd be better keeping up with play than combing your hair.'

But don't think Steel was an anti-hero. He wasn't. And today I am saddened that heroes and heroics have gone out of fashion. In a world in which instinctive action is abhorred, the advent of a new D'Artagnan, Brigadier Gerard or Scarlet Pimpernel would be greeted with embarrassment not cheers. This is indeed the age of the anti-hero, the man whose patriotism is tinged with every-day ruthlessness, cynicism and vice. Unlike the Greeks, who endowed their historical heroes with supernatural qualities and deeds, we cannot protect our great men from destructive analysis. Indeed, we don't want to; we want to think our heroes have our own unworthy qualities, their valour being merely an odd quirk.

And that's a pity: perhaps the real source of many of the ills of the world. For I believe, with Thomas Carlyle, that society is founded on hero-worship. Heroes bring colour and glamour to a dull society. If there are no heroes, where is the incentive? What boy wants to be a dingy, impoverished spy? What lad seeks to be a cunning politician or avaricious businessman who reaches the peak by stealth and kniving?

Thus I worry about football, which has become all the duller with the introduction of method play. The wrecker, the man whose main job is to stop the opposition at all costs, has come to the fore – and is all too often hailed as the saviour of his side instead of being heartily hooted as a villain, the reception he would certainly have received in the old days.

Anyhow, I still do not accept the destroyer in football. I do not want my soccer stars to have the less admirable traits of a James Bond. I want them to have the theatrical heroism of less sophisti-cated times. I want them to be men of red blood and impulsive action and also I want them to be graceful and poised. I want them to be match-winners, men who, like Rob Roy or Robin Hood or John Wayne, defied overwhelming odds by sheer force of physique, skill and imagination and achieved the seemingly impossible. I want them to be master strategists.

If they have faults I want them to be the failings of a Bulldog Drummond, not the studied, cruel revenges taken by a Bond.

Most of all, however, I want to see the return of . . . yes, that's right . . . a Sharp, a Williamson, a Grierson, a Hamilton. The thoughtful men. The graceful men. The men whose swerve was breathtaking. The men whose passing was audacious and so beautifully directed.

I truly believe that if football is to become again the favourite sport, we must restore to the inside forward the liberty to direct, to make the game poetic, to engineer.

They were unassuming, those splendid inside-men who made halcyon my early days in football. But they taught the greatest lesson in football: in true art, simplicity is all.

It may be said that, in those days, football was a simple game played for simple people . . . but if we had more of those wonderful inside-men in their slightly old-fashioned rigouts in action today, a sun would shine so radiantly on the sombre scene that even the terracing louts would be so dazzled that they would at last be constrained from thuggery to pay tribute to endearing skill.

### FIREWORKS

up cumzthi wee man
beats three men
slingzowra crackir

an Lennux
aw yi wahntia seenim
coolizza queue cumbir

bump
rightnthi riggin
poastij stamp
a rockit

that wuzzit
that wuzthi end

finisht

Tom Leonard

## CRACK

cuts inty thi box
croass cumzthi centre hoff
    a right big animull

crack

doon goes Dalgleesh
ref waves play on
nay penahlti

so McNeill complainzty im
oot cumzthi book

tipical
wan mair upfurthi luj

Tom Leonard

## YON NIGHT

yonwuz sum night
thi Leeds gemmit Hamdin
a hunnirn thurty four thousan
aw singin
yilnivir wok alone

wee burdnma wurk then
nutsnur a wuz
but she wuzny intristid
yi no thi wey

well there wuzza stonnin
ana wuz thaht happy
ana wuz thaht fed up
hoffa mi wuz greetnaboot Celtic
anhoffa mi wuz greetnaboot hur

big wain thata wuz
a kin laffitit noo

Tom Leonard

# The Men with the Educated Feet

BOB BROWN

My mother's brother, Willie Jackson, a great Shettleston Juniors
committee man who would slip off to Ibrox if the *Town* were
idle, from these twin pinnacles of non-comprehension used to
pull my leg long after I ceased being a lad about our family
devotion to Queen's Park. Uncle Willie Jackson claimed we dashed
out to buy each three of Glasgow's evening sports editions, to
read all about it throughout those Saturday nights when Queen's
Park were celebrating a memorable victory. Of course, he was about
right, whether we had actually been present to observe the event or
not. But to be mocked about the *Jolly Old Spiders* was sometimes
more than my passion could endure. By the mid-thirties Queen's
Park were finding the going distinctly slippery because the ancient
war against professionalism that opened for them in the 1880s
was showing ominous signs of today's near fatal conclusion.

My tender days on what the era's football scribes loved to call
*The Classic Slopes*, as different storm cones were hoisting elsewhere in Europe, too often saw the heroes flounder when such
as Alec Anderson, Hutton, Bremner, Willie Lyon, Tommy Souter
and Willie Martin were eternally off to Parkhead, Ibrox, Tynecastle or wherever. Taking the professional ticket from Hampden
Park (as the scribes also put it) had been endemic for decades
before my time, but the disease was not funny when you were a
wee fellah trying on the bowler hat and striking your colours to
the mast in Eastbank Academy XIs by wearing your own jersey
outside the pants in Queen's distinctive and traditional style.

After all, it was less than ten years since Hampden wept over
the dismemberment of the last truly talented team of amateur
footballers to occupy commanding heights anywhere in the world
within the thoroughly professionalized game. That was the Queen's

Park side of lyric poets: J D Harkness; T K Campbell and W
Wiseman; J McDonald, R Gillespie and W S King; J Crawford,
W S Chalmers, D McLelland, J B McAlpine and W G Nicholson.
Jack Harkness, supreme in an immense line of gifted Hampden
'keepers, guarded the sticks for the *Wembley Wizards* and thereby
lives forever. His Wembley medal for being the only amateur was
presented by him later to adorn Queen's Park priceless chain of
presidential office. Bob Gillespie invented the Third Back Game
which revolutionized field strategy and in 1933 was installed the
ultimate amateur, last to captain Scotland against the ageless
enemy. Six of them all told wore Scotland shirts which the immortal McAlpine was denied by the merest accident of English
birth, a fate, like the dark side of an aristocratic blanket, that now
and again kept favourite Scottish sons from entering into their
inheritance. Those lucky enough to be around Hampden in Gillespie and McAlpine's day watched and applauded genius; and
my father ever afterwards, even when Queen's playing skills failed
to sustain the claim, invariably clapped his hands as the famous
black and white hoops emerged from the pavilion tunnel and
declared: 'Here they come then, the men with the educated feet.'

Down the years Queen's Park and Hampden have coalesced
semantically as well as in the *realpolitik* of Scotland's football,
sometimes to the glory and sometimes to the confusion of it all.
If Queen's have been esoteric and idiosyncratic, Hampden Park
with its measured capacity for well over 150,000 spectators has
become internationally identified as the headquarters, seedbed
and clangorous cockpit of the Scottish game and *Hampden Roar*.
The additional fact is that Queen's Park are Scotland's oldest
club and in adversity in the seventies still retain much of their
customary hauteur. They remain amateur still at Hampden, whatever private anguish may increasingly disturb the governing breast,
and hold fast by the first article of their original constitution:
*This club shall be called the Queen's Park Football Club and its
object shall be the recreation and amusement of its members.*

Long before the twentieth century was born they had organized
in Glasgow in 1872 the world's first international between Scotland
and England, and provided the entire Scottish team which merited

more than its goalless draw; they had won the Scottish FA cup ten times in twenty years; they had given one of their meagre guineas towards the purchase of the FA cup and lost two of its controversial finals to Blackburn Rovers. If all this is old hat from soccer's mists of time, it is also the club's immemorial lineage. Geoffrey Green, that eclectic cavalier of *The Times* footballing columns and historian of the FA, properly saluted them as 'Historic Queen's Park, father and mother of the game north of the Border.'

In truth they were even more, missionaries and midwives throughout Scotland and much of England in football's formative years, helping to discipline it from the chaos of the gutter, to unify its laws and to perfect techniques clearly recognizable today when, irregularly, the club carries the gospel on safari to outpost foreign fields. Now, more than a century on from 1867, from the beginnings for the Scots on Queen's Park Recreation Ground at Langside (which is only a hefty punt or two from modern Hampden) the *Jolly Old Spiders* are debilitated by pernicious anaemia and gasping to survive. Some in Scotland's football hierarchy, with sensitivity, hold them in affection yet as endearing anachronisms lurking behind the Latin elegance of the motto from their matriculated arms which proclaims how they play the game for the game's sake. Some others see them (as some others have always done) as the perennial bloody nuisances of the people's game who perpetuate their legend and claim immortality on the strength of Hampden Park. But it was Queen's Park, visionaries ever, and they alone, who laid down Hampden more than seventy years ago while the timid marvelled. It was third in its line and the prototype for all the massive stadia of modern times.

'Hampden Park is dying,' Mr W P Allan, Secretary of the Scottish FA, said sadly four years ago. That tragic utterance made official what had been openly muttered. Once it had been declared, it could no longer be dismissed by Queen's Park who own it, by its friends who revere it or by faithful *afficionados* like myself who, despite all, scarcely comprehend how the playground of the gods can be falling into disrepute. For this is the arena in which history is made, the battlefield of triumph and disaster, where Alec Cheyne's corner kick vanquished England in 1929, where Delaney's dying seconds winner electrified the Victory International, where Baxter tormented the Saxons in '62 and where (my father always insisted) Queen's own Harold Paul before the Kaiser's War scored the finest goal Hampden ever saw, a thunderbolt from far out on the left touchline that toppled Corinthians and produced its testamentary evening paper headline: *Paul's Epistle to the Corinthians.*

Yet Hampden is dying for the sufficient reason that, as inflation bites and costs rise and professional football develops its own nasty symptoms of impending death, Queen's Park have become unable to muster enough cash flow for basic maintenance, far less embark on their confident old habits of modernization and improvement. Five million Scots in their day have been obsessed with many things; with complex issues of national identity amidst encroaching Anglicization, with concepts of international brotherhood in which Marx and Burns mingle, with stark economics and infighting for a decent job and steady job, with taking one side or another vis-a-vis the demon drink, but perhaps above all in this century of the common man with the nation's footballing destiny and the beauty of the ba'. Hence Hampden stands four square with Bannockburn in the Scottish psyche, a shrine of the nation despite being indirectly named for the Saxon patriot. Hampden for the Scots is emotionally irreplaceable.

All this Scotsmen know for, as any of us will tell you, we are the most perceptive of the world's peoples. All this Scotsmen know, and not just the endless band of pilgrims who make their roistering yet holy passage along Cathcart Road to Mount Florida's caravanserai on those International occasions of surging adrenalin which, I am inclined to think, have been consistent always with the gut exultation of Glasgow's earlier socialism or, over the past decade, brought Scotland's dormant springs of post-Union nationalism briskly to the boil. The same, of course, goes for cup final and similar festivals when the Old Firm pair, Rangers and Celtic, are so often involved. Then different and darker passions can be aroused and that (as with its half-true, half-phoney reputation for political unrest) is what a wondering world seems to reckon Glasgow to be peculiarly about. Sometimes Glasgow's canni-

B

balistic tendencies to exuberant violence concerning the fitba' strike black despair even in Glasgow hearts, its passionate dedication above anything Rio or Madrid, Milan or Liverpool contrives.

Hampden has more than a Mecca mystique or a fateful role in the intense devotions of the masses; there is a continuing imperative for it in season to house huge crowds which, as the stadium visibly ages, invokes crisis headlines which question its very future. Let none doubt that some Saturday, somebody will say, as has always been asked around two o'clock of a stranger in a Glasgow pub, 'Are ye fur the gemme, then, Jimmy', – and incredibly there may be no Hampden fur the gemme to go to.

So Glasgow is different and Hampden is magic. The Government absorbed the message in 1973 and appointed a Working Party of wise and sensitive men to sit down and consider how best to go about restoring its health and prosperity. The Working Party recently reported with imaginative proposals for Hampden's £15-£20 million reconstruction as Scotland's national football and atheletics centre and indoor sports complex (while listing also a couple of reserve schemes, less costly, less favoured). The Working Party was led by Mr Laurie Liddell, chairman of the Scottish Sports Council, who was largely instrumental in having Edinburgh's Meadowbank Stadium transmogrified in time for the 1970 Commonwealth Games; and Laurie Liddell stated Hampden's situation so eloquently that his words should be graven above Somerville Drive's old main gates, whatever the eventual outcome: 'We are hoping for the best possible solution. Scottish football deserves it and, God knows, if our recommendations are followed through there are very special opportunities in this area to do more than just put up another form of football stadium. We have an opportunity to do a great deal for social and community welfare, for the health and life of nearly half of Scotland's population within travelling distance. Hampden today is run down, a bit worried about itself, needing recovery. But it is a jewel with great potential. If we don't take this chance, we will have thrown something very special away.'

Nobody knows if Government in tough times for the British economy (however much reminded that the Treasury picked up its rickety to support essential ground improvements for England's 1966 World Cup) will sanction the bulk of that vast expenditure the Working Party's plans desire. Nobody knows if Queen's Park, disdaining as ever to bewail their own and Hampden's problems in the belief that such matters are the concern of the club alone, will abdicate their landlord's role. But the longer the dialogue proceeds, the higher the costs will soar from £15 to £20 million and the weaker will become Queen's Park's bargaining capacity – short of the suicidal last-ditch throw which, exchanging Hampden's asset for developer's millions, would also sentence the club swiftly and irretrievably to soccer oblivion. Suddenly within the decade at Hampden the name of the game has changed. The stadium is no more an automatic visa for Queen's Park to exert power and prestige, nor can it ever be again; instead, it will be a miasmic epitaph for doomed eccentrics unless the club itself seeks a decisive way out.

Contemporary Hampden's financial equations are altogether too much for Queen's Park. They add up to astronomical funding against the outlay of £10,000 that purchased the original twelve acres, opened on Hallowe'en 1903 with a 1-0 Scottish League victory over a Celtic side of Homeric dimensions invoked by the mere presence of Barney Battles, Dunn Hay, Alec Bennett, Jimmy McMenemy and Jimmy Quinn. Soon Hampden's twelve acres spread to thirty-three, encompassing Lesser Hampden, practice grounds, car parks and approach roads – and the lot cost £18,156. Capital projects have been constant since then but at a bargain basement aggregate investment of around £300,000 which, pre-1939, saw the North Stand built and terracings extended. In the sixties, the pavilion was modernized, the enclosure covered and floodlights erected. Financial agreements are operated with the Scottish FA and League, which allocates the club up to twenty per cent of the £130,000 or so that can now accrue from major matches. But Queen's themselves could attract 65,000 spectators against Partick Thistle in the twenties, never mind their 40,000 to watch Corinthians, 28,000 for Kilmarnock in 1950 and a steady 10,000 during the last promotion season twenty years ago. Now the normal attendance for their Division II fixtures has slumped derisively to around 600 which, in agonizingly real terms, speaks again of 1867 when the founding fathers launched Scottish soccer – but levied sixpence a head to buy the ball.

Queens Park's 600 loyal adherents who trickle into Hampden today have no entitlement, beyond their Jacobite nostalgia or positive concern for what an uncertain future holds, to make known their views on how things might be done. Queens Park the institution is like the Catholic Church, nobody gets into the hierarchy unless they have been first ordained (and, as though that was not enough, the support is too respectably bourgeois to demonstrate behind the stand like distraught fans in other places). True, the rules have been bent a mite in recent years to permit discreet infiltration but the club remains a club of members, overwhelmingly an exclusive brotherhood of players and former players – those who donned the colours and for whatever reason did not defect for pay. My own reaction to Hampden's desperate plight remains ambiguous. There is no good reason that I can see to go along with Lord Poole's lapidary words: 'In politics it is easier to see the problem than the solution. That is because there is no solution.' To agree would induce the same despair that overcame George IV on first being confronted with Caroline, his destined queen: 'I am not well, pray get me a glass of brandy.' Such despair is unthinkable.

Political solution in Hampden's case is emphatically possible, brandy is not clinically necessary. The key lies in the exclusiveness of Queens themselves which, perhaps understandably, makes it difficult to surrender their title to Hampden's soil. Yet this is exactly what must be done. Then the case could surge ahead for Government aid in line with the Working Party's proposals. Already the Scottish Development Agency is emerging with a £300 million budget heftily earmarked for the restoration of Clydeside's crucial role in Scotland's economy. Clydeside has long been an economic slum and its main requirement is for industrial and mercantile initiatives to underpin its faltering strength. And if Clydeside is a social slum then it can only be revived when amenities like Scottish Opera, the Strathclyde regional park, a Burrell gallery and an arts complex to house the Scottish National

Orchestra – but above all the brave new Hampden envisaged by the Working Party – are symbolically refashioned to demonstrate that Clydeside's future is to be neither despised nor despaired. This may be a lofty vision but it is the kind Queen's Park have also been accustomed to see.

Football, like fighting and fornication, I have come to appreciate is a fundamental Caledonian sub-culture, whether drink is taken or not, whether the terracings are sedate or erupting with urine-loaded beer cans. It is only Glasgow that is fitba' daft and that is substantially to do with the obfuscated rivalries that distinguish Rangers and Celtic, who wage Boyne's ceaseless battle by the bonnie banks of Clyde. How odd that Glasgow, rooting its reputation for soccer turbulence in the Old Firm's Hampden Riot nearly seventy years ago, should have sired in Queen's Park the northern Olympians whose success, influence and verve forced England consciously to create Corinthians. Queen's Park were always regarded in Scottish football as middle-class elitists, sporting buffs and gentlemanly exponents of the hard and clever, and many used to wish they would turn professional to dish both Celtic and the Rangers. Celtic, as it happened, by an almost unspoken law of friendship and respect, scarcely ever sought a Queen's Park player, but Rangers used Hampden shamelessly as an inexhaustible pool of talent. They took the incomparable R S McColl; they took Alan Morton who spent seven Hampden seasons learning to be the *Wee Blue Devil*; and their plundering reached its peak post-1945 when at one stage no fewer than six ex-amateurs wore Ibrox first team blue, among them the later Scotland managers, Ian McColl and Bobby Brown.

The Scots as a race indeed care, darkly, passionately, metaphysically, about Hampden Park and what becomes of it. Yet nowadays the sad fact is that the terracings see Queen's Park the club, those *Jolly Old Spiders* of legend and romance, to be of the merest significance, much in the same class of wayside teams that Airdrie's Jock Ewart in earlier days would have dubbed Brechin City, Stenhousemuir or Meadowbank's fledgling Thistle. Mighty Queen's Park have fallen, less from pride or grace as vanished silently by their own impotence into a sea of indifference. Nobody really takes them seriously any more. Sentimentally this is difficult to accept when, along with lots of other potential revivalists, I have to resist mixing today's reality with old men's memories that rise with Walter Arnott and set on Charlie Church. Arnott, with ten consecutive caps against England in the 1880s, was an unsurpassed defender in his age; the dashing Church in the 1950s was conceivably Hampden's best loved son, scoring impossibly to compensate for missing incredibly, flighting those beautiful balls that sparked the stand alight, giving his all for the jerseys and epitomizing in every ninety minutes the tantalizing vagaries of Queen's ever fickle ways.

'It's a complex fate being an American', sighed Henry James and, as fates go, it must be still more complex to serve on Queen's Park General Committee which oversees all and meets in the Hampden pavilion monthly on Mondays for high tea as the first of sixty or so signed players arrive to start the week's training. The General Committee are Hampden's palace guard. For a decade or more the club has almost appeared to have lost the will to live, surrendering the old fighting spirit and settling abjectly for the half-dozen final places in the lowest league as though it was natural habitat. Too often the jerseys leave the tunnel as if they too received this message from on high. My guess is that most of the 600 who stand today on Hampden touchlines, stoically patient but dreadfully depressed, would share my view that Queen's Park's urgent and clamant need is to claw their way back into the game itself by gladly relinquishing that overall responsibility for managing Hampden Park which has helped to drag them down. But first they must secure right of access for much of the time to the new stadium's main playing arena for their League programme and, of course, their own club accommodation must be guaranteed as a substantial and inviolate part of future Hampden's greater whole.

That, with luck, would clear their head of bankruptcy mists, clarify the vision and concentrate the mind on the supreme question of the club's actual survival. It immediately raises the parallel matter of whether Queen's Park continue to hold fast by a century's tradition of steadfast amateurism or elect at last to cross the ultimate divide and embrace the heresy of pay. This, as has been rightly said by R A Crampsey, the club historian, is the seminal issue which in the seventies can be ignored no longer. Queen's Park resolutely faced a lesser dilemma before 1914 when, among a handful of others, R S McColl obtained reinstatement as an amateur from the Scottish FA, after sojourning with Rangers and Newcastle United, and was thereafter permitted to regain his spiritual home. But not without much frenzied and schismatic debate, since when the club has remained inflexibly amateur despite the game's sly folklore of secret fivers tucked in Hampden boots as countless stalwarts stripped for Saturday's fray. Like so many other legends concerning the legendary Queen's the myth of the fivers slowly withered, its potency emasculated first by that interminable post-war exodus to the professionals, and finally by their own diminishing skills across the past decade. Player after player, team upon team, silently stole away.

In 1945-46 they were fielding a side whose excellence almost matched Gillespie's and with such reserve in the Strollers XI that, when a top man was injured, his absence was scarcely noticed. The team usually comprised R Brown; J McColl and W Galbraith; D Letham, J Whigham and A Cross; J Farquhar; J R Harris, C Liddell, K Chisholm and J Aitkenhead. Unlike Gillespie's when a mere three defected, only David Letham and Alec Cross did not in time go pro; but the replacements were off too – Ronnie Simpson to his eventual European Cup-winners' badge with Celtic, Archie McAulay, Billy McPhail, Alan Boyd, Derek Grierson and the legions of their successors. Now professional scouts haunt the place less since Bobby Clark to Pittodrie, Derek Parlane to Rangers, became virtually the last of the mighty amateurs to depart in search of fame, fortune and the fabled Scotland shirt.

Now professional football everywhere is at a frightening watershed of cooling ardour, and Queen's Park with it. Now the economics of international soccer are in a crazy mess, and question upon question relevant to the conflicts of its future pound in on the game like some remorseless surf. Who knows the answers when the magic elixir of the turnstiles' click is replaced by social club cabaret and drinking, development association bingo and the bank manager's fateful verdict on the degree of overdraft? Who in Scotland can tell whether Rangers and Celtic will yet be forced to swap their comforting League dominance for the capricious hazards of permanent competition in Britain or Europe? Who knows if Scotland's domestic football will be left to Heart of Midlothian, Hibernian, Motherwell, Dundee and the lesser rest, all delusions of grandeur gone in the imperative of settling for the quasi-professional (and often near amateur) structure that Austria, Scandinavia and much of Europe already knows? Probably the Scots (outside of Parkhead and Ibrox) must reconcile themselves before long to saying farewell to fulltime football, and to their astonishment they may even find the game the better for it. Probably this is the impending scenario for Scottish football, the backdrop against which Queen's Park must shortly endure Bob Crampsey's seminal examination to decide where and after what fashion their future lies – or, for that matter, if they are to possess a future anywhere from top to toe within the likely shape of Scotland's coming game. Perhaps semi-professionalism in the style of other clubs, whatever Queen's Park purists shudder to think, is rapidly focussing as their last-ditch hope for sheer survival; perhaps Queen's next challenge is simply to exist and, by doing so, to keep alive in Scottish soccer some flavour of those noble amateur traditions which otherwise will die.

Glasgow's South Side may turn out to be part of the Hampden equation, surburban territory which Queen's Park shared for practically a century with their famous neighbours from over the hill at Cathkin Park, Third Lanark FC, who were hounded to boardroom liquidation a few years ago amidst universal consternation. The South Side's neighbourhood affection for Thirds was as warm as its regard for Queen's. Some hold their panache to be even stronger since many Thirds fans, disposed to congregate at Cathkin largely to blether with friends along the terracings, were apt to look on victory as something of a bonus. This charismatic atmosphere pervaded Hampden too, and countless South Siders found no difficulty on alternative Saturdays in cheering the colours at either ground.

Third Lanark's eclipse left a void like a family death which has never been adequately filled, partly because Queen's Park's ebbing struggle in evil times was shorn of those epic proportions the South Side needed to arouse its partisan emotion. Today's 600 Hampden loyalists include two-thirds who confess to the hardening arteries of fifty years. But 200 youngsters go regularly garbed in black and white, full of the contemporary fitba' cult and singing the hymns from more magnetic terracings, 'We'll support you evermore,' which some of them do from Forfar to Stranraer. My impression is that if Queen's Park's loins can spawn a further generation of Hampden faithful, they are more liable to classify themselves as *afficionados* of a South Side team than as twenty-first-century inheritors of Queen's unique traditions of robust and skilful football which helped establish Scotland's style when all the world was young.

If Queen's youthful supporters are aware of their amateur lineage, they do not seem to lean on it as their fathers did. The same can almost certainly be said of most who actually pull the black and white hoops over their heads. Nowadays Queen's Park also find the going hard to recruit high-quality playing members of the club willing to devote their years to Hampden as did the present President, R L Cromar, or Willie Ormond, Ian Harnett, Willie Hastie and Frank Crampsey who were bulwarks of the last memorable eleven; that splendid championship side of 1955-56 which held its head high in Division I the following season. Then the ranks were sorely depleted again as Valentine, Robb, Glen, Herd, McEwan absconded in turn and the club tumbled sadly to Division II obscurity. Perhaps Queen's Park already know, but are reluctant to admit, that the exclusive days are over when the club could constantly replenish its total strength from playing members. It is difficult to imagine any permanent solution for Queen's Park which does not involve voluntary abdication of its ancient exclusiveness by throwing club membership open in order to enrol 5,000 or so pro-Hampden South Siders, reinforced by friendly affiliates from elsewhere, capable of injecting between them a much needed dynamism to the running of affairs. This stands high alongside abandoning Hampden's management. These are crucial decisions which cannot be much delayed and it would further enhance the moral justice of the club's claim for special status within the community-oriented Hampden Park which the Working Party's plans imply. Given a crumb of luck that could help keep Queen's Park amateur still and, for thousands like myself for whom fitba' is nothing if it is not fun, that is a consummation devoutly to be wished.

Fitba' should be fun but it should also be the disciplined fun which demands and receives from those who play it that maximum dedication that ennobles Borders Rugby and, in earlier days at Hampden, distilled a Queen's Park pride which never remotely entertained the notion that to be amateur, somehow, was to be second rate. I believe all this to be so, as I believe that Queen's Park in the recent past have shown signs of being weary of the world, of settling for the worst of all alternatives, of perpetuating near fatal mistakes from the best of motives. The club, haunted by Hampden's accounts, have allowed a Division II mentality to develop in boardroom and dressing room, apparently assuming Division I to be a dream beyond attainment. Players have been invited to join in quantity rather than on quality, thereby adulterating that sensible preference for recruiting lads from professional homes which, if it confirmed Scotland in its smouldering suspicions of elitism, at least reduced the pace at which the gladiators quit for pay. But, beyond all reason, Queen's Park have failed to soak their every influx of players in ageless mystique, which meant that amateurism for most youngsters was a ludicrous creed to stand against their cynical appraisal of Hampden as the temple wherein to flaunt their wares and pray for bids.

Possibly too much is for conjecture as Queen's face the perplexing decisions they must boldly begin to take; possibly the tide will turn at last should football's dwindling economics indeed work for them within the changing alchemy of the people's sport. Whatever the future shape for Scottish soccer, its heroic age is over. My own best hope is that Queen's Park are about to survive immortal and pursue their honoured course in the mainstream of Scotland's game. That way Hampden may raise the bowler hats again in sweet acclaim for the educated feet.

# Play up, Play up
# and Get Tore in

GEORGE MACDONALD FRASER

The native Highlanders, the Englishmen, and the Lowlanders played football on Saturday afternoons and talked about it on Saturday evenings, but the Glaswegians, men apart in this as in most things, played, slept, ate, drank, and lived it seven days a week. Some soldiering they did because even a peace-time battalion in North Africa makes occasional calls on its personnel, but that was incidental; they were just waiting for the five minutes when they could fall out crying: 'Haw, Wully, sees a ba'.'

From the moment when the drums beat *Johnnie Cope* at sunrise until it became too dark to see in the evening, the steady thump-thump of a boot on a ball could be heard somewhere in the barracks. It was tolerated because there was no alternative; even the parade ground was not sacred from the small shuffling figures of the Glasgow men, their bonnets pulled down over their eyes, kicking, trapping, swerving and passing, and occasionally intoning, like ugly little high priests, their ritual cries of 'Way-ull' and 'Aw haw-hey'. The simile is apt, for it was almost a religious exercise, to be interrupted only if the Colonel happened to stroll by. Then they would wait, relaxed, one of them with the ball underfoot, until the majestic figure had gone past, flicking his brow in acknowledgment, and at the soft signal, 'Right, Wully,' the ball would be off again.

I used to watch them wheeling like gulls, absorbed in their wonderful fitba'. They weren't in Africa or the Army any longer; in imagination they were running on the green turf of Ibrox or Paradise, hearing instead of bugle calls the rumble and roar of a hundred thousand voices; this was their common daydream, to play (according to religion) either for Celtic or Rangers. All except Daft Bob Brown, the battalion idiot; in his fantasy he was playing for Partick Thistle.

They were frighteningly skilful. As sports officer I was expected actually to play the game and I have shameful recollections still of a Company practice match in which I was pitted against a tiny, wizened creature who in happier days had played wing-half for Bridgeton Waverley. What a monkey he made out of me. He was quicksilver with a glottal stop, nipping past, round, and away from me, trailing the ball tantalizingly close and magnetizing it away again. The only reason he didn't run between my legs was that he didn't think of it. It could have been bad for discipline, but it wasn't. When he was making me look the biggest clown since Grock I wasn't his platoon commander any more; I was just an opponent to beat.

With all this talent to choose from – the battalion was seventy-five percent Glasgow men – it followed that the regimental team was something special. In later years more than half of them went on to play for professional teams, and one was capped for Scotland, but never in their careers did they have the opportunity for perfecting their skill that they had in that battalion. They were young and as fit as a recent war had made them; they practised together constantly in a Mediterranean climate; they had no worries; they loved their game. At their peak, when they were murdering the opposition from Tobruk to the Algerian border, they were a team that could have given most club sides in the world a little trouble, if nothing more.

The Colonel didn't speak their language, but his attitude to them was more than one of paternal affection for his soldiers. He respected their peculiar talent, and would sit in the stand at games crying 'Play up!' and 'Oh, dear, McIlhatton!' When they won, as they invariably did, he would beam and patronize the other colonels, and when they brought home the Command Cup he was almost as proud as he was of the Battle Honours.

In his pride he became ambitious. 'Look, young Dand,' he said. 'Any reason why they shouldn't go on tour? You know, round the Med, play the garrison teams, eh? I mean, they'd win, wouldn't they?'

I said they ought to be far too strong for most regimental sides.

'Good, good,' he said, full of the spirit that made British sportsmanship what it is. 'Wallop the lot of them, excellent. Right, I'll organize it.'

When the Colonel organized something, it was organized; within a couple of weeks I was on my way to the docks armed with warrants and a suitcase full of cash, and in the back of the truck were the battalion team, plus reserves, all beautiful in their best tartans, sitting with their arms folded and their bonnets, as usual, over their faces.

When I lined them up on the quayside, preparatory to boarding one of HM coastal craft, I was struck again by their lack of size. They were extremely neat men, as Glaswegians usually are, quick, nervous, and deft as monkeys, but they were undoubtedly small. A century of life – of living, at any rate – in the hell's kitchen of industrial Glasgow, has cut the stature and mighty physique of the Scotch-Irish people pitifully; Glasgow is full of little men today, but at least they are stouter and sleeker than my team was. They were the children of the hungry thirties, hard-eyed and wiry; only one of them was near my size, a fair, dreamy youth called McGlinchy, one of the reserves. He was a useless, beautiful player, a Stanley Matthews for five minutes of each game, and for the rest of the time an indolent passenger who strolled about the left wing, humming to himself. Thus he was normally in the second eleven. ('He's got fitba',' the corporal who captained the first team would say, 'but whit the hell, he's no' a' there; he's wandered.')

The other odd man out in the party was Private McAuslan, the dirtiest soldier in the world, who acted as linesman and baggage-master, God help us. The Colonel had wanted to keep him behind, and send someone more fit for human inspection, but the team had protested violently. They were just men, and McAuslan was their linesman, foul as he was. In fairness I had backed them up, and now I was regretting it, for McAuslan is not the kind of ornament that you want to advertise your team in Mediterranean capitals. He stood there with the baggage, grimy and dishevelled showing a tasteful strip of grey vest between kilt and tunic, and with his hosetops wrinkling towards his ankles.

'All right, children,' I said, 'get aboard,' and as they chattered up the gangplank I went to look for the man in charge. I found him in a passageway below decks, leaning with his forehead against a pipe, singing *The Ash Grove* and fuming of gin. I addressed him, and he looked at me. Possibly the sight of a man in Highland dress was too much for him, what with the heat, for he put his hands over his eyes and said, 'Oh dear, oh dear,' but I convinced him that I was real, and he came to quite briskly. We got off to a fine start with the following memorable exchange.

Me: Excuse me, can you tell me when this boat starts?

He: It's not a boat, it's a ship.

Me: Oh, sorry. Well have you any idea, when it starts?

He: If I hadn't, I wouldn't be the bloody captain, would I?

Now that we were chatting like old friends, I introduced myself. He was a Welshman, stocky and middle-aged, with the bland, open face of a cherub and a heart as black as Satan's waistcoat. His name was Samuels, and he was very evil, as I discovered. At the moment, he was not pleased to see me, but he offered me gin, muttering about the indignity of having his fine vessel used as a floating hotel for a lot of blasted pongoes, and Scotch pongoes at that. I excused myself, went to see that my Highlanders were comfortably installed – I found them ranged solemnly on a platform in the engine room, looking at the engines – and having shepherded them to their quarters and prevented McAuslan falling over the side. I went to my cabin. There I counted the money – it was a month's pay for the party – and before I had finished the ship began to vibrate and we were away, like Hannibal, to invade the North.

I am no judge of naval behaviour, but looking back I should say that if the much-maligned William Bligh had been half as offensive as Lieutenant Samuels the *Bounty* would never have got the length of Land's End, let alone Tahiti. At the first meal in the ward-room – which consisted for him of gin and chocolate biscuits – he snarled at his officers, bullied the stewards, and cross-examined me with a hackle-raising mixture of contempt and curiosity. We were going to the Grand Island, he knew; and what did we think we were going to do there? Play football, was it? Was that all pongoes had to do? And who were we going to play then?

Keeping my temper I told him we had several matches arranged against Service and civilian teams on the island, and he chose to make light of our chances. He had seen my team aboard; they were midgets, and anyway who had they ever beaten?

At this one of his officers said he had seen us play, and we were good, very good. Samuels glared at him, but later he became thoughtful, applying himself to his gin, and when the meal ended he was still sitting there, brooding darkly. His officers looked nervous; they seemed to know the signs.

Next morning the African coast was still in view. I was surprised enough to ask Samuels about this, and he laughed and looked at me slantendicular.

'We're not goin' straight to the Island, Jocko,' he explained. 'Got to look in at Derna first, to pick up supplies. Don't worry, it won't take long.' He seemed oddly excited, but distinctly pleased with himself.

I didn't mind, and when Samuels suggested that we take the opportunity to go ashore at Derna so that my boys could have a practice kick-about, I was all for it. He went further; having vanished mysteriously into the town to conclude his official business, he returned to say that he was in a position to fix up a practice match against the local garrison side – 'thought you boys might like a try-out against some easy opposition, like; some not bad footballers yere, give you a game, anyway.'

Since we had several hours before we sailed it seemed not a bad idea; I consulted with the corporal-captain, and we told Samuels to go ahead. And then things started happening.

First of all, Samuels suggested we change into football kit on the ship. There was nothing odd about that, but when we went to the baggage-room the team's fine yellow jerseys with the little tartan badge were missing; it transpired that through some inexplicable mix-up they were now in the ship's laundry, being washed. Not to worry, said Samuels, we'll lend you some blue shirts, which he did.

He took personal charge of our party when we went ashore –
I was playing myself, as it was an unimportant game, and I wanted
to rest our left half, who had been slightly seasick. We played on
a mud-baked pitch near the harbour, and coasted to a very gentle
7–0 win. Afterwards the garrison team invited us for drinks and
supper, but Samuels interrupted my acceptance to say we hadn't
time; we had to catch the tide, or the wind, or something, and
we were bundled into the truck and hurried back to the harbour.
But one remark the garrison captain let fall in parting, and it
puzzled me.

'It's odd,' he said, 'to find so many Scotsmen in one ship's
crew.'

I mentioned this to Samuels, back on board, and he sniggered
wickedly.

'Well, now, natural enuff,' he said. 'He thought you was all in
the ship's company.'

A horrid suspicion was forming in my mind as I asked him to
explain.

'Well, see now,' he said, 'I 'ad an idea. When I went ashore
first, I looks in on the garrison an' starts talkin' football. "Got a
pretty fair team yere, 'aven't you?" I says. "District champions,"
says they. "Couldn't beat my ship's company," I says – cuttin'
a long story short, you understand. "Couldn't what?" says they.
"You want to bet?" says I.' He sat back, beaming wickedly at me.
'So I got on a little bet.'

I gaped at the man. 'You mean you passed off my team, under
false pretenses . . . You little shark! You could get the jail for this.'

'Grow up, boyo,' said Samuels. 'Lissen, it's a gold mine. I was
just tryin' it out before lettin' you in. Look, we can't go wrong. We
can clean up the whole coast, an' then you can do your tour on
the Island. Who knows your Jocks aren't my matelots? And
they'll bite every time; what's a mingy little coaster, they'll say, it
can't have no football team.' He cackled and drank gin. 'Oh boy!
They don't know we've got the next best thing to the Arsenal on
board!'

'Right,' I said. 'Give me the money you won.' He stared at me.
'It's going back to the garrison,' I explained.

'You gone nuts, boyo?'

'No, I haven't. Certainly not nuts enough to let you get away with using my boys, my regiment, dammit, to feather your little nest. Come on, cough up.'

But he wouldn't, and the longer we argued the less it seemed I could do anything about it. To expose the swindle would be as embarrassing for me and my team as for Samuels. So in the end I had to drop it, and got some satisfaction from telling him that it was his first and last killing as far as we were concerned. He cursed a bit, for he had planned the most plunderous operation seen in the Med since the Barbary corsairs, but later he brightened up.

'I'll still win a packet on you on the island,' he said. 'You're good, Jocko. Them boys of yours are the sweetest thing this side of Ninian Park. Football is an art, is it? But you're missin' a great opportunity. I thought Scotsmen were sharp, too.'

That disposed of, it was a pleasant enough voyage, marred only by two fights between McAuslan on the one hand and members of the crew, who had criticized his unsanitary appearance, on the other. I straightened them out, upbraided McAuslan, and instructed him how to behave.

'You're a guest, you horrible article,' I said. 'Be nice to the sailors; they are your friends. Fraternize with them; they were on our side in the war, you know? And for that matter, when we get to the island, I shall expect a higher standard than ever from all of you. Be a credit to the regiment, and keep moderately sober after the games. Above all, don't fight. Cut out the Garscube Road stuff or I'll blitz you.'

Just how my simple, manly words affected them you could see from the glazed look in their eyes, and I led them down the gangplank at Grand Island feeling just a mite apprehensive. They were good enough boys, but as wild as the next, and it was more than usually important that they keep out of trouble because the Military Governor, who had been instrumental in fixing the tour, was formerly of a Highland regiment, and would expect us not only to win our games but to win golden opinions for deportment.

He was there to meet us, with aides and minions, a stately

man of much charm who shook hands with the lads and then departed in a Rolls, having assured me that he was going to be at every game. Then the Press descended on us, I was interviewed about our chances, and we were all lined up and photographed. The result, as seen in the evening paper, was mixed. The team were standing there in their kilts, frowning suspiciously, with me at one end grinning inanely. At the other end crouched an anthropoid figure, dressed apparently in old sacking; at first I thought an Arab mendicant had strayed into the picture, but closer inspection identified it as McAuslan showing, as one of the team remarked, his good side.

Incidentally, it seemed from the paper's comments that we were not highly rated. The hint seemed to be that we were being given a big build-up simply because we were from the Governor's old brigade, but that when the garrison teams – and I knew they were good teams – got us, we would be pretty easy meat. This suited me, and it obviously didn't worry the team. They were near enough professional to know that games aren't won in newspaper columns.

We trained for two days and had our first game against the German prisoners-of-war. They were men still waiting to be repatriated, ex-Africa Korps, big and tough, and they had played together since they went into the bag in '42. Some of our team wore the Africa Star, and you could feel the tension higher than usual in the dressing-room beforehand. The corporal, dapper and wiry, stamped his boots on the concrete, bounced the ball, and said, 'Awright fellas, let's get stuck intae these Huns,' and out they trotted.

(I should say at this point that this final exhortation varied only according to our opponents. Years later, when he led a famous league side out to play Celtic, this same corporal, having said his Hail Mary and fingered his crucifix, instructed his team, 'Awright, fellas, let's get stuck intae these Papes.' There is a lesson in team spirit there, if you think about it.)

The Germans were good, but not good enough. They were clever for their size, but our boys kept the ball down and the game close, and ran them into a sweat before half-time. We should have won by about four clear goals, but the breaks didn't come, and we had to be content with 2-0. Personally I was exhausted: I had had to sit beside the Governor, who had played rugby, but if I had tried to explain the finer points he wouldn't have heard them anyway. He worked himself into a state of nervous frenzy, wrenching his handkerchief in his fingers and giving antique yelps of 'Off your side!' and 'We claim foul!' which contrasted oddly with the raucous support of our reserve players, whose repertoire was more varied and included 'Dig a hole for 'im!', 'Sink 'im!' and the inevitable 'Get tore intae these people!' At the end the Germans cried 'Hoch! hoch!' and we gave three cheers, and both sides came off hating each other.

Present in body and also in raw spirit was Lieutenant Samuels, who accosted me after the game with many a wink and leer. It seemed he had cleaned up again.

'An' I'll tell you, boyo, I'll do even better. The Artillery beat the Germans easy, so they figure to be favourites against you. But I seen your boys playin' at half-steam today. We'll murder 'em.' He nudged me. 'Want me to get a little bet on for you, hey? Money for old rope, man.'

Knowing him, I seemed to understand Sir Henry Morgan and Lloyd George better than I had ever done.

So the tour progressed, and the Island sat up a little straighter with each game. We came away strongly against the Engineers, 6-0, beat the top civilian team 3-0, and on one of those dreadful off-days just scraped home against the Armoured Corps, 1-0. It was scored by McGlinchy, playing his first game and playing abysmally. Then late on he ambled on to a loose ball on the edge of the penalty circle, tossed the hair out of his eyes, flicked the ball from left foot to right to left without letting it touch the ground, and suddenly unleashed the most unholy piledriver you ever saw. It hit the underside of the bar from twenty-five yards out and glanced into the net with the goalkeeper standing still, and you could almost hear McGlinchy sigh as he trotted back absently to his wing, scratching his ear.

'Wandered!' said the corporal bitterly afterwards. 'Away wi' the fairies! He does that, and for the rest o' the game he might

as well be in his bed. He's a genius, sir, but no' near often enough.
Ye jist daurnae risk 'im again.'

I agreed with him. So far we hadn't lost a goal, and although
I had no illusions about preserving that record, I was beginning
to hope that we would get through the tour unbeaten. The
Governor, whose excitement was increasing with every game, was
heard to express the opinion that we were the sharpest thing in the
whole Middle East; either he was getting pot-valiant or hysterical,
I wasn't sure which, but he went about bragging at dinners until
his commanders got sick of him, and us.

But the public liked us, and so did the Press, and when we
took the Artillery to the cleaners, 3-2, in one of the fastest and
most frantic games I have ever seen, amateur or pro, they were
turning crowds away from the stadium. The Governor was like
an antelope full of adrenalin, eating his handkerchief and shivering about in his seat, crying, 'Oh, my goodness gracious me!' and
'Ah, hah, he has, he hasn't, oh my God!' and flopping back,
exhausted. I was too busy to steady him; I was watching (it
dawned on me) a really fine football team. They moved like a
machine out there, my wiry, tireless wee keelies, and it wasn't
just their speed, their trickiness, or their accuracy; it was their
cool, impregnable assurance. What gets into a man, who is
nervous when a sergeant barks at him, but who, when he is put
out in front of 20,000 shouting spectators, and asked to juggle
an elusive leather ball, reacts with all the poise and certainty of an
acrobat on a high wire?

I didn't need to tell them they were good. They knew it, and perhaps some of them knew it too well. Following the Artillery game,
two of them got picked up by the MPs, fighting drunk and out of
bounds, and I had to pull out all the stops to save their necks. I
dropped them from the next game (which we won narrowly, 4-3),
and then came our final match, and we won it 4-0, and that was
it. I relaxed, the Governor took to his bed for a couple of days,
wheezing like a deflating balloon, Lieutenant Samuels danced on
the bar at the Officers' Club ('Jocko, boy, you're luv-ley, an' all
your little Scotch Pongoes are luv-ley, hoots mon, an' I've won a
dirty, great, big, luv-ley packet. You know what? I 'ad all the

ship's funds as well as my own money on 'em for the Artillery game') and my team took it easy at last. That is to say that during the day they punted the ball about on the practice pitch, crying 'Way-ull' and 'Aw-haw-hey,' and at night they sat in the bars, drinking beer and eyeing the talent, and keeping their bonnets over their eyes.

With the pressure off they drank more and ate more, and I was not surprised when, a few days before we were due to leave the island, two of them came down with one of those bugs which inhabit melons in foreign parts and give you gyppy tummy, or as they call it in India, Delhi Belly. They were packed off to bed and I read the others a lecture on the perils of over-indulgence. It was good, strong stuff, and so influenced me personally that I declined to join Lieutenant Samuels in the celebratory dinner which he tried to press on me at the Officers' Club that night.

I regarded him with distaste. 'Why aren't you out sinking submarines or something?'

'This is peacetime, boyo,' said he. 'Anyway, we're gettin' a refit; we'll be yere for weeks. I can stand it, I'm tellin' you.' I doubted whether he could; the gin was obviously lapping against his palate and his complexion was like a desert sunrise. He insisted loudly on buying me a drink at least, and I was finishing it and trying not to listen to his gloating account of how he would spend the filthy amount of money he had won, when I was called to the phone.

It was the Governor, excited but brisk. 'MacNeill,' he said. 'How's your team?'

Wondering, I said they were fine.

'Excellent, capital. I think I can arrange another game for them, farewell appearance, y'know. That all right with you?'

I was about to mention the two men in hospital, and that we wouldn't be at full strength, but after all, we were here to play, not to make excuses. So I said, 'Splendid, any time,' and before I could ask about our opponents and the where and when, he had said he would ring me later and hung up.

Samuels, now fully lit, was delighted. 'It never rains but it pours,' he exclaimed gleefully. 'Send it down, David. Let's see, put a packet on your boys – who they playin'? doesn't matter – collect on that, crikee, Jocko, what a killin'! I'll plank the bet first thing . . . trouble is, they're gettin' to know me. Ne'mind, I'll get my clerk to put it on, he can go in mufti.' He crowed and rubbed his hands. 'Luv-ley little pongoes; best cargo I ever had!'

It seemed to me he was taking a lot for granted; after all, our opponents might be somebody really good. But we'd beaten the best in the Island, so he probably couldn't go wrong.

So I thought, until I heard from the Governor's aide late that night. 'Two-thirty, at the Stadium,' he said. 'Full uniform for you, of course, and *do* see, old man, that your Jocks are respectable. Can't you get them to wear their hats on the *tops* of their heads? They tend rather to look like coalmen.'

'Sure, sure. Who are we playing?'

'Mmh? Oh, the other lot? The Fleet.'

For a moment I didn't follow. He explained.

'The Fleet. The Navy. *You* know, chaps in ships with blue trousers.' He began to sing *Heart of Oak*.

'But . . . but . . . but,' I said. 'That's like playing the Army. I mean, there are thousands of them. They'll be all-professional . . . they'll murder us . . . they . . .'

'That's what the Admiral thought,' said the aide, 'but our Chief wouldn't see it. Got rather excited actually; they're still arguing in there; can't you hear 'em? Amazing,' he went on, 'how the Chief's manner changes when he gets worked up about a thing like this; he sounds positively Scotch. What's a sumph, by the way?'

I wasn't listening any longer. I was sweating. It wasn't panic, or the fear of defeat. After all, we had done well, and no one could expect us to hold the Navy; we would just have to put on a good show. I was just concentrating on details – get the boys to bed quickly, two men in hospital, choose the team, balance it as well as possible. I ran over the reserves: Beattie, Forbes, McGlinchy, myself . . . Lord, the Fleet! And I had fourteen to choose from. Well, barring miracles, we would lose. The Governor would be in mourning; that was his hard luck, if he didn't know better than to pit us against a side that would be half First

Division pros, and possibly even an internationalist. Suddenly I felt elated. Suppose . . . oh, well, we'd give them something to remember us by.

I simply told the boys at bedtime who they were playing, and they digested it, and the corporal said:

'Aw-haw-hey. Think they're any good, sir?'

'Not as good as we are.'

'We're the wee boys,' said the corporal, and the wee boys cried 'Way-ull,' mocking themselves. They were pleased at the thought of another game, that was all. I doubt if their reaction would have been different if their opponents had been Moscow Dynamo or the Eye Infirmary.

The corporal and I pored over the team all morning; the one doubtful spot was left wing, and after much heart-searching we fixed on McGlinchy, but the corporal didn't like it. He at least knew what we were up against 'an' we cannae afford a passenger. If Ah thought he'd wake up mebbe half the match, OK, but no' kiddin', sir, yon yin's no' a' there.'

'He's all we've got,' I said. 'Beattie's a half back, and I'm just not good enough. It's got to be McGlinchy.'

'Aye, weel,' said the corporal, 'that's so. But by half-time I'll bet we're wishin' we'd picked . . . McAuslan, even.'

In the unlikely event that we had been daft enough to do just that, we would have been disappointed. For when we embussed for the stadium McAuslan was mysteriously absent. We waited and swore, but he didn't appear, so Beattie was detailed to run the touchline, and off we went. With any luck McAuslan had fallen in the harbour.

The dressing-room was hot and sunny under the stand as we sat around waiting. The boys chewed gum and McGlinchy played 'wee heidies' against the wall – nodding a ball against the partition like a boxer hitting a punch-ball. ('Close-mooth, tanner-ba' merchant,' muttered the corporal.) Outside we could hear the growing rumble of the crowd, and then there was the peep of a whistle, and the referee's step in the passage, and the boys shifted and said, 'Way-ull, way-ull,' and boots stamped and shorts were hitched, and outside a brass band was thumping out *Heart of Oak* and a great thunder of voices was rolling up as the Fleet came out, and the corporal sniffed and said:

'Awright, fellas, let's get stuck intae these matlows,' and I was left alone in the dressing-room.

I went out by the street door and was walking along to the grandstand entrance when I came face to face with Samuels in the crowd that was still pouring into the ground. It was a shock: I hadn't given him a thought since last night. Before I could say anything, he slapped me on the back, addressed me as Old Jocko, and said I was luv-ley.

'Goin' up to watch the slaughter?' he shouted. He was well ginned up. 'The massacre of the innocents, hey?'

'I like that,' I said. 'You've won enough off them; you could at least show some sympathy.'

'Who for?' he guffawed. 'The other lot?'

A horrible cold hand suddenly laid itself on the base of my spine.

'The other lot,' I said. 'You know who we're playing?'

'Been on the ship all mornin', checkin' stores,' he said, shaking his head. 'Who's the unfortunate party?'

'Tell me,' I said carefully. 'Have you put a bet on?'

'Have I, boyo? The lot, you bet. The sub-cheese. The bundle.'

I looked at my watch. It was two minutes to kick-off.

'Phone the bookie,' I said. 'Get it off. No matter what, cancel that bet.'

He didn't seem to be receiving me. 'The whole lot,' he said. 'Boyo, I cleaned out the safe. I shot the works. I'm tellin' . . .'

'Shut up, you Welsh oaf,' I shouted. 'Don't you understand? We're playing the Fleet, the Navy, all the great horrible battle-ships and aircraft carriers, millions of talented sailors. They will eat us alive. Your bet, if you let it ride, will go down the nick. Get it off.'

In all the world there is no sight so poignant as that of the confident mug when he feels the first sharp bite of the hook and realizes it is going to sink inexorably home. His face went from sweating red to dry grey, and he seemed to crumple.

'You're drunk, boyo,' he croaked.

'I'm drunk? Look who's talking. Look, Taffy, you'll have to cancel . . .' And just then what he had said came home to me. 'You say you cleaned out the safe? The ship's safe? But you've got two weeks of my Jocks' pay in there . . . Oh, brother.' I just stared at him. This was death, court-martial, ruin, and disaster. He was cooked. Unless the bet was scrubbed.

'It's no use,' he said. 'I cannot do it.' Odd, I thought, he says cannot, not can't. 'I didn't place it myself, see? The clerk did. Peterson. I gave him half a dozen addresses. I dunno where he is, now.'

The crowd was moving in, the last of it. There was nothing to be done. The band had stopped. I left him standing there, like a busted flush, and climbed the stairs to the stand. Poor Samuels, I thought. Idiot, mad Samuels. Of all the . . .

The roar hit me in the face as I came out into the stand. I sat at the back of the main box; down front the Governor was starting work on his first handkerchief of the game, and beside him was a massive, grizzled hero in blue, with gold lace up to his armpits. That would be the Admiral. Their henchmen were about them, full of well-bred enthusiasm; the stadium was jammed, and every second man seemed to be a sailor. Our support was confined to a handful of khaki down below the box: our own reserves and a few associates.

'Flee-eet!' rolled across the brown, iron-hard pitch, and I saw the concentration of yellow shirts down near one goal: the Navy were attacking, powerful dark-blue figures with red stockings. They smacked the ball about with that tough assurance that is the mark of the professional; I saw the corporal slide in to tackle, and red stockings deftly side-stepped and swept the ball past him. The roar mounted, there was a surge in our goalmouth, and then the ball was trickling past into the crowd. I felt slightly sick.

'Get tore intae these people!' came from in front of the box, to be drowned in the Navy roar. Yes, I thought, get tore in. It's your pay and Samuels' reputation you're playing for. Then I thought, no, the heck with that, it's just for yourselves, that's all.

And they played. The hard ground and the light ball were on our side, for we were ball-players first and last; on grass the

Navy would have been just too strong. They didn't rush things; they passed with deliberation and looked for their men, unlike our team, who were used to fast, short passing controlled by some sort of telepathy. If we played at their pace we were done for, so we didn't. The doll-like yellow figures moved and ran as though they were at practice, easy and confident.

We scored in the sixth minute, a zig-zag of passes down the middle that left Campbell, the centre, clear of the defence, and he lofted the ball over the Navy goalkeeper's head as he came out. There was a shocked roar from the crowd, a neigh of triumph from the Governor, a perceptible empurpling of the Admiral's neck, and an exulting 'Aw-haw-hey!' from below the box.

Two minutes later Campbell had the ball in the net again, but was ruled offside. Then he headed against the cross-bar, and we forced three corners in a row. But you could feel it slackening; the Fleet were as steady as ever, and presently they came away, swinging long passes through the open spaces, using their extra length of leg, keeping the ball up where their height counted. They *were* good; in their way. And for a moment, as they broke through on the left and centred and their inside right chose his spot in the net and banged in the equalizer, they were imposing that way.

There was worse to come. The Fleet went ahead with a penalty, when the corporal, in a momentary lapse into close-mouth warfare, obeyed our supporters' behest to 'Ca' the feet fae 'im,' and brought down a Navy forward close to goal. It was a critical point: when we kicked off again the Navy, one goal up, came storming through. Their centre got away and side-footed the ball past the advancing goalkeeper. It was rolling home, but the corporal came from nowhere and stopped it on the line. And then he did the ridiculous, unspeakable thing. I can still see him, the stocky yellow figure with his foot on top of the ball, watching three blue jerseys tearing down on him; alone, in his own goal. Bobby Moore himself would have belted it away for touch and been thankful. But not our boy. He shifted his hips, beat the first Navy forward on a sixpence, showed the ball to the other two, feinted amidst agonized yells of 'Get rid of it!' stepped over a scything foot, looked about him, and patted the ball into the hands of the goalkeeper, who was so stricken with anxiety that he nearly dropped it.

It was perhaps the cheekiest piece of ball-juggling that I've ever seen; it shook the Fleet momentarily for it seemed to indicate a careless contempt. It said, more clearly than words could have done, that there was no sense of panic in this defence. The Admiral roared with laughter, and I hoped again.

We scored again, just before the interval, a goal against the run of play headed in from a long, free kick, and the teams came off and the Marine band marched up and down playing *Iolanthe*. I stayed where I was, listening to the Governor chattering Good game, good game, my goodness, and the Admiral's bass rumble, and staring out at the sunlight on the great crowd lining the saucer of the arena. There was no point in my going down to the dressing-room; we were doing well, and nothing I could say could make it better.

The second half began disastrously. A high ball went into our goalmouth, the centre half and the Fleet centre went up for it; the sailor came down on his feet and our man on his back. He lay still, and my heart turned over. I watched them lifting him, crowding around, but his head hung forward, and presently they took him behind the goal. 'Dirty, dirty!' came the cry from down front, drowned in the answering roar of 'Wheel 'im off!' from the Navy. The referee bounced the ball to restart the game, and as the injured man was supported towards the dressing-room I was bounding down the stairs.

He was slightly concussed, the doctor said; he wanted to go back on, but the doctor said it was out of the question. I watched while they bandaged his head, and told him – what I honestly felt – that it didn't matter a damn about the game. His face took on that look of whining rage that the Glaswegian wears in times of stress, and he said, 'We had them bate. We'd've sorted them this half.'

Maybe we would, I thought; with ten men it was certain that we wouldn't now. The doctor broke in to say that he ought to go to bed, and as they took him away I went back to the stand.

Dimly I had been aware of the distant roar swelling and dying; when I climbed into my seat we were kicking off again. We were down 4-2.

The Fleet were out for blood now. Even the Admiral was joining in the roar, and the Governor was just sitting eating his hankie. Ten men don't look very different on the field from eleven; for a time they may even play above themselves, but they don't win. They never deserve to lose, but they lose.

Oddly enough, we held our own now, and with the tension gone I began to take in details. McGlinchy was playing like an elderly horse; he hadn't seen much of the ball in the first half, and now he was using it as if it was a land-mine, shying away from it, stumbling, and generally living up to the corporal's expectations. His inside man, little Forbes, was obviously cursing himself hoarse. The crowd enjoyed it.

'Windy!' roared the Fleet.

'Ah, you sharrap! Get back on the front o' the Players packet!'

'Turn blue, pongoes!'

'Play up,' cried the Governor. 'Come along, come along.'

The Admiral said something to him, and they both laughed, and I watched the handkerchief being twisted. There were about fifteen minutes left.

Then it happened, and you can read about it in the files of the Island's leading daily paper.

McGlinchy got the ball and lost it; it came back to him and he fell over it and it went into touch. The Navy threw in, the ball ran to McGlinchy again, and for once he beat his man and was moving down the wing when a sailor whipped the heels from him. The crowd roared, McGlinchy got up hopping painfully, the Governor exclaimed, 'Oh, I say,' and little Forbes went scurrying in, fists clenched, to avenge the foul. Oh no, I said, please God, don't let Forbes hit him, not out there with everyone looking. Please don't, Forbes. But the referee was in between, shaking his finger, Forbes was hustled away by his mates, and the referee gave a free kick – against McGlinchy.

It was taken amid much hubbub, and I watched McGlinchy, standing looking puzzled, too surprised to protest, and then his head lifted, and the ball was running towards him. He stopped it, turned, swerved past the half back, and was away. He could run when he wanted; he swerved in field, then out again towards the flag. The back went sliding in and McGlinchy side-stepped him and came in along the by-line, teasing that he was going to cross the ball, but holding it, like Matthews in his good years.

'Get rid of it!' cried an unhappy voice, but he held it, sand-dancing, looking up, and then he made a dart towards the near post, with the back straining at his heels, and he passed across and back when he couldn't have been more than three yards out, and Forbes had the empty goal in front of him.

The net shook, and the Admiral pounded his fist amidst the uproar, and the Governor made strange sounds, and I could see the corporal slapping McGlinchy's back and upbraiding him for holding on so long, and I thought regretfully that that had been McGlinchy's one brilliant flash. He was trotting back thoughtfully to his wing, with the applause dying down. It was 4-3 for the Navy and perhaps twelve minutes to go.

Then he did it again. Or very nearly. He went down the touch-line and then cut square across the field, beating two men on the way. He had an opening towards goal, with the Fleet defence floundering, but being McGlinchy he back-heeled the ball to nobody and it was cleared. I saw the corporal beating his breast, the Governor tore his handkerchief across, the Admiral bellowed jovially – and McGlinchy got the second chance he didn't deserve. The back's clearance hit a Fleet man and ran loose. McGlinchy, still in midfield, fastened on and this time went straight ahead, turned out to the left as the centre half closed in, and centred hard and high. Duff, the right winger, met it at the post with his head, and I realized that I was making ridiculous noises of tri-umph and delight. It was 4-4, the Fleet defence were gesturing at each other, and the little knot of yellow shirts was hurrying back towards the centre circle, embracing as they ran.

Then the Navy showed how good they were. They attacked, and for the first time in my experience of them I saw my team panicked. They had snatched a possible draw from certain defeat, and they were scared stiff of slipping back. They were wild; they fouled twice, once perilously close to the eighteen-yard line, and I could see, although I couldn't hear, the corporal barking at them, swearing horribly, no doubt, steadying them. He was wise, that corporal; whenever he got the ball he looked for McGlinchy. He sensed, like me, that he was in the presence of a phenomenon; it couldn't last, but he knew to use it while it was there. 'Feed him, feed him, he's bewitched,' I found myself saying, and McGlinchy went off down the wing, fair hair flying – I made a note to make him get it cut – and was tackled and the ball ran out.

He clapped his hands for it, trapped it as it was thrown in, back-heeled it through an opponent's legs, and ran on to it. He stopped, on the edge of the centre circle, foot on the ball, looking round. And for a split second the sound died. Then:

'Coom to 'im, man!' in a great Yorkshire voice.

'Get rid o' it, mac! See the winger.'

The roar swelled up, and he swerved away, dummied past a half back, reached the penalty circle, slid heaven knows how between two defenders, almost lost the ball, scratched for it, flushed it forward, feinted to shoot, swerved again, and now he was on the penalty spot, with the blue jerseys converging, and little Forbes screaming for the ball, unmarked, and Campbell on the other side of him beating his hands. But he went on, the Admiral covered his face, the Governor rose to his feet cramming his handkerchief into his mouth, McGlinchy had one sailor at his elbow and another lunging desperately in front of him; he checked and side-stepped, looked at Forbes, shoved the ball under the tackler's leg, went after it, and just for a split second was clear, with every sailor except Lord Nelson thundering in on him, the goalkeeper diving at his feet, and then the blue flood swept down on him.

'Get rid o' it!'

'Kill him!' bawled the Admiral, decency forgotten.

'Get tore in!' cried the Governor.

He went down in a heap of navy jerseys, and a sudden bellow went up from behind the goal. I couldn't see why, and then I saw why. The ball was lying, rolling just a little, a foot over the goal-line. It came to rest in the net, just inside the post.

At such times, when all around is bedlam, the man of mark is distinguished by his nonchalance and detachment. Calmly I took out my cigarette case, selected a cigarette, struck a match, set fire to my sporran, roared aloud, dropped cigarettes, case, and matches, and scrambled on my knees along the floor of the box trying to beat the flames out. By the time I had succeeded the box was full of smoke and a most disgusting stench, one of the Admiral's aides was looking round muttering that expressions of triumph were all very well, but the line should be drawn somewhere, and the Fleet were kicking off in a last attempt to retrieve the game.

They didn't make it, but it was a near thing. There was one appeal for a penalty when the corporal seemed to handle – if I'd been the referee I believe I'd have given it – but the claim was disallowed, and then the long whistle blew. We had won, 5-4, and I found myself face to face with a red-faced petty officer who was exclaiming, 'By, you were lucky! I say, you were lucky! By!'

I made deprecating noises and shot downstairs. They were trooping into the dressing-room, chattering indignantly – it was their curious way not to be exultant over what had gone right, but aggrieved over what had gone wrong. I gathered that at least two of the Fleet should have been ordered off, that the referee had been ignorant of the offside law, that we should have had a penalty when . . . and so on. Never mind, I said, we won, it had all come out all right. Oh, aye, but . . .

The Governor looked in, beaming congratulation, and there was a lot of noise and far too many people in the dressing-room. The team were pulling off their jerseys and trying to escape to the showers; clothes were falling on the floor and bare feet were being stepped on; the Governor was saying to Forbes, Well done, well played indeed, and Forbes was saying See yon big, dirty, ignorant full back, and at last the door was shut and we were alone with the smell of sweat and embrocation and steam and happy weariness.

'Well done, kids,' I said, and the corporal said, 'No' sae bad,' and rumpled McGlinchy's hair, and everyone laughed. Through in the showers someone began to make mouth-music to the tune of *The Black Bear*, and at the appropriate moment the feet stamped in unison and the towel-clad figures shuffled, clapping and humming.

'Not too loud,' I said. 'Don't let the Navy hear.'

I went over to McGlinchy, who was drying his hair and whistling. I wanted to ask: What gets into you? Why don't you play like that all the time? But I didn't. I knew I wouldn't ever find out.

For no reason I suddenly thought of Samuels, and realized that he was off the hook. Resentment quickly followed relief; he was not only in the clear, he had probably made a small fortune. How lucky, how undeservedly lucky can you get, I thought bitterly: but for McGlinchy's inexplicable brilliance Samuels would now be facing the certainty of court-martial and dismissal, possibly even prison. As it was he was riding high.

Or so I thought until that evening, when I was summoned to the local bastille at the request of the provost-Marshal, to identify a soldier, one McAuslan, who had been arrested during the afternoon. It appeared that he and an anonymous sailor had been making a tour of all the bars in town, and the sailor had eventually passed out in the street. McAuslan's primitive efforts to minister to him had excited attention, and the pair of them had been hauled off by the redcaps.

They brought him out of his cell, looking abominable but apparently sober. I demanded to know what he thought he had been doing.

Well, it was like this, he and his friend the sailor had gone for a wee hauf, and then they had had anither, and . . .

'He'll be singing *I belong to Glasgow* in a minute,' observed the redcap corporal. 'Stand to attention, you thing, you.'

'Who was the sailor?' I asked, puzzled, for I remembered McAuslan's antipathy to the ship's crew.

'Wan o' the boys off the ship. Fella Peterson. He was gaun tae the toon, an' Ah offered tae staun' 'im a drink. Ye remember,' he went on earnestly, 'ye told me tae fraternize. Well, we fraternized, an' he got fu'. Awfy quick, he got fu',' McAuslan went on, and it was plain to see that his companion's incapacity offended him. 'He drank the drink Ah bought 'im, and it made 'im fleein', and then he was buyin' drink himsel' at an awfy rate . . .'

'That was the thing, sir,' explained the redcap. 'This sailor had more money than you've ever seen; he looked like he'd robbed a bank. That was really why we pulled them in, sir, for protection. Weedy little chap, the sailor, but he had hundreds of pounds worth of lire on him.'

Suddenly a great light dawned. Peterson was the name of Samuels' clerk, who had been going to place his bets for him, and McAuslan had obviously encountered him beforehand, and full of good fellowship had bought him liquor, and Peterson, the weedy little chap, must have been unused to strong waters, and had forgotten responsibility and duty and his captain's orders, and had proceeded to go on an almighty toot. So it seemed obvious that whatever custom the bookies had attracted that day, Samuels' had not been part of it. His money (and the ship's funds and my Jocks' pay) was safely in the military police office safe, less what McAuslan and Peterson had expended with crying 'Bring in!' Samuels could make that up himself, and serve him right. Also, he could have fun explaining to the MPs just how one of his sailors came to be rolling about town with all that cash on his person.

'McAuslan,' I said, 'in your own way you're a great man. Tell me,' I asked the redcap, 'are you going to charge him?'

'Well,' said the redcap, 'he wasn't what you'd call incapably stinking, just happy. It was the sailor who was paralytic. He still is. So . . .'

'Thank you,' I said. 'Look, McAuslan, you're a lucky man. You shouldn't go about getting little sailors stotius . . .'

'I was jist fraternizin', honest . . .'

'Right. You can fraternize some more. What I want you to do is go over to the ship, look out Lieutenant Samuels, and tell him, in your own well-chosen words, what happened today. Tell him the money's in the MP safe. And then you might offer to buy him a drink; he'll probably need one. And McAuslan, if he tries to hit you, you're not to clock him one, understand? Remember, be fraternal and polite; he's your superior officer and you wouldn't want to hurt his feelings.'

C

We took our leave of the civil redcaps, and I watched McAuslan striding purposefully towards the harbour, bonnet down over his eyes, to break the glad news to Samuels. It was growing dusk, and all in all, it had been quite a day.

I saw McGlinchy many years after, from the top of a Glasgow bus. Although his fair hair was fading and receding, and his face looked middle-aged and tired, there was no mistaking the loose-jointed, untidy walk. He was carrying a string bag, and he looked of no account at all in his stained raincoat and old shoes. And then the bus took me past. I wondered if he remembered those few minutes out in the sunlight. Perhaps not; he wasn't the kind who would think twice about it. But I remember McGlinchy when . . .

From *The General Danced at Dawn* (Barrie and Jenkins 1970)

# Out of the East

JOHN FAIRGRIEVE

It has long been accepted, by men of perception, that those who follow such clubs as Hearts, Partick Thistle and Queen's Park are of a special breed. It is easy, after all, to follow the likes of Celtic and Rangers, who have a distasteful habit of winning things just about every year. It is also easy to support the smaller outfits, which never do win anything, and are not expected to do so; in this, geography is usually the deciding factor.

But while I can, in all honesty, speak with no great authority as to what constitutes a Partick or Queen's supporter, there are very few around able to give me any lessons, so far as Hearts are concerned.

Heredity matters. So does environment, naturally. Then there is a long apprenticeship, during which one goes through the fire. Hearts always have great expectations, which, with crushing inevitability, fall in ruins, usually just before or just after the New Year.

Occasionally, very occasionally, a cup or a title does come to Tynecastle, and belief is temporarily suspended. When they were scoring all those goals in the late 1950s, we celebrated well enough, but, somehow, deep down, there was this strange disappointment. It was as if we feared Hearts might become mere pot-hunters, like the people at Ibrox and Parkhead. Soon enough, however, everything returned to normal, and we were able to relax.

Yet had we not gone through that ordeal of apprenticeship in the art of supporting a great club and a team barely above average, we could not have survived. A civilized philosophy has to be developed in that time. Many fall by the wayside. Some even go to Easter Road, and if, suitably ashamed, they come creeping back later to their accustomed spot, are forgiven but not forgotten. They have not failed: nor have they passed, with flying colours. They are flawed. We do not ostracize them, as I have said, for we are kindly men, but we remember.

There were three reasons why I became a Hearts fan . . . and why I achieved a pass-mark that can only be described as triumphant. One was my maternal grandfather, one was my father, and the other was Tommy Walker. Since I first saw Tommy play, I think it must have been in 1938, it has been cautiously suggested to me, now and again, that maybe he wasn't the best inside forward of them all, and that's when my mind closes. I listen courteously, then change the subject, which is not worthy of intelligent discussion. I take my legends seriously and, anyway, that was a legend with plenty of basis in truth.

When he was appointed manager of Hearts in the middle 1950s, the club reached its pinnacle. We had our share of the goodies, then let others take their turn with good grace. But on 28 September 1966, Hearts sacked Tommy Walker. That was a bad day.

I was in Glasgow at the time, and saw the teasing placard for an evening newspaper. 'Tommy Walker shock', it said. The words I wrote that evening were full of rage and sorrow. My refuge was the thought that those who had done such a thing were mere stewards, and rotten ones, at that. They had no right to be where they were, no right at all. Who the hell did they think they were?

Tommy Walker telephoned, and said thanks, but he wouldn't say a word of criticism about the board. I thought about that, too, and realized that this was the last, and cruellest exam of the apprenticeship.

He is on the board himself now but, of course, even before he was recalled, I was back in the fold. Indeed I had never left, not truly. Well, you don't, do you?

## RANGERS COMING OUT

The hubbub of the terracing dies down to a wilderness
of pure stillness.

More silent than Meribah when Moses stood before the
rock.

Up bubbles a tiny cry that fades as soon . . .

*Crack*! and in that jubilant ascension,

Blue wave on blue wave of Rangers' blue springs and
springs out to the joyous thunder and thundering joy
of their blue-splashed host.

James T R Ritchie

## 'MCEWAN'

From 'The Singing Street' by James T R Ritchie (Oliver and Boyd 1964)

'There was this fellie coorin' doon on the terracing and some'dy said "What are ye feared for?" an' he said "Thae empty beer bottles fleein' aboot!" "Away!" said the man, "dinnie be daft, ye've nae chance o' bein' hit by a bottle. Your name has to be on it." "Aye, that's jist ma trouble," said the fellie, "ma name's M'Ewan!"'

# The Old Firm

## CLIFFORD HANLEY

In fact, I didn't know there were any other teams than Rangers and Celtic. When we kicked a tanner ball about, or more often a complicated artifact made of crumpled newspaper and string, somebody was Rangers and somebody else was Celtic. If I had been able to spell the word, I would have called it the great Glasgow dichotomy.

There is no way of getting away from this in Glasgow. We dichotomize with the compulsive urge of amoebae to split into separate amoebae. Here's an odd thing: when my family moved to Shettleston, there were suddenly two local teams to support – Shettleston, and Shettleston Celtic. How could a speck on the map like Shettleston support two whole football teams, each with its own park? The explanation is simple. Shettleston, like the Glasgow macrocosm, couldn't live without something to hate.

We'll get to Celtic and Rangers in a minute, after I have exorcized Shettleston. I got into Well Park illegally – at the time, I could walk under a turnstile without stooping – because sneaking into Well Park was one of the challenges of my generation. Everybody else did it, so I did it. I don't remember who the home team was playing, I don't remember the game, I was bored up to the oxters because I realized I was almost totally immune to football. But I did shout for The Town because I knew what was expected of me. They lost, I think.

There must be something treasonous and decadent about a Glasgow kid who is not hooked on football, and that is what this is really about. Well, I am still here, and Well Park is not. Later on, at Eastbank Academy I weasled out of playing football, because I kept being sandwiched between two twelve-stone oafs with granite skulls, and I switched to hockey, where every man's stick is the same weight.

And before I get to Celtic and Rangers, or Rangers and Celtic, I can say that I was a whizz at hockey. At five feet and seven stone I could run like a bullet, and apart from a broken ankle delivered by a hysterical football player on temporary secondment to the sissy sport, I survived the game without scathe.

Sometimes we played the girls' team, and there was a very good female player, a splendid long lassie with legs up to her ribs, who was so incensed at not being able to catch me on the wing that I had to marry her in the end.

So I am perhaps uniquely qualified to talk about the Old Firm, because I spent my life standing above and apart from it, with my hockey stick at the ready. I have this bizarre and antisocial deficiency – I have hardly ever been able to be a member of a crowd. When everybody is screaming Hang the Kaiser, or Murder the Ref, or Thingummy the Pope, or Unhorse King Billy, I am the Martian in the background taking notes.

Once I saw a film about the great lemming race, in which the wee souls were galloping for the great event of the decade, a mad breenge into the North Atlantic, and I noticed there was one lemming who fell out of parade and sat peching behind a rock.

I could understand what his cousins were saying to him – 'Come on, Charlie, the water's going to be great, pow pow!' while he muttered, 'Yeah, in a minute, I'm just tying my lace,' or 'See you later, I'm dying for a fag.' Meaning, 'Okay, Fred, I can hear the bugle as well, but I'll think about it till tomorrow, and I can't stand overcrowding.'

What on earth can be wrong with me? I've just got the instinct to survive, that's what. I was born in the Gallowgate, no more than a beer-bottle's throw from Celtic Park, and it never occurred to me to make the short pilgrimage. The whole Rangers-Celtic thing seeped into my childhood like swamp-water, and I hated swamp-water, even in whisky.

The football bit was no more than froth on the surface, hinting at a more savage poison below. On the twelfth of July ('Twelfth of July, the Papes will die') kids who couldn't have recited the

First Commandment roamed the streets like demented Vigilantes mouthing the challenge, 'A Billy or a Dan or an auld tin can?' They were seeking out their enemies so that they could smash their faces in, in the name of the gentle Nazarene and in propagation of the doctrine of Christian brotherhood. I always identified myself as an auld tin can, like Peter denying his Lord ere the cock crew thrice. I was a stout Presbyterian, but I also had this staunch and rugged hatred of having my face bashed in.

Rangers and Celtic were not football teams, they were banners under which Glaswegians could foam at the mouth. There was a period when I felt I ought in all conscience to join the Rangers mob because I knew that the Catholic Church was the Scarlet Woman of Rome, and I had a very odd dream about nuns when I was about six. But I somehow couldn't raise the polemical energy to sign up.

I mean, what if Celtic were quite nice? I would be shouting imprecations at people who had never done me any harm, and although I rather enjoyed the imprecations themselves, I thought it would be better to save them up for somebody I genuinely disliked.

At the age of five I found myself wandering footloose in Cubie Street, and became aware of distant music, followed by pennants and marching feet emerging from the mirk of Bridgeton and advancing like, well, like either the Crusaders or the Saracen hordes. I can tell you, I didn't wait to inquire which. I ran. It was my first whiff of the Church Militant, or the Orange Walk as we call it in Glasgow, and I had the precocious certainty that these boys were going to do whatever they wanted to do and ask questions later, if they could sober up in time.

But it was impossible to evade the knowledge that the Celts and the 'Gers were the world's greatest. Eccentrics might support the Bully Wee, stoic pessimists might cling despairingly to the Jags, but real football meant two teams and two teams only. They were the stuff of legend, of lore and song.

> 'Come along the Rangers, buckle up your belts
> You'll mebbe beat the Hearts but you'll never
> beat the Celts.'

The songs were pretty rotten, but they were memorable and singable. Follow follow, we will follow Rangers, everywhere, up the stair, we will follow on. Definitely not Eurovision material. Well, now I think of the Eurovision songs of recent years, maybe I'm wrong. When I was writing a column for a Beaverbrook newspaper which has now vanished (perhaps as a result of that column), I provoked a monstrous postbag of contempt because I got a name wrong in the ancient rune. 'Oh, Charlie Shaw, he never saw, where Alan Morton put the baw.'

How was I to know it was Charlie and not Jimmy? The names meant nothing to me but noises heard on the wind.

But the names of the Celts and the 'Gers were inescapable. The veriest auld tin can couldn't help knowing that Patsy Gallacher was above powers and principalities. He had the knack of putting people up in the air, it seemed, and I quite fancied that, if I hadn't to play football at the same time. Jimmy McGrory figured in a very rude quatrain, coupled with the name of the Holy Father. There was the legendary Jimmy McMenemy, and his son John McMenemy – these were all Celts, of course, and when I met John McMenemy in the flesh many years later I was flabbergasted to find that he was a helluva nice fellow.

For that matter, the shadow of Willie ('Boss') Maley lay over the world football scene throughout my childhood, and many years later I met him too. He was so genial and kindly that I suspect the fire had gone out of him by then. Maley made Celtic great. Well, he made Celtic a great football team, but I was never sure if that was the point of the exercise.

Indeed, I made the brief acquaintance of John Lawrence, who had become the chairman of Rangers, and I thought he was a most mild and humane man, applying the lessons of his hard early years to the business of being a tycoon without callousness. But there is an essential callousness about the Old Firm that few men can shake off.

Ah, there was the great tragedy of football, and it had to involve Rangers and Celtic. On a September afternoon in 1931, Sam English of Rangers got the ball and made for goal, where young Johnny Thomson was waiting to block the shot. Thomson suddenly hurled himself horizontally at the ball, crashed into English's knee, and fell bleeding while the shot bounced off a post. He died that day without regaining consciousness.

You didn't have to be an Old Firm fan to feel the horror of that moment. Kids are all hooked on bizarre deaths anyway, and this ranked with the bloodcurdling tale of how Jack Johnson had killed a man in the ring. English was a Ranger. Thomson was a Celt. Strangely. I never heard a song about the death of Thomson.

Let me leap momentarily to recent times, when Rangers had another disaster, in which the spectators died, crushed and trampled as the crowd left Ibrox too fast, and I made a lot of enemies without even having been there.

I had seen only one Rangers game before then, when the 'Gers played Moscow Dynamo to a 2-2 draw. In truth, I didn't see a lot of the game, because there was a very large man standing in front of me on the terracing, and I had to do the best I could with the view of a herringbone jacket. But at the end of the game, when the philosophic fans started making their exit, I was genuinely terrified. The people in my part of the crowd were crying Slow down, while the people farther back were crying Speed up. ('Those behind cried forward, and those in front cried back.')

Nobody was actually crushed, but my own feet didn't reach the ground for about twenty yards, women and children were having quite legitimate hysterics, and I was glad to find myself in the street with all limbs accounted for. It was the last big game I ever attended, or ever will.

Well, when the disaster did come, and people did die, there was a prompt fund, and kindly people poured their money into it, and I had the bad taste to write a newspaper article advising them not to. It wasn't that I objected to charity. I was simply incensed by the fact that people who were killed on the roads, or at home, or work, in single numbers were ignored, and that if you wanted your widow to get a handout you had to arrange to die in a mass accident.

We were talking, however, about the teams themselves. My instinct as a born Protestant (or, as a childhood acquaintance pithily described it, a Proddy-dog) should have been to favour Rangers. But when we played cowboys and Indians, I was always by choice an Indian, and I tended to go for Celtic out of sheer perverseness. That was long before I realized that all human aspirations are vain, and started rooting for Partick Thistle accordingly.

My perverseness was justified as wisdom and knowledge oozed into me later. I hadn't realized then that Celtic, set up as a charity-raising organization to give hot soup to deadbeats, was Roman Catholic but not stubborn about it. They didn't scruple to play Proddy-dogs, or Muslims if available, and this created its own legends, which may even be true.

One is the tale of a Protestant newly signed for Celtic who came into the dressing room at half-time with his veins bulging and his nostrils white because a Rangers fan kept barracking him as a dirty Fenian swine. Jimmy McGrory, or maybe Patsy Gallacher, soothed the fellow down by saying 'They call me that all the time.' 'That's all right for you – you *are* a Fenian swine!'

Another is the story, certainly untrue but all the better for it, about the day when Celtic trounced Rangers on New Year's Day, and John Lawrence excused the defeat by pointing out to Bob Kelly that the Celts had two Protestants in the team. 'Aye, but you've got eleven,' said Kelly.

True, true. Rangers always has eleven Protestants, or at least non-Catholics, on the field, and no crucifix ever darkens Ibrox's doors. At times, they do very well, in football terms, with this line-up, and they too have their legendary names which burn into the brain of even an apathetic child. Meiklejohn and Wee Blue Devil Morton, and Torry Gillick and Willie Thornton and Willie Waddell and Big Geordie Young, who is also an okay guy and runs a very nice pub, and McPhail and Baxter and the rest. At times they have done very badly, and the fans really feel it.

Oh my brethren, do they feel it! Not being an afficionado, or yet an encyclopaedia, I will not try to recall the team or the year, but I do know that when I worked on the *Daily Record*, I knew a sports writer who was fairly pro-Rangers (what I mean is that he got his eyes dyed blue for his birthday) and the great 'Gers were beaten seven to one by some obscure set of upstarts. I actually tried to josh him about it, and he strode past me with unseeing eyes and blood squirting out of his ears. And that was a month after the game.

I also gained the suspicion that he didn't like Roman Catholics, because when I was getting married he exhorted me to have fifteen kids as part of the crusade to outnumber the bastards. I told him I was a Buddhist, and he said that was fine, as long as I wasn't a Fenian Buddhist.

So that was what it was all about, really. It wasn't two football teams, it was two living symbols of that cleft in Glasgow's consciousness, the grand canyon separating Prod from Pape.

Maybe that's all right. I wouldn't want everybody in Glasgow, or even in Shettleston, to think the same way or believe the same things. There is much to be said for and against the Roman Church, and much to be said for and against John Knox and John Calvin – or King Billy. One thing to be said for King Billy, or William of Orange to the historians, is that he didn't give a tinker's damn. He was generous to monasteries and convents, and the Pope couldn't have been more pleased when he won the Battle of the Boyne because the Pope had gone off the Stuart dynasty as well.

Never mind, no staunch Proddy is going to swallow that. Notice the adjective. In Glasgow, a Protestant is staunch, a Catholic is bitter.

Was it possible, is it possible, that the existence of Rangers and Celtic provides a fairly harmless outlet, a safety valve, for pent-up hostilities that would blow the lid off otherwise? Or is it that they create a venturi tube, a forced draught, to embers that would otherwise die a natural death?

I don't know, and only a fool could be sure. With the moralistic surface of my mind, I sternly deplore the whole thing. Football should be football and religion should be religion and ne'er the twain should meet. But since I'm sceptical about my moralistic postures, I wonder if that needle is essential to provoke men to great deeds. Since we are by nature evil and violent, maybe we need a bit of football that gives our hostility a wee holiday by adding the fire of sectarian ferocity.

You will not get me anywhere near a Rangers-Celtic game, because I would feel too much of an alien and somebody might say a rude word to me or accidentally stand in my teeth. But while I sometimes make the pilgrimage to Firhill to relish the gentle melancholy of yet another disaster, and enjoy the wittiest patter and the best pies in the football game, I know that there's another, bigger, fiercer, more terrible, more poetic kind of football, and as the pendulum swings, it's the football people get from Rangers or Celtic.

I grew up between them, and whether I like it or not, Rangers and Celtic have helped to make me what I am, and make Glasgow what it is.

Thoreau, in one of his presumptuous moments, proclaimed, 'I accept the universe.' And Thomas Carlyle riposted, 'Egad, he's got to!'

Well, I accept Rangers and Celtic. Because Egad, I've got to.

# Priest Butted on Nose and Sabbath

BRIAN WILSON

A Uist football match ended in amazing scenes on Sunday with a priest being butted in the face by a soldier. The game, between North End and the Army, ended in total disarray.

The priest, Father Colin MacInnes, was playing for North End, which he also manages. The North End Team is an amalgamation of the old Iochdar and Bornish sides and is composed almost entirely of young players – some of them still at school.

Sunday's trouble began when the appointed referee failed to turn up and one of the spectators volunteered. 'From the outset it was a battle between the referee and the Army,' said Father MacInnes on Wednesday. 'They just refused to accept his decisions.'

It seems that, going by the form-book, the Army should have been good for the two points. And so their humour was not helped when the young North End side forged into a two-goal lead. As proceedings degenerated the referee, Mr Donald Mac-Askill, attempted to send Army players off – but they refused to go.

Abandonment should have followed at this stage – but the game went on its ever-more ferocious way. At half-time there was talk of abandonment, but it was decided eventually to continue. 'In the second half the Army just got wilder and wilder,' said Father MacInnes. 'My boys were very good – they didn't retaliate at all.'

The Army tactics paid off and they drew level and then went ahead. It was at this stage that the final incident took place. An Army player butted the priest on the nose, drawing a lot of blood. It appears that he accompanied the action with the words:

'That's what I think of your team.' Father MacInnes said: 'That was it – the game had to be stopped.'

It remains unclear whether the game was in fact abandoned or if it will go down as a North End walk-off. Father MacInnes said that he was hoping for a special league meeting, either this weekend or early next week. He was concerned about the general organization of the South Uist and Barra League as well as the specific incident. He said he would not be making a complaint to the Army 'though I understand someone's coming to see me.' His interest lay in sorting the matter out with the League Management Committee and in avoiding a repetition.

An Army spokesman at Benbecula said that he had heard of the incident. He understood that the referee might have been 'under the influence' (this was refuted by Father MacInnes) and that the priest's conduct was 'unbecoming of a man of the cloth.' He said that no disciplinary action had yet been taken against the man who butted Father MacInnes, since no complaint had been made.

From the *West Highland Free Press*

# People, Places . . . and Press boxes

JOHN MacKENZIE

Round about the time I was drawing my weekly subsistence from
His Majesty's paymasters, a strip-tease dancer with considerable
and noticeable assets, who did not believe in concealing them
overmuch, was billing herself as 'The Girl the Lord Chamberlain
banned'.

I have very little in common with the unclad Phyllis Dixie,
except that we were in the same business . . . exposure. She was
selling a much more attractive package. However, there was a
night in May 1967 when I had a notion of how she felt. The Lord
Chamberlain has never taken exception to anything I have written,
and that makes him unique. But lesser mortals have risen up in
outraged dignity on various occasions to inform me that I was
banned from something or other.

Ignoring the fact that in my earlier, formative years as a critic,
St Mirren, Raith Rovers, Celtic and Airdrie had begged me not to
darken their doors again, the first outraged citizen of any note was
the late Willie Allison, PRO to Rangers, whose main claim to fame
was that he would never use one word where a dozen or so would do.

Rangers had just lost in the final of the European Cup Winners'
Cup to Bayern Munchen, in Nuremberg, a crime that was com-
pounded by the fact that their ancient rivals from the other side
of the city, Celtic, had won the European Cup by beating Inter
Milan in Lisbon just one week earlier. But that ill-fated trip to
the city famous for the trial of war criminals had earned a place
in history as much for the exploits of the club chairman off the
field, as for those of the players on it.

In common with one or two of my less inhibited colleagues,
I had fired a momentous broadside at Mr John Lawrence after
statements he had made at a press conference on the day before

the final. In a few well-chosen words, he accepted that Rangers were second-best to Celtic, and criticized his manager Scot Symon who was forty miles away with his players for fielding a forward line full of half backs. And he did little for the morale of the chosen players by assuring one or two of them that they would certainly be replaced by better players next season.

I did not expect to win popularity by having a go, but I had been hovering around the relegation area in that respect with Rangers for a long time in any case. But neither did I expect the letter that dropped on my desk an hour after arriving home from Nuremberg. Willie Allison must have had a fast car waiting to take him to the nearest typewriter. There was I, sitting behind my own machine in Albion Street, dredging the bottom of a barrel or two in a bid to find a kind word to say about a team that had a European Cup in its grasp, only to throw away the chance, when the letter dropped on my desk.

The letter was short and to the point, which was surprising considering the author. It informed me that I would no longer be welcome at Ibrox Stadium. A few life-long Rangers' supporters of that era assured me that the club had done me a favour. I was certainly left in no doubt that the honour of risking a coronary by climbing the spiral staircase . . . now thankfully replaced . . . to the Ibrox pressbox was no longer to be mine.

Willie Allison had signed the letter himself, under his official title of PRO, a title most people found misleading to say the least. If it meant Public Relations Officer, the public knew nothing about it. It presumably meant Press Relations Officer, but since he always kept the press at arm's length, a position they were happy to occupy, his function was always a little obscure.

John Lawrence is never going to believe it, but even around the time when he kept calling press conferences that led to trouble, I quite liked the benign old gent who had wandered from the building industry, almost unwittingly, into a cut-throat rat-race where he always looked more than a little out of place. He was often badly advised, and never knew enough about the day-to-day politics of the game to realize it. The Nuremberg affair was typical.

The press conference was set up by the PRO who provided the

answer to all the questions, a simple task since he had planted most of the questions in the first place. Mr Allison later claimed that the conference had been a huge success, and that the sports writers could not get to their telephones fast enough when it finished. You bet your life they moved fast . . . and the group included several foreign correspondents who seldom found such manna dropping from heaven into their ever-ready notebooks.

When the horrified Mr Allison discovered how the story had been handled, he made a big issue of the fact that I, and one or two others who were critical, were in Nuremberg's famous Turkish Baths at the time the conference was taking place, and were reporting second hand.

Perfectly true! But the *Scottish Daily Express*, which tended to send task forces to these major football occasions, was more than adequately covered. Jim Rodger, now with the *Daily Mirror*, who, in between taking phone calls from various Government ministers and vetting the Honours List, is one of the most conscientious leg men in the business, was at the meeting. For good measure, the *Express* team also included Jimmy Sanderson, now also with the *Daily Mirror*, and Willie Waddell, who is now General Manager and Vice-Chairman of Rangers.

Jim Rodger produced an accurate report of the meeting, and my job was to comment on it. And I did, with encouragement, I may say, from my colleagues, including the future Rangers' boss. But since I never believe in attack without securing the lines of retreat, I took the potentially explosive piece to the Grande Hotel, where John Lawrence was comfortably ensconced in Suite 241. I felt he had the right to know what was coming, and having explained what I intended doing, I put it to him that he had been, at the best, more than a teeny little bit indiscreet. I suggested that I agreed with much of what he had said, but that the timing would have done credit to a Bob Hope. He not only refused to withdraw a single word, but he expanded on the theme at considerable length. That at least absolved me from accusations of reporting second-hand material.

That was a remarkable interview, in its way. On the way to Suite 241 I bumped into Hal Stewart, manager, publicity man, import and export agent for Morton, who had a six o'clock appointment with Mr Lawrence. He offered to let me go first.

'I'm probably killing off any chance I had of getting a favour by letting you in first,' he assured me. I never discovered if he ever got his favour. And it was in Suite 241, after failing to convince him that he had been ill-advised, that John Lawrence went on to name the next Rangers' manager. It was a strange coincidence, since the man concerned, Dave White, then manager of Clyde, was at that moment sitting in my room back in the Mercur hotel in his underpants, waiting for his trousers to be pressed. Mr Lawrence told me that Rangers were contemplating asking Dave White to become assistant to manager Scot Symon, to secure the line of succession, and give him time to work and study under Mr Symon for a year or two. When I hinted to Dave White later that an early move from Clyde seemed indicated, he revealed that the initial move had already come from Rangers.

Little did he know that Scot Symon would be fired within a few months, leaving him as manager before he was ready, and that he too would be fired just two years later.

I re-wrote the damning article about the press conference with a future Rangers' manager in Dave White sitting in the room . . . I admit he flinched several times when he heard it read over the phone . . . and *his successor*, Willie Waddell, in the next room. The reaction was not unexpected, really. I dropped to the bottom of the Ibrox popularity poll, not that it was a long drop. And it took just an hour after arrival home for the axe to fall. Hugh Taylor, of the *Daily Record*, who had dipped into his astonishing vocabulary of colourful phrases to write an equally critical piece, was not banned, and phoned Willie Allison to complain. He was told I was a persistent offender.

The game itself is history. Rangers lost in extra time, and the one real chance that came their way fell to Roger Hynd, a stout-hearted but awkward centre half playing at centre forward for the night. He missed from about six yards . . . a miss it was claimed later, that left John Lawrence just six yards away from a knighthood, since Bob Kelly was knighted following Celtic's European Cup win in the same year.

A final word on that incident, to demonstrate the vagaries of the little men behind the scenes in football . . . the members of the board. At the airport in Nuremberg, on the way home, one of the Rangers directors sidled up to me and whispered: 'You were quite right. I am on your side.' Less than five minutes later, I heard him say to another director: 'Mackenzie has gone too far this time. He's got to go.' And when the ban was lifted before the start of the following season, the same director offered me a couple of complimentary tickets for their opening game at Aberdeen!

John Lawrence was really more sinned against than sinning. He just did not know what it was all about. It was said of him at one time that when Celtic found an open space, they used it to create a winning move, but when Rangers found one, John Lawrence built a bungalow on it. Things have changed at Ibrox, and with the directors fulfilling only a social and financial role, relationships are almost cordial.

People . . . places . . . and press boxes. That, really, is what football is all about for the man who looks at the game over the top of a typewriter. And mostly about people.

It all started for me when I joined the *Scottish Daily Express* more than twenty years ago as 'The Man in the Crowd', a faceless character who, apart from mingling on the terracing, and covering a match as the crowd saw it, rather than through his own eyes, went out and about every Monday morning seeking supporters of a particular club, looking for criticisms and suggestions. The criticism was usually hard, and the suggestions verging on the criminal.

Having interviewed the alleged supporters, I then headed nonchalantly for the office of the manager, for his answers and comments. The nonchalance was born of innocence. I did not know my managers. Most of them, unfortunately, had at least heard about me. The welcome was often warm, but never cordial. Since I was employed by a sports editor with a sadistic touch, who did not believe in pampering newcomers, the first expedition was handpicked. I was sent to Stirling, where some of the fans seemed to be let out of their cages to waylay me, and where the awesome figure of the late Tam Fergusson waited for me.

The insults directed at Tam by his own supporters were choice. No group of fans has ever dragged up such an impressive vocabulary of vituperation to describe a manager . . . or managing director as Tam called himself. He owned the club. He ran Stirling Albion, not with a rod of iron, but with a walking stick that earned a place in the Football Hall of Fame, or should have done. The trouble was that no one had told me what to expect, and the half hour in his twelve foot-square coal-masters' office in Stirling became an experience I will never forget. I spent most of it trying to stay out of reach of his walking stick, and not always succeeding.

He left the Stirling Albion supporters without a name, and then invented a few for them. He dug out a few choice descriptive phrases about me as well, before chasing me out into the coal yard using his walking stick like a sabre. In full flight, in spite of the limp, he was an impressive figure. A few of his players also felt the weight of that stick when his displeasure was at its height, which was often, since Stirling were not exactly noted for winning matches at that time.

However, he provided sound training for the confrontations that lay ahead. Malcolm McDonald, manager of Kilmarnock, never had any need for a stick. Nor did he use words. He just talked without saying anything, which is a highly effective weapon when dealing with reporters. He was one of the all-time greats in that line. Malcolm, nice fellow though he was, was never one of my favourites. I fell out with him, which came easy to me, after I gave the inside story, with the referee as the obvious source of information, about a penalty kick awarded to Partick Thistle about a minute from time, from which they scored the winning goal against Kilmarnock at Rugby Park. He called me a referees' stool pigeon, and told me not to come back to Rugby Park.

He moved to Brentford, and returned to Kilmarnock as manager many years later. I went down to see him, with the object of building up a forthcoming European cup-tie, to be greeted in the entrance hall with the words: 'I thought I told you not to come back here.'

Scot Symon was next. The man who invented the phrase 'No

comment' was a formidable obstacle, but at least this time I knew what to expect. Rangers were going through a bad time, which meant in newspaper terms in those days that they had lost a couple of games, and their gates were down to around 40,000. It was never easy to locate their fans without their scarves and banners, because their support is so widespread. I tried Govan, but for every blue-nose I spoke to, I stopped three Tims who were only too happy to tell me what was wrong with Rangers. The Ibrox fans I did find must have been lying in wait with the most awkward questions imaginable. I eventually climbed the famous marble staircase, after going through the front-door preliminaries, which in those days stopped short only of passwords, countersigns and visas. Suddenly I was in the presence.

Without even looking up from his blotter . . . blue, of course . . . while I wondered whether to sit uninvited in one of the chairs available, or to die standing up with my boots on, he said:

'I know who you are, so spare me the introductions. I have no time for writers who hide behind ridiculous pen-names.' Not bad for openers, and as it happened, one of the longest speeches he ever made.

'I have some comments from your supporters . . .' I started tentatively.

'Rangers have supporters. I have no supporters.' Never a word wasted, and no chance of a come-back.

'Can I read them to you . . . ?' I was cut off in mid-sentence.

'You'll be printing them, no doubt?'

'I will.'

'Then I'll read them in the paper. Good morning.'

I learned in one not-so-easy lesson that Scot Symon was a hard man to get through to. But he was the most blue-blooded, blue-nosed, fanatical Rangers' man I have ever known, and probably still is under the Partick Thistle exterior he now wears.

I had other confrontations with him that are worth recording, notably in Seville, when Rangers went to defend a 4-0 lead in the Cup Winners' Cup. It started out as a promising trip. A few minutes after the team checked in at the hotel, I was standing on the steps with director John Wilson, now back on the board after an absence, when a Spaniard sidled up and asked how many players there were in the party. In those days before five substitutes were allowed on the bench, Rangers had fourteen men with them. Inside ten minutes the friendly local citizen was back with three taxis, and fourteen luscious Spanish birds. He was chased for his life, birds and all.

There was an open-air banquet at midnight that night at which the hospitality was so liberal that Andy Stewart, a life-long Rangers' fan, gave one of his less memorable performances of 'A Scottish Soldier'. But that was the beginning. The match itself was chaotic, not least for the few sports writers who were there. It was the night of the Barcelona floods, telephone lines were down all over the place, and calls, if they ever arrived, were limited to six minutes. Six minutes, for the most astonishing scenes I had seen on a football field up to that point! Newcastle and Barcelona were still in the future.

Rangers lost 2-0, but still qualified, and it ended with 22 players throwing punches at each other. Willie Henderson broke a sprint record when Canario chased him with mayhem in his heart. Billy Ritchie may have saved the wee man's life by bringing Canario down in a rugby tackle. Scot Symon, trainer David Kinnear and reserve Doug Baillie kept trying to get out of the dug-out, whether to join in the fight or to try and stop it I never found out, but the local police kept kicking them back into it. It was not a pretty sight.

Getting that lot across in six minutes left my nerves in a slightly shredded condition, but it was not yet time for Andy Stewart to give out with another of his hit songs . . . 'The Battle's O'er'. There was still the banquet to come, and by this time the team got there, Scot Symon was visibly very upset and operating on a hair trigger, and I was about ready to blow up. There was still work to be done, checking on possible injuries sustained in the battle, still another attempt to be made at getting a call through to Glasgow. Maybe I made the mistake of going to trainer David Kinnear instead of going direct to Scot Symon at the top table. Whatever the reason, by the time I got to him, and before I had a chance to open my mouth, his finger slipped on the trigger and the balloon went up in public, to the delight and astonishment of the Spanish officials. I stood up to an attack that made my modest war experiences seem totally insignificant. The Ibrox boss tore painful strips off me in public.

I was conceding about six inches in height, and a couple of stones in weight, although that gap has been closed considerably since then, so I have always been glad of the quick intervention that stopped the verbal onslaught from taking on a more physical look.

There was a temporary reconciliation at the hotel later, where Mr Symon came as close to apologizing as he was ever likely to get, and we settled down in the lounge for a long football discussion, as if nothing had ever happened. Then he realized suddenly that as we talked, players were tip-toeing across the floor behind him, out into the night, although they were under curfew. He moved faster than I would have believed possible, and caught one of them on the front steps. And from the withering look I got as he convoyed his players back to their rooms, I was left in little doubt that he was convinced my job was to keep him occupied while the players sneaked out.

The ex-Rangers boss can be thanked, however, for one memorable experience that came my way, even if it was never meant to work out that way. We set out for Yugoslavia, to spy on Red Star Belgrade, next European opponents for Rangers. And Mr Symon was so intent on avoiding me, that I had to take the only unoccupied seat left on the plane at London. As it happened, the next seat was occupied by that charming and talented actress Yvonne Mitchell, who was filming in Yugoslavia at the time. She not only made an interesting travelling companion, but when we reached Zagreb, where incoming travellers go through immigration procedure, she shepherded me through with a smile at the guards, while Scot Symon and his companion had to queue.

And when we returned to Belgrade two weeks later for the game, I had dinner with her in the Metropole, and met her co-stars Omar Shariff and Kenneth Cope. However, back to the spy trip, which became memorable for other reasons. It was the trip home that will be remembered. Dr Obradovic, manager of Red Star, and one of the nicest fellows I ever met on the European circuit, insisted that we should fly from Sarajevo to Belgrade with his team, instead of taking the overnight sleeper. Since I had spent the previous night sharing a garlic-impregnated sleeper with three of the local inhabitants, I was amenable to a change in travel plans. So was Mr Symon.

But when we learned that the ancient DC-3 which was to take us was already full, and was about to take off from a grass runway in the twilight without the assistance of runway lights, I was ready to trade the flight for another helping of garlic. Dr Obradovic was having none of it. To make room for us, he sent his goalkeeper forward to sit in the spare pilot's seat. What happened to the spare pilot if there ever was one, I never found out. Another player was ordered into the toilet for the duration of the flight, which made life difficult for anyone suffering from the trots, for which Scot Symon and myself were both candidates by this time. A third player had to sit on a hamper in the corridor, and a flight that defied all the rules of air safety somehow tottered off the ground and into the air, to fly without further incident to Belgrade.

There were unbelievable and memorable trips with Celtic round about that time as well, even if some would be better forgotten.

When the Parkhead club were drawn to play against Dynamo Kiev in the European Cup, trouble was hiding just round the corner from the minute the late Sir Robert Kelly and his board took on the Kremlin and won looking round. Kiev at that time happened to be conveniently buried under about three feet of snow, a substance that was to become very familiar to Celtic before the trip was over, and since FIFA have still to acknowledge snowshoes as an acceptable item of football equipment, the Russians transferred to Tbilisi, in the deep south, where Rangers had played in a friendly some years earlier.

The trouble began when the Russians decreed that Celtic must fly in a Russian jet. Celtic thumbed their noses at the Kremlin, and demanded the right to take their own charter aircraft into Russia. The story made headlines throughout the world, and Celtic won the battle, not just for themselves, but for every other European team for future years. But the fun had just started.

Celtic won the first game at Parkhead comfortably, with Bobby

Murdoch scoring twice, and Tommy Gemmell adding a third. The Russians had lost a couple of battles but they were still waging war. Celtic's charter plane was forced to take the long way round via the north, instead of slipping in quietly through the backdoor in the south. It added a few hundred miles to the trip, but there was no depression in the Celtic ranks when the party took off from Prestwick on a January Sunday morning. The first leg took the team to Copenhagen, and two Russian navigators came on board to take over guidance of the plane to Moscow Airport. Then just twenty minutes out from Copenhagen's Kastrup Airport came the announcement that quietened the party and turned a few faces a sickly shade of grey.

The captain announced that a warning light indicated that the undercarriage had failed to lock in place, and that he was turning back to Copenhagen. He did not warn us that he intended to circle Kastrup Airport in the dark for an hour and a half to use up fuel. It was an agonizing performance, and when the plane finally headed for the runway, a few beads were being counted here and there, with even the 'Proddies' were hoping they would work. Cushions were used as personal shock-absorbers, and seat belts were never more tightly fastened. The plane drifted down on to the runway in a glorious anti-climax, and roared along with fire-engines and ambulances, blue lights flashing, as an escort.

A few hours later and the plane was back in the air, and arrived safely in Moscow where the temperature was minus twenty degrees centigrade, and the charter plane was flying no farther that night. The pilot, whose name was Sean Conway, which is as close as you can get to James Bond without looking down the barrel of a gun, had flown his allotted number of hours, and not even 007 could have persuaded him to take the plane into Tbilisi after dark. Next morning there was time for a brief look at the Bolshoi Theatre, and a walk round Red Square where dozens of elderly women were clearing the snow, and fighting a losing battle since it was coming down harder than they could shift it. At least it kept the unemployment figures down.

Although every English language paper had been confiscated before we were allowed to leave the plane ... I remember since it was Sunday, wondering what Kruschev would make of Oor Wullie and Hen Broon in the *Sunday Post* . . . I was allowed to take cine film unhindered, and at one point took a shot of Alex Cameron, then with the *Daily Mail*, posing in front of a political poster, making funny faces.

Two jovial Russian policemen enjoyed the joke, not that there were all that many jovial faces around in Moscow.

It took a couple of hours to defrost the BAC-111 enough to let it fly south into a different world, where smiling faces replaced the dourness of the north, where the sun shone, and the clothes were colourful, with delighted old men wearing the huge scone bonnets peculiar to that region. There were hundreds at the airport to look at the first British jet ever to fly in there, and after the party had disembarked, they stood in orderly queues to see over the plane, in through the back door and out at the front. And the Celtic baggage astonished them.

Apart from the four huge green trunks that carried the playing kit, the porters had to unload a dozen big cardboard containers. Celtic had taken with them four dozen prime Angus Steaks, one dozen chickens, 30 pounds of gammon, 64 lbs of assorted fruit, plus tea, butter, orange juice, cornflakes and cans of soup. And for much of the time spent in a far from luxurious hotel, Sean Fallon was in the kitchen supervising.

Russia, I have to admit, is not my favourite country for telephonic communications, and a host of other things not quite so important to a sports writer. Without a telephone, a football correspondent is a dead duck. There were a few dead, or nearly dead ducks lying around Tbilisi. In civilized hotels there is a central switchboard, with a line into every bedroom, and there is no problem in being paged around the hotel if you happen to be absent from the room when your call comes in.

Not in Russia. Not in a country that can carry on conversations with men in outer space. Every single room has its own telephone number. The call from a Scottish newspaper office goes through a series of international exchanges direct to a bedroom somewhere, and if the unhappy reporter who has waited hours for the call happens to have been caught short, an occupational hazard in the circumstances, and disappeared to the john for ten minutes, his luck is right out.

Another custom peculiar to Russia is the madame who holds court on every floor, sitting at a desk just outside the lift, as custodian of the keys. There is no central porter's desk. Come to think of it, there are no porters. Madame, usually stout, always dressed in black, never leaves her post, lets no one pass without handing in a key, and is always on the watch for undesirable visitors. Had the same system applied in Copenhagen, one or two players might still be allowed to play for Scotland instead of being banned for life.

In most hotels there are small bars on each floor, where hard booze by the glass or bottle, beer and soft drinks can be bought. Room service had not been invented yet, and the endless wait for calls which sometimes did not arrive at all, meant for some of the reporters a cliff-hanging existence spent mainly in the bar close to his room, to which the door was kept wide open. For a reporter, the phone that never rings is the first step towards dipsomania. A few first steps in that direction were taken in Tbilisi, where, by the end of the second day, most of the small party of pressmen had been reduced to a group of nervous near-alcoholics. The sight of one of the elder statesmen, a writer with many years of experience, rampaging around the hotel in shirt sleeves, red braces flying like danger signals, will never be forgotten by the others present.

It had taken the journalist concerned a lifetime in the game to build up his image as the unflappable, easy-going, nerveless type. It took three days to destroy the illusion for all time.

After 36 hours without a single call, he was reduced to sitting in the service bar next to his room, drawing on the local firewater for solace. The locals, in spite of the language barrier, caught the drama of the situation, and were ready to drink in sympathy, not that the Georgians ever needed an excuse anyway.

When the telephone finally did ring after hours of shattering silence, our now rapidly ageing colleague leapt off his stool, and dived for his room, only to find the door locked. The Celtic official with whom he shared the room was out on a shopping expedition with the key in his pocket! The Russian brandy took another beating. Out of such experiences are nervous breakdowns fashioned.

The game became secondary to the circumstances surrounding it. Celtic never looked like losing their three-goal lead, and when Tommy Gemmell equalized the goal scored earlier by Sabo, there was nothing left but the long flight home, and that was plenty. The temperature in Moscow was even lower than it had been on the way out, a shivering minus reading that put even brass monkeys at grave risk. The plane sat outside the terminal building, with two gun-toting, unsmiling Russian soldiers at each exit. They could only have been there to stop their own countrymen defecting to the West, because there was no danger of the Celtic boys slipping out to defect to the East. At that point Jock Stein cracked: 'The soldiers would defect, but they know they won't get far travelling with this party.' He didn't realize how right he was.

Hours later the plane took off for Copenhagen, and taking off for it was as close as we were going to get to that delightful city . . . it was in the days before unrestricted pornography. The flight had reached a point where every single announcement on the public address system became an adventure, or at the least, a surprise. The undercarriage barely had time to tuck itself into place . . . and lock properly this time . . . before the captain was telling everyone that Copenhagen was snowbound, and that the plane was now heading for Stockholm, which was also snowbound but not quite so badly. We got the uncomfortable feeling that we could be drifting around aimlessly with the snowflakes looking for a place to land until the aircraft ran out of fuel. Stockholm certainly was snowbound, and the party wondered what Copenhagen looked like because the drifts in Stockholm were six feet deep, and getting deeper all the time. However, 007 up front made it into the airport a darned sight easier than he was ever going to get out of it again.

The press corps dived for telephones, and since we were back in a civilized region, it was comparatively easy to get through to Glasgow even from a coin-box. Chairman Bob Kelly knew the problems, and insisted that no matter how long it took to get stories through, the plane was not taking off until we had finished. He could have saved his breath. Nobody was going anywhere that night, or for most of the next day. Twice the party was led out through the snowstorm, and twice back into the warmth of the lounge. The hydraulic systems were frozen up, the runways were losing the battle to stay clear, and the captain cheered everyone up when he said that an attempted take-off could lead to another Manchester United-Munich situation.

The night was spent in the Grand Hotel, and then back to the airport next morning to go through it all again. The nightmare of near take-offs and cancellations began all over again until Bob Kelly shouted enough. He dug in his heels and told the skipper that if he ever succeeded in getting his plane off the ground, which he doubted, Celtic Football Club would not be on board. He demanded a replacement aircraft, and got it. A plane due to fly from Frankfurt to Dublin was diverted to pick up the party, but the fates had not yet finished with Celtic.

The plane that had caused all the trouble took off empty long before the replacement, and had landed safely in Dublin hours before Celtic reached Prestwick after midnight. And having arrived safely after more than 36 hours of frustration and worry, the plane flew on to Dublin without unloading the Celtic kit hampers.

If Russia holds its terrors for sportswriters, there have been nasty moments in more attractive countries. Show me a football writer who has covered a game in Lisbon, and I'll show you a guy with ulcers. They do have a telephone system in Portugal, but I have never been convinced that the instrument sitting in front of me on a ledge in the press-box is connected to anywhere else in the world. And somehow in this city where contact with Glasgow becomes a matter for prayer and crossed fingers, there is always drama that should be pouring back over the hot line. Celtic's most famous occasion, the European Cup Final against Inter Milan, was comparatively straightforward, because it kicked off in late afternoon and there was time to spare, all of it needed. The telephone that cost the *Daily Express* £30 to install has still to ring, but there was telex as a stand-by.

But night games in the Portuguese capital start usually around ten o'clock, and few of the men charged with the responsibility of keeping the Scottish public informed will forget the night Celtic played Benfica, with a comfortable three-goal lead to defend. It was a nostalgic return, staying in the Palaccio Hotel again, the Estoril HQ for the historic final a year or two earlier. I got off to a bad start, in bed with a chill after risking a dip in an allegedly heated swimming pool, in the month of November. When Jock Stein, with some camp followers, visited my bedroom carrying a huge bunch of flowers borrowed from the lounge, and singing 'Nearer my God to Thee' it did nothing to help my recovery.

But I made it to the match and often wished I hadn't. Eusebio and Graca scored before half-time to put Celtic on a tightrope, and there was a miracle . . . the phones were working. Political intervention somewhere along the line had guaranteed uninterrupted service for the duration of the match. Celtic fought a rear-guard action throughout the second half, but two minutes into injury time Diamintino pushed the ball over the line. In the press-box, nobody knew whether the referee's whistle had signalled a goal or the end of the game. Were Celtic through or not? There was no way of knowing until the teams came back out to play an extra half-hour. It was then the writers realized that every phone in the press-box was dead. Service had been guaranteed for the duration of the game and nobody in the international exchange had ever heard of extra time.

Fingernails were nibbled down to the knuckle, and faces got whiter and whiter as the 30 minutes dragged on, with no further score. And the phones were still dead while the drama continued in the referee's room below the stand. It was a toss-up.

Billy McNeill, Jock Stein, Coluna and Otto Gloria, the Benfica boss, gathered round the referee. In those days there was no question of replays, or penalty kick deciders. The referee explained that he would toss the coin twice. The first toss would decide who had the right to call first in the toss that really mattered. He asked if everyone understood. Jock Stein said he did, but it was the first thing the referee had done all night that he understood. Billy McNeill won the first toss. Next-time up, the coin hit the floor, rolled against the referee's boot, and then round in a full circle before falling over. And it fell the right way for Celtic. To complicate the issue for the writers who were still trying frantically to contact Glasgow, a roar from the crowd seemed to indicate that Benfica had won. The phones started working again just in time to get the facts across, but a few writers cut their life expectancy by a year or two that night.

By the time Rangers got to the same city to play Sporting Lisbon, the rules had been changed, but someone forgot to tell the Dutch referee Van Ravens. Not only did away goals count double, as they had done for some time, but the rule had recently been changed so that goals scored away from home in extra time also counted double. Rangers travelled with a 3-2 lead, having been three up at one stage at Ibrox before slipping near the end. Sporting Lisbon went ahead twice, and twice Colin Stein equalized, to keep Rangers ahead on aggregate. Then Ronnie McKinnon was carried off with a broken leg, and Gomez headed in the winner in the 64th minute, to make them level over the two games.

It was back to the ulcers for the men in the press-box as the game went into extra time.

Willie Henderson scored after ten minutes. Perez equalized from the penalty spot five minutes later. When the final whistle blew with the score still level, the referee put himself into the history books, and Rangers into the quiz books, by ordering penalty kicks to be taken, and the reporting gang died a thousand deaths. I knew the referee was wrong, having studied the change in rules just before setting out on the trip. I asked the office to contact SFA secretary Willie Allan for confirmation, but he could not give it because he did not have the rules with him at home. Meantime Rangers were going through the most miserable five minutes of their history. They missed five penalties. Tommy McLean even got two chances because the keeper moved the first time, and he missed both times. That is what put the new question into the quiz books ... which team missed five penalties and still won the tie?'

Because Rangers had certainly won, in spite of Mr Van Ravens. Willie Waddell showed him the rule book without shaking him. It was next day before UEFA finally confirmed that the referee had been wrong, and Rangers were through to the next round.

Rangers, of course, went on to beat Bayern Munchen and Moscow Dynamo in the infamous Barcelona final, which was another trip to remember. I sat in the open press-box that night after the field had been invaded, and Rangers' fans had fought their running battle with the police, thumping bravely at a typewriter, surrounded by hostile fans . . . hostile because the only story they wanted sent back to Glasgow was that of Rangers' triumph, and not the bloody aftermath. Every time I reached the end of the first paragraph, a hand came over my shoulder, pulled the paper out of the machine and a gruff voice informed me that there was no way I would send that back to Glasgow.

In the end I had to lift the phone and dictate a story to Glasgow in the quietest voice they could possibly hear. Meantime, down in the press-room below the stand, colleague Jimmy Sanderson had won a battle to get himself a telephone, and in totally chaotic circumstances, with hundreds milling around, and the story changing every minute, was sending a front page news story back to Glasgow. He had to fight off competitors who wanted to use the phone, and knowing Jimmy, they probably included the fellow who belonged to the instrument in the first place. The noise was unbelievable. And he was suddenly interrupted.

Our sports editor, now retired, had travelled to the game on a charter flight, simply as a spectator. In the middle of the maelstrom in the press-room, he suddenly appeared at Jimmy Sanderson's side, and heaven knows how he got there. He tried to speak to Jimmy, but had to give up. A few minutes later Jimmy found a note stuck under his nose. It said simply . . . : 'why no lap of honour.' To his credit Jimmy did not even stop in mid-sentence. His look was enough, and the boss melted away quietly into the crowd.

A new legend emerges from almost every trip. Young men grow old, older men grow still older. Ulcers are born, and the foundations of coronaries are laid. Friendships are sometimes strained, and tempers lost.

But it is still better than working.

# Heads We Win

JOHN FAIRGRIEVE

There are peaks of nobility to which I would not aspire, and so it was with admiration, awe and envy that I noted the tale about the youth who took part in a rugby match as both player and referee, and permitted his own side to lose.

The occasion was a third-fifteen match, true, but that doesn't make a lot of difference. The appointed referee didn't turn up. The player in question, apparently the senior man present, assumed two parts, wing-three-quarter and ref. It could only have happened in rugby. His own side was beaten 11-18, and, so far as is known, there were no recriminations afterwards.

Now it is well enough recognized that, for every man of stature, there are a thousand Lilliputians hopefully hanging around with the grappling-irons, and I would counsel that player-referee to beware. He has set himself a standard which, in later life, will be difficult to maintain.

I speak from experience. I, too, have both played and refereed in the same match, though, not simultaneously, and in the authorized version of the game, which means the ball was round. It would be inaccurate of me to say that I failed to resist the obvious temptation. It was less a temptation than a golden opportunity.

The match was an inter-village one in the Lothians, and there was considerable ill-feeling about at the time. By assiduous flattery of our captain, a face-worker of the highest calibre, and a centre half eminently capable of worrying a Sherman tank, I was picked at outside right, where it was thought I could do little real harm.

I wore rubber gym-shoes, a common gamble in such matches. These had an obvious advantage over pit-boots in the matter of pace, but the odds remained no better than evens. Implicit in the gamble was the necessity for avoiding physical contact at all costs, for, by some weird but apparently immutable quirk of fate, one's immediate opponent would invariably choose rotten great boots.

I lost, because their centre half, moving across with terrifying speed, though shod like a deep-sea diver, got me very early, as he was perfectly entitled to do. It was clear to me that the left back entertained ambitions about an encore, and for the remainder of the half, my interest in the proceedings was academic.

Half-time came with the score 3-2 for them. We were playing Seven Up, which meant that the first side to score seven were the winners. Unorthodox, no doubt, but nobody had a watch.

It was while everyone was lying down, smoking Woodbines, that I suggested refereeing the second half, seeing that my left leg felt broken.

This put the opposition in a dilemma. They could and did – without loss of face – ask what we wanted a referee for, but they could hardly have expressed undue suspicion. That would have been interpreted as fear of defeat, and by ten men, at that. They agreed. They were surly about it, but they agreed. I took over, with a Boy Scout whistle.

The equalizer was easy enough, for it was expected that goalkeepers should be charged into the net: unlike nowadays, when referees are brainwashed into penalizing a centre who dares to look nastily at a goalie. They weren't too pleased, admittedly. They made the point that their goalkeeper had been about three feet in the air, and on the way down with the ball, when our inside-left hit him, but I waved them away brusquely.

The rot set in, I suppose, with the penalty. What annoyed them was the fact that I was in the other penalty-area, being puffed, at the moment of giving the award. Their goalkeeper called me a silly blind bugger, but I sorted him out when he saved the kick. 'Take it again,' I ordered. 'He moved.'

'I bugger-all moved,' he said. Maybe he didn't have much of a vocabulary, but he was a wiry, mean-looking lad and known for an ability to de-cap bottles with his teeth. I became a little concerned but, encouraged by the whole-hearted approval of our captain, persevered. He didn't save, the second time.

That made the score 4-3, and there didn't seem much point in half-measures now. A few minutes later, I made it 5-3.

Frankly, it looked a good enough goal, anyway. A trifle high, perhaps, but there was no cross-bar, and if there was a doubt, I knew who was getting the benefit of it.

They had now reached the conclusion that they were definitely struggling, and about the only thing they couldn't say was that they were playing twelve men.

They said many other things.

It was that goalkeeper who spoiled it. In our next attack, he ignored the ball completely, and kicked our centre on the kneecap. 'Off,' I said, with dignity. He then came for me at a dead run, and was halted only because the centre, though hopping, managed to get him on the side of the head with a swinging right.

The game was now past saving, but the contest continued. We had the best of it, mainly because the captain's two brothers, hitherto frustrated spectators, came on to the park and helped out.

Nobody was badly hurt, however, which was just as well; the National Coal Board had just started a system of paying six shifts for every five worked. I heard later that some busybody phoned the local copper, who was no fool and preferred to consider the affair a private quarrel.

My happiest memory of the whole day is that I was never blamed personally by either side, it being felt that I had done my duty as I saw it. The replay was held the following Sunday, and they let me watch.

# World Cup '74

IAN ARCHER

It has to start somewhere for everyone, this daft, wild, extra-ordinary notion that happiness is a Scottish lap of honour and that the greatest, most hysterical happiness would be a Scottish lap of honour on a World Cup final day, England having just retired to the dressing rooms, not just beaten, but destroyed, humiliated, thrashed, gubbed. It is possible to put a personal date to an obsession which has scarred too much of a lifetime already.

On 26 September 1961, Scotland played Czechoslovakia at Hampden Park and St Paul saw no greater light on the road to Damascus. I took a girl who meant a lot to that match which sort of proves how innocent you can be, how much you need to know about what is right and proper about this game. We stood holding hands high on the terraces, but that lovers grip was separated three times when those tiny dots in dark blue went up the far end of the pitch and scored.

She went out of my life. That team, arranged in traditional syntax, stayed – Brown, McKay and Caldow, Crerand, McNeill and Baxter, Scott, White, St John, Law and Wilson. Law started one goal in his own penalty area, scored it in the other and while I can't – although I sometimes want to – remember the exact outline of that girl's neck, then every caress of that goal intrudes upon the consciousness at least once a month. It was a World Cup qualifying game, two months later Scotland bungled the play-off in Brussels and Czechoslovakia were the beaten finalists in Chile the following year (Brazil 3 Czechoslovakia 1, in Santiago, Amarildo, Zito, Vava for Brazil, Masopust for the Czechs).

Two years later, on the attainment of my majority and through the courtesy of an Uncle's five-pound note, that interest hardened to addiction. I reached Wembley sober, the last time the nerve has permitted such a luxury, and Scotland beat England 2-1. They, the people who decant on to overnight trains, wobble to Wembley, throw whisky into empty stomachs and fall down six of those steep terracing steps at a time, continue to say it was Jim Baxter's match. He shuffled past Armfield for the first and soft-footed a penalty for the second goal but for all that, it wasn't his game. It was Davie Wilson's. Pressed into full back service after Smith's tackle had broken Eric Caldow's leg, he was magnificent. (Years later, I gave him a lift from Edinburgh to Glasgow and was too shy to ask about it – and why, when grown men meet a footballer do they gaze in awe, stammer with embarrassment and then steal off to share with others the secret of close, real, proximity to a hero?)

So I was 21 and nowhere to go, except Ibrox the occasional Saturday to watch Baxter, who could dance on eggshells and make the ball laugh, tease like a toreador and who once, in his early Rangers days, caused the subway to be stopped outside Copland Road. 'That yin couldnae tackle a plate of mince and tatties' said one who had not been initiated into the mysteries of Baxter's vision of his craft while others fell upon him fighting and throwing bottles.

In 1967, Jim Baxter went to Wembley again for Bobby Brown's first match as manager and in the dressing room Brown, anxious, nervous and desperate to succeed, started giving a tactics talk as long, as complex and as well meaning as a last tutorial before final exams. The man whom Willie McNaught had discovered lay about reading the *Daily Express* and ultimately the manager, knowing the unbeaten World Champions were tying their laces across the corridor, asked: 'Anything to add, Jim.'

'Aye, see this English lot, they can play nane.'

Five years later, there was a bad match against England at Hampden Park. Bremner and Ball seemed intent not so much on going over the ball, but over the man as well. Scotland lost, which is always bad, but the match was sour enough to be deeply offensive. The lines of retreat led to Paisley Road West, where Baxter runs a bar which cascades with beer, football talk and lines of men just gazing at the owner, standing in the corner drinking and keeping a tidy eye on the profits. We talked of friends and things when a man with an English rosette came in and considering the company and his uniform, made the boldest advance through a minefield since the Normandy landings. 'I couldn't leave Scotland without shaking your hand,' he said and shook hands and went and the bevying, good, wholesome, any Saturday and not England-day bevying, began in earnest.

Which all mattered when the taxi, a clapped out twenty-year-old Plymouth Sedan without springs, driven by an Egyptian called Kelly, turned off the main Cairo-Alexandria road and took the last three miles to a place called Damanhour, a small town among the irrigated heartlands of the Nile Delta. Scotland, after all those years, were in the World Cup and so, too, were Zaire, who were playing Guinea at this God forsaken place. Willie Ormond, the manager, had come to watch them. He sat down in the front row, took out his diary, marked in it headings like 'Team Plan', 'Blend', 'Skills', and watched these aloof Africans. Ten minutes later he snapped it shut, wiped the sweat from his forehead in a temperature the hot side of a hundred, and smiled. 'They cannae play,' he said. It was the start of the best and the worst time for Scottish football.

Scottish football is all about what the soul of the country needs, its heart remembers and its mind cares to forget. Round its western industrial belt, where they dig coal, build ships and make iron, they made the playing and the watching of this game their own towards the end of the last century, a Saturday afternoon something, a bitter, narrow dedication by hard men on open ground, a release and a commitment. They coined grand romantic names for clubs throughout the country, Queen of the South, Heart of Midlothian, Third Lanark, Partick Thistle. They had an idea that if the bruising of life could be placed in straight conjunction with the freedom of the birds to fly, then man could be ennobled. It needed a ba' for a tanner, a group of comrades, a

real or imagined enemy, later a shout of 'We Arra Peepel' and they
were away.

Soon, some 60,000 were watching when Scotland played England, always, to their minds, an effete country, represented on
the field by those old Corinthians, la-de-da, amateurs, worthless.
And as time went by and England prospered from that industrial
revolution, in Scotland, half a country, half a hostile reservation,
neglected, deprived, besotted, ill-housed, the pangs of nationalism
– the right to self-government – began to rear at Hampden. 'Not
a country, eh? We'll fucking show youse. Fitba, that's all we
know or get. Bastards. It's oor oil. See the English. Nae worth
a barrowload of shite.'

To a background of such dulcet encouragement, Scotland
qualified for this 1974 World Cup after an absence of sixteen
years in which the trophy had been held in turn by Brazil twice,
and England, who had cheated to acquire it. In the qualifying
stages Denmark had been beaten twice, and on a climactic night
in Glasgow, that old score had been settled against Czechoslovakia
with a winning goal from Joe Jordan and a nostalgic, worthwhile
contribution from Denis Law, once a gazelle. The 82,000 had
screeched 'Bonnie Scotland'. Willie Ormond, who had inherited
the job from Tommy Docherty, was hoisted shoulder high and
every last one on the terraces promised to pay his dues and come
to West Germany for the final stages – and many kept that pledge.

(Three weeks later, on the same night that Scotland were com-
pleting the formality of the section in Bratislava, the joy was
complete when England failed to qualify. The team watched that
match on television in their hotel. Law could not suffer the
closing minutes as the English battered on the doors of the Polish
goal. He went to the cludgie and when an English journalist came
in at the end to tell him the news, he said 'That's bad luck.' And
when the English journalist went out and only three Scots were
left by the wash-hand basins, he screamed: 'You———beauty.')
It was going to be us, Jummy, on our own suh, against all thae
Huns, ken, and 'Six foot two, eyes of blue, big Jim Holton's after
you – da-da-DA-DA-da-da-da DA-da.'

Scotland's World Cup squad left for the competition on the last day of May 1974. They were to play Belgium and Norway en route. Ten days earlier there had been one of those marvellously funny and painful incidents which haunt our game. At Largs, where the squad was staying before the English match at Hampden, early morning strollers had noticed a small boat heading in the direction of Millport, containing a small man who was said to be holding a single oar above his head shouting 'Scotland, Scotland.' Soon the lifeguards were called and at roughly 6 am, almost the entire World Cup squad were on the beach persuading Jimmy Johnstone that the task in hand was the winning of a little tournament in West Germany and not a singlehanded crossing of the Atlantic. It was a cartoonist's delight, a silly story out of the silly season and the more perceptive watchers realized that it boded well. On the Saturday, England were beaten by two clear goals, Johnstone made a gesture to the press box as he retired, and on such an amicable note, the Scottish caravan departed on a British Airways charter flight weighed down by champagne for Ghent, Oslo, and later Frankfurt. Some said that there was a certain lack of professionalism shown at Largs and that footballers should be in their beds at six o'clock in the morning, but the truth is that these events were Scottish and good. If your average Glaswegian was asked to climb mount Everest in a fortnight's time, he'd go and have a few drinks, turn up at Base Camp wearing nothing but a Rangers' scarf and a pair of jeans, bum a packet of fags and then start climbing. Scotland's footballers never really believed they were in a World Cup until they saw the whites of Zairois eyes in the first match and by then, it was a bit too late. There is no other way.

Scotland stayed at 'The Holiday Inn', Ghent, before their first warm-up match, a suitable choice of boarding house considering the Largs business. It happened to be in the middle of a Spaghetti Junction, Ormond had a row over the lack of porters to carry in the hundred-weights of equipment and on the next night the side lost 2-1 to Belgium. Raymond Goethals, manager of the enemy, covered his eyes at the end of the match and said: 'That is how Scotland played – like blind men.' Our Mr Ormond said:

'The referee was a homer and the linesman was terrible.' The party then left, early Sunday June 2nd for Norway, and British Airways, sensing the tastes of the hangers-on, broke all records for champagne serving.

The hotel in Oslo was named 'The Panorama' and was soon christened 'The Paranoia' for it was really a students' hostel with one wing converted for visitors, who slept in beds which were all constructed in the belief that no one grows bigger than Jimmy Johnstone. Scotland were due to play Norway on the Thursday and much happened in this small hiatus.

On Sunday afternoon, Jimmy Johnstone and Billy Bremner shared a refreshment in the downstair's bar of the hotel, a not exceptional occurrence among footballers at that time of the week. When Ormond was called from his tea, both were in melodious form and some unfriendly remarks were aimed by the manager to the men. The next day, the Scottish Football Association severely reprimanded both of them, who in turn offered their 'profuse apologies'. With a glass of fresh orange juice costing £1.25 in that bar and a pint of lager some 60p it seemed to one onlooker that the captain and winger had shown some canniness in quenching their thirst.

This all meant good lively copy for homesick journalists and every sub-editor bound to a desk back home it seemed wanted to know whether Scotland were wandering about Europe in a state of alcoholic oblivion. Some were – but they were not players. Copies of the different papers reaching Oslo then started causing trouble because the manager banned the press from a training session, instructed his players not to talk to the typewriting brigade, told one journalist – John Mackenzie – that what he had written was a 'disgrace' and the same dour reporter was officially banned by the SFA. A brewery (it had to be a brewery) flew out and offered the squad £110,000 if they won the World Cup.

On the Thursday, Scotland did manage a win against Norway, Kenny Dalglish, coming on as substitute, scoring the winning goal to add to Jordan's earlier header. Back in the bar, most of the squad enjoyed a quiet drink and sang some supporters' songs.

I kept dropping things. We had been away a week and were wondering if the money would last. There was brandy in a high heidyins room at four in the morning and when someone remembered there was a World Cup starting in a week's time, the chorus was 'Easy, Easy, we'll skoosh it.'

Scotland's World Cup party reached Frankfurt on Friday June 7th to find the competition under siege. Forty uniformed guards stood around the aircraft, while 40 more, dressed in mufti with tell-tale bulges under their left armpits stood around the terminal building. A garish charabanc drove them some 30 miles to a grand hotel called the Erbismuhle in a valley among the Taunus Hills. It was a secret place and the bomb squad had checked every bedroom before they arrived. Zaire were far to the north in the Rhineland but Brazil and Yugoslavia, the other group opponents, were near at hand. The team met Adolf, the security guard who was to make sure that the Israeli incident of the 1972 Olympics did not happen again. Adolf was a playful man: 'Hit me there,' he would ask Billy Bremner, pulling his tee shirt up to expose a hard gut. Bremner would do so. Adolf would then laugh.

Ormond seemed overawed. He had been chosen as Scottish manager after Tommy Docherty left for Manchester United and Willie Cunningham of Falkirk had declined the job. The events in Oslo had taken some revenge on the stomach and the nerve of a wee patriot from Musselburgh, a friend of the fishermen there, a good listener to other people's renditions of the Burns ballads. He was missing Margaret, his wife.

The squad was greeted with champagne cocktails, the camera shutters clicked and a Brazilian journalist asked: 'Are they sober today?' There was a week of waiting, of patient training, of last-minute commercial bargaining, of sleepless nights and long, unending afternoons around the scrabble Board, the ping-pong table and the sun terrace. The Scotland squad went deathless quiet that week, upset by the publicity, aggrieved by the amount of sponsored money they were missing, unsure of their global status.

Here, in the long length of a risen country, the great had established themselves. Brazil, with a paterfamilias for every player, possessed Rivelino, Jairzinho. They were backed by millions of government money and acted like kings on the throne. Holland had brought Cruyff and thousands were waiting to cross the border in orange support. West Germany's footballers could not go to the toilet off-the-record and there were smashing photographs of Mr Beckenbauer at home, clean and pressed, surrounded by his family, a man of substance, part of an economic miracle. And who were we?

In that waiting week, Scots came to think of themselves as just a bunch of scrubbers and so the last, much needed ingredient – the imagined insult – was added to the team's equipment. So, we're not a country, we haven't got our own stamps, they won't accept our money, we haven't even got our own anthem. Who cares? 'We arra peepel.' Piss up a close, ye cannae shove your grannie aff a bus, these are my mountains and this is my glen, Bonnie Scotland, we'll support you ever more. Gie us another drink hen, a bigyin, we'll take a few down WITH us, so we wull. See those fans, mortal, stocious, miroculous, steamboats, magic. Zaire – black bastards, Brazil, coons, Yugoslavs, gipsies. They'll never get that plane down at Abbotsinch with the Cup. So help me, I'll lie on the runway. This Hun tells me to leave so I banjo him don't I. Who won the war?

On Sunday Ormond took the team down to the Wald Stadium Frankfurt, where the later group matches were to be played. He hoped for a private session, but word got out and the man who used to stop every day at Glenfarg for his bacon sandwich before training started at St Johnstone said: 'We've never had a crowd like this at Muirton, except for Old Firm games.'

On Tuesday, the nerves showed in public. The team trained on a little local pitch in the mountains. They would not start until a fee had been negotiated with a television company whose ironic representative was Billy Wright, the English yeoman. When they stripped they started a match as coarse as any in the Ayrshire junior world. John Blackley cut Jimmy Johnstone down, Jim Holton lunged at Peter Cormack while Martin Buchan (the quiet one with the guitar) locked limbs with Joe Jordan in a spectacularly uncivil meeting. 'It shows the needle's in,' Ormond said afterwards, the best omen since Johnstone's Hampden Park V-sign.

Wednesday was easy and Billy Bremner, publicly quiet but quietly hopping since Oslo, was persuaded to issue a formal call to arms. 'If I didn't think Scotland would win this World Cup, do you think I'd be here? I'd be on a beach in Majorca. I'm not a raging Scottish Nationalist saying that. I'm hard heided, me. We'll win it.' The team left the Taunus for Dortmund and Friday's match while the World Cup opened with a dull, predictable draw between Brazil and Yugoslavia in Frankfurt, a bad game and a poor result for Scotland. There, a Glasgow voice shouted as the teams trooped off – 'Rubbish.'

Dortmund was an agony. The cool of recent days gave way to a hot sticky evening. The mouths of the Scottish players went dry as they warmed up outside the main stadium and some could not run at all. Stomachs were bare and every breath seemed to rub angrily against the wall of the lungs. From nowhere, fans started appearing in kilts but no shirts, trailing the banners, drinking that city's famous beer out of plastic cups, filing into the ground behind a piper and they too were nervous, out of place, guests at a posh party in the wrong dress before the first loosening refreshment.

Ormond had named his strongest side. Harvey of the English accent and chickens in his back yard, kept goal. Jardine, the smart Ranger, and McGrain, the shy Celt, were the full backs. Bremner looked pale and drawn, suddenly old, suddenly responsible, the man from Stirling. Big Jim Holton from Lesmahagow, breathed in deeply as the Scots fans gave 'God Save the Queen' some desperate laldy. Blackley's red hair stood on end. Lorimer looked the quiet professional, Dalglish inscrutable, Jordan and Hay impassive. Denis Law was loving it because soon he would be gone.

The Zairois stood with their arms across chests for their own anthem, wearing simmets under their green jerseys and who knows what went through their minds, so far from home, cold on this humid night. Only they did not look like totems, this team of Kazadis, Mukombos and Kakakos. What followed was a strange, unreal match as the eyes focused not on the broad global sweep of the event itself, but the small rituals of the playing surface. It was, at last, fitba.

'They cannae play,' Ormond had said those weeks previously in Damanhour, but in parts of the match they gave a fair impression of having absorbed the basic lessons, south of the equator. In the 26th minute Scotland took the lead when McGrain's cross found Jordan's head and Lorimer, screwing his body round finally disposed of the ball into the back of the net. A few minutes later Jordan ran through unchallenged and maybe offside to give Scotland its second goal from a Bremner free kick. 'Easy, Easy,' Scotland's unofficial World Cup anthem, was shouted by the fans – but it wasn't.

In the second half Zaire came across the Sahara desert in football terms and we wondered if those rumours about a witch doctor in the camp were correct. Something had happened in the dressing room. Harvey needed to make two horizontal saves from Mayanga and Ndaye to protect the lead and Bremner ignored instructions to go for more goals in order to stop the match and find safety in collective midfield numbers.

That decision is still debated when the World Cup is relived. We needed goals, but it was hot and well, these Africans were playing a bit and the captain did what he thought best. 2-0 didn't look enough on the night and wasn't later, but Bremner was brought up in a hard school where points come first and embellishments later. It was Scotland's first ever victory in the World Cup, we had won, we had argued, we had aged, and back in the Taunus the following day, we relaxed. Scotland now belonged to this tournament.

The programme announced the next match on the Wednesday as 'Brasilien v Schottland'. Christ, I could hardly write the next three days, but dribbled on about a tie between South America's most admired country and Europe's most misunderstood nation. On Tuesday, 24 hours before the match, eating was impossible, the doctor dispensed the sleeping pills. There were rude noises made when we discovered Harold Wilson would be present in the Wald Stadium, we discussed Calvinism, the booze, and the burden that those Scottish players would carry into that tree-lined park.

We should have been adult enough to dismiss such theories, to have reminded ourselves it was just a match, but we knew that defeat would send us home bitter inward-looking and with another grudge to hold. We wanted victory so that the cry would be heard: 'IT'S US. WE'RE HERE.' Scots by the thousands were arriving down town, plastering the city with their shouts, apologizing that they had no passports, roistering in the red light Kaiserstrasse, waiting.

One moment we considered Brazil in its historical football context, World Cup winners in 1958, 1962 and 1970, permanent possessors of the Old Jules Rimet trophy, now replaced by a little piece of solid goldware. We thought of Pele, Tostao, Gerson, Vava, others of the past. They had taken from Hampden Park the all-time world crowd record when Maracana was erected and filled. Then we were either despondent or braggart.

The next moment we noticed the Gods had gone, that even with Jairzinho and Rivelino Brazil had played poorly at Hampden Park twelve months previously, that they had looked uncertain in that opening match, that the samba bands were making not much noise in this oompah land. Then we were quietly confident.

It was the second view that the team and manager held. Having dipped their toe in the water against Zaire, they now felt they could swim the Channel. It was almost a modest side which tackled Brazil, a side suddenly grown in stature that believed not so much in a country and a cause, but preferred to recall its own tradesworthiness, a conscious belief that years of training, learning, playing would serve them well enough to win. At the Erbismuhle, the mood changed imperceptibly from one of cocksure defiance to sedate assessment. Correctly, properly and in due course, they said they would win.

It was one hell of a long dry day, just waiting. Lunch seemed to last hours and nothing was eaten. A full three hours before the match started, we were standing outside the ground like bairns: 'Please let us in Muster'. Those fans came from every corner, looking heavy eyed, awkward, as if they had already played a game. Slowly the ground filled . . . and three hours later my night was finished with this dispatch.

Scotland o Brazil o

Scotland the Brave . . . but Scotland the bitterly disappointed. They played all the old tunes of glory here tonight but somehow could not force Brazil to abdicate the crown they have worn since they became World Champions in Mexico four years ago.

After a time no patriot will ever forget, a solitary piper now plays a final skirl in a deserted stadium and somehow the slow sad cadences that echo around the empty terraces seem to match the mood of a people who came, competed and so nearly conquered.

Scotland should have beaten Brazil in this Wald Stadium and beaten them by the width of the Atlantic Ocean which separates the one country who learned the game so quickly and another nation who copied the lesson so well. It remains a mystery why they did not do so.

To the tales of folklore which football people hand down so carefully from generation to succeeding generation, we must add the events of this day in 1974 to a list which stretches over a century. During a second half of astonishing intensity, Scotland battered at the gates of Heaven as if they were sinners determined to be allowed to pass. But no one would open them.

During that time, Peter Lorimer could have won this match three times over and the ball bobbed about the Brazilian goalmouth so frequently that some South American magic was being used to keep it the wrong side of that important white line. We shuffled in our seats, rose from them in expectancy on numerous occasions but were eventually and cruelly not to be rewarded.

Only a statement more often heard on a cold and windy Saturday afternoon at Firhill or Shawfield rather than in a sophisticated European stadium sums up our attitude – at the end of the night as the floodlights dim and the cool wind sends litter shuffling up and down the terraces: 'We wiz robbed.' Of all the men who almost fashioned the greatest result in Scottish footballing history, I pick Billy Bremner, the greatest of a long line of captains who wear their hearts on a dark blue jersey. Involved, impassioned and irrational, he almost single-handedly reduced Brazil's declining standards into a raggle taggle collection of dispirited players.

He played, quite simply, the best match of his brilliant career, but there were ten others. Harvey was solidly reliable in goal, Jardine and McGrain conscientious full backs and constant over-lappers. Before the match, the fans chanted of our centre half as they stared cold-eyed into the faces of the Brazilians, who were tangoing in the stands to the tunes of their home-made bands: 'Six foot two, eyes of blue, big Jim Holton will eat you'. An hour later, he had had the entire Brazilian attack for dinner.

Buchan patrolled Jairzinho so heavily as to render him in-visible, while, just forward of that battle, Hay was enormously virile, snapping at heels, and shooting almost as frequently and as powerfully as Lorimer. Dalglish and Morgan were the quiet ones but they, in fairness, chased every ball as if it were their last, harried Brazilians into elementary mistakes of technique and generally deserved a place which Willie Ormond might have given to others.

In attack, Lorimer's presence was almost murderous as three times the Brazilian goalkeeper Leao saved shots and then in-spected his hands and looked anxiously towards the touchline as if calling for splints to mend his damaged fingers. Jordan seemed to climb up every time the ball was aimed across the goalmouth, as if trying to reach the helicopters which hovered about the ground on their various security missions.

'With a little luck, we would have won,' Willie Ormond said after the match and that statement is undeniably true. There has been a strange miscarriage of justice in front of an audience which rose to only one team at the end. Proudly, one can say that they were not applauding Brazil, now the discredited world cup champions. They were sympathizing with Scotland who had been abused by all the Fates.

The ref was terrible. Oh, Davie Hay, one of those shots should have gone in, son. Oh, Billy, when that ball went off your knee just wide, I died a thousand deaths. Oh, Peter, that keeper was a diddy, yet he got all of your shots. How did he do it? Did you hear about Billy at the end. This big Pereira comes up and says 'You Prima'. Billy's going to do him. Their full back speaks English. 'No' he says, 'He means you're the best': 'Great' says Billy 'Tell the black man he can play a bit himself.' I want to go home. I want a drink. No, I don't want to go home, no I don't want a drink. Absofuckinglutely diafuckingbolical.

That night was the best and the worst moment of the best and the worst time for Scottish football. The team came back to their hotel, sad, proud, big and still in the World Cup. It was down to the one equation that a Scot can understand. One match, one victory, qualification and, of course, the taken-for-granted business of winning the cup a little later. Only Yugoslavia barred the way on Saturday.

They were entertained back at the Erbismuhle by Billy Connolly, that Glasgow comedian who had died, like 10,000 others, on the terraces. Bremner impersonated Sinatra, Johnstone sang 'Amazing Grace', his tune, and Ormond had his well deserved bucket. A few hours' sleep and Thursday became the tournament's most convivial day, a little Sabbatical.

We sat on the terrace at the hotel, supping giant pints. Jim Holton passed by and we kidded him on about one precious moment when he had killed a kick-out stone dead, lassooing the ball to his foot. 'I always told you gentlemen, class will tell.' Ormond, for the first time, publicly said that Scotland should have its own national anthem and revealed that his after-match talk was short and sweet: 'You're the greatest'. His wife was due on a charter. He had come to West Germany secretly wondering if Musselburgh to Munich was too long a distance to travel in too short a time. Now he sat back and relaxed, opening at random some of the 1,000 telegrams from Scotland which said they had cried the previous night.

All Scotland was now infested with a kind of certain madness. Work had stopped and one newspaper had carried a picture of Argyle Street Glasgow during the Brazil match. It was as totally deserted as it would be if the missiles were on their way from Russia with love. Thousands wondered just how a photographer could have been found to take the snapshot.

The Scottish National Party claimed that if an election was due the following week, they would win in a landslide and if custom posts were needed at Carlisle, there would have been no shortage of volunteers. Billy Bremner became the housewives' choice, so small, looking a little undernourished, always seen on the television in action as if saying 'It's ma ba'.' In their hundreds fans trooped through Glasgow airport, were poured on to planes and poured off again at Frankfurt, growing taller and more dignified by the passing minute, there for history to be enacted.

This was not to be war against the Yugoslavs, but merely the singing ceremony that would put Scotland on the world stage which, in the view of the punters, had not been the way of things since the signing of the Act of Union in 1707. Some flew, a lot drove (one van was completely covered in tartan wallpaper) and a few hitched, like the man who had been at Hamilton Races, come up with a treble, given his wife a week's housekeeping, walked across to the nearby M74 and started begging his way south.

At the Erbismuhle, all the players talked to all the journalists, autographs were signed by the bookful, and a threat, later found out to be a hoax, by the IRA to kill the team was not allowed to disturb the calm of cool warriors about to go into battle. There was much joking about it and a head count of Protestants and Catholics among the team taken. 'And do you know,' someone said: 'You could get the Protestants in this lot into a minicab.' The atmosphere was pleasant, restrained, comfortable and out-of-character.

Yugoslavia were one of the feared countries in the 1974 World Cup. West Germany, Holland and Poland – all of whom were safely qualifying for the last eight as this Scottish pageant was unfolding – believed they would be a severe obstacle placed in the way of the eventual winners. Miljan Miljanic, afterwards to go to Real Madrid, was a shrewd and abrasive manager. Oblak was their Bremner. Dzajic on the wing was mentioned as one of Europe's best. They were promised the support of those thousands of their own immigrants in West Germany and in a way there was some spirit of friendship, a connection, with the Scots, another deprived people.

We were courteously met when we wandered to their hotel and the national coach Milovan Ciric said: 'We have a genuine complex about Scottish football. Four times we have played you – and we are still to win. We fear Bremner. You know Pele the other night called him a great leader of men. And Jordan is the best header of a ball in the tournament. We like the way you play hard – because so do we.' We came back from Konigstein certain of a difficult match, but believing it was no hopeless task. Again the period of waiting began.

Saturday dawned crystal clear and many Scots saw that dawn because there was no way they could sleep. Breakfast this time was an endless meal of many coffees and one slice of bread and apricot preserve. Soon the charabancs were ready for the team, the journalists and the officials. The first sign that this was to be, by any standards, an afternoon unusual and grim, came when the team hopped out of their hotel into the waiting coach.

At the same time a helicopter rose from the grounds of the hotel and as we looked up, we saw a dozen troopers hanging out of it, their legs dangling while they cradled submachine guns in their arms. Adolf gave a little speech to Scotland's group of footballers on the way to the most important match of their lives: 'In the event of a terrorist attack, you are to exit by the back door which vill open automatically. You must go out von by von and seek the nearest cover.' Jimmy Johnstone shrunk to about three-foot-six as he snuggled down in his seat.

That helicopter patrolled the team as it rushed down to a Wald Stadium looking very decorous, its car parks and its trees laid out in neat rows, a whole five acres set aside for the fans containing enough electronic equipment to take this match not just to the four corners of the globe but to every planet if necessary. Ormond hung about in one of the many corridors in the place with no one to talk to as the minutes ticked away to kick off.

I had decided to leave the arid technicalities of the press box and go to a seat in the stands. Hughie Taylor, the only man alive to have seen every World Cup match that Scotland has contested, came as well. He was a sore, lovely, trial as the afternoon wore on. We noticed many Scots freely surrendering their carry-outs at the gates for hard drink was not allowed on the slopes of this park. George Mulholland, from Scotstoun and now Toronto, a Rangers fan, appeared behind us. We need a lot of Coca Cola and there were no backs to the seats. Not a drop of the hard stuff had touched our lips.

We had all rung home for courage and sustenance, mumbling into telephones. 'It's only a match, it's only a match,' I kept saying. Hughie kept hissing and pulling at his moustache as he does when his stomach is churning. George had lost his voice against Brazil and was, therefore, out of the game. Some 12,000 were in it, up to their epiglottis's. From distant corners came the sounds of 'Bonnie Scotland, We'll Support you Evermore, we'll Support you ever more.' The teams came out, which was great, because we were getting used to this World Cup business and the nerves departed.

There followed a coarse, hard, definitively European game, the extra defenders shutting off space, the wingers unable to beat full backs and the midfield humping up and down like navvies. For long periods, as they say, nothing continued to happen and you didn't quite know whether to be pleased that Scotland were still level instead of behind, or whether to be sad because they had not scored the goal that would carry them onwards. Hughie said at half time 'They can do it.' There was too long a queue at the Coca Cola stand.

Dzajic at least is impotent, still not recovered from a car crash. Oblak is in Bremner's pocket. Katalinski dishes it out, but so do some of ours. It becomes very hot all of a sudden as the sun kisses this World Cup for the first time. Much of the chanting and shouting from the terraces is in deference to the occasion rather than because the play on the field warrants high excitement. We get on top for a while, the Yugoslavs hold us and it's pawn to queen five in an orthodox middle game. The minutes pass away, it's almost domino, goodnight Munich and the boys have played great and they did their best and it's not a very good era for Scottish goalscorers and Hughie says it's better than 1954 and 1958 all rolled together and we were never much good at this game and it's absolutely bloody crazy that grown men should behave like this and that he's heard of a boat trip up the Rhine, only 50 marks and should we have a little donner at it on Tuesday.

Yugoslavia go up the park with five minutes left. Dzajic crosses for the first time and Karasi heads past Harvey. The defence is nowhere as it's looking for a goal at the other end. Hughie throws his arms all about me and I can feel hot tears, not three seconds later, all the way through my shirt and on to my shoulders. He stays that way for a long time, sobbing, heaving, muttering 'No, No, No.' I'm getting no sensation at all from my legs.

Behind us there's a man and a woman, not married, never met. He's crying too, snuggling into her and talking as well. 'The last time I cried it was at my father's funeral.' George's head is between his knees. No one's thrown anything yet, I think. There is a deep, bitter, unbelieving silence and our flags have come down. I want home, now, this minute, on one of those time machines that can take me there in a split second.

Scotland go up the park, desperate, chilled, not comprehending. The ball is in Yugoslavia's penalty area, Jordan kicks and slowly it rolls into the net. 'Who scored?' 'Let me see Hughie'. Does it matter? Have we won, have we lost, just what the hell is that bloody American doing standing in front of me, it's not his game – but is it ours? The referee blows his whistle, they all shake hands and our lot start crying. End Game.

There is still a straw of a chance that Scotland have qualified if Zaire restrict Brazil to two goals in Gelsenkirchen and this statistical fact is passed around the terraces, but soon the electronic scoreboard pings out Brazil 3 Zaire 0 and we've now really no place to go, we've been locked out, unchosen, dismissed, told to geraff this competition. No one wants to throw anything and Hughie is fumbling with his spectacles.

There are a few plastic cups to kick on our way round to the other side of the ground and you would think that you'd want to look round at the other Scots about the place, for we're abroad and there might be someone you know and would like to talk to. But all heads and eyes are down, they are shuffling away and this is a grief too deep for any words.

Showing our passes, we get to see Ormond. Margaret's weeping a few yards away. He's blind with tears that refuse to drop. We're too embarrassed to even shake hands so we just look at each other, long, hard, affectionately. This time I want to cry for it may be all of Scotland that this day is about, but for me, it's this little man, who has endured it, slept it, drunk it, butterflied it for months and *he is* Scotland standing there, small, pawky, unwanted, done in. And maybe he sees this because he smiles.

We all stand about for a long time, waiting for a bus to take us home. Miljanic, in passing, says we 'are good players, but, better, good sports.' Ormond has been into the Yugoslavian dressing room to congratulate the winners and qualifiers and that deeply impresses this big Stein of a man, who says nothing nicer will happen in the competition. Then we notice a strange movement inside this room towards the window and people are looking out on the most beautiful sight in this dreadful experience.

A group of about 200 Scots has gathered around the team coach, as they do every Saturday at places like Brockville, Dens Park, Cappielow for that, too, is part of our own thing. They start singing slowly, not the supporters' songs but the songs of a people who want to be a nation 'Flower of Scotland', 'The Road and the Miles to Bonnie Dundee', 'The Star of Rabbie Burns'. When the players come out, smart now and spruce, they cheer, softly. And they end by singing 'We're on our way to Argentina, we shall not be moved.' It is the stuff of legends, the cry of the undefeated. They are singing love songs.

A totally silent journey takes us back to the Erbismuhle, where players buy us drinks. Sandy Jardine says: 'Do you know, when that Yugoslavian goal went in, I just didn't care. It's the first time in my career I just didn't care. That's terrible, isn't it.' He says it was 82 out there and the only way he could breathe in the second half was by shoving ice cubes down his throat. Jim Holton selects a record on the juke box. It is Frank Sinatra and 'My Way'. He listens a bit '. . . the record shows, I took the blows, and did it my way.' Jardine whispers 'That's it, that's our story, isn't it?'

Bremner holds court. His temper is sharper than others and consequently he recovers from bad times that much quicker. He is talking tactics, techniques and the beer bottles are being juggled across the table to prove the point. He smiles.

Willie Ormond is telling a story or two. 'I've died a thousand deaths on this trip but when I got back to the hotel, I saw Adolf's machinery lying about and I looked at the revolvers and I could have shot myself.' (Adolf is being instructed in the highland fling on the dance floor.) We ask the manager what did happen when he met the Prime Minister after the Brazil match for there have been rumours about it. 'Well *he* says that I should have used Lorimer wide instead of down the middle and I say to him. "You look after your job and let me look after mine." He's looking forward to going home.

And so to bed for the only World Cup squad which, in the history of the competition, will be going home undefeated to a delirious welcome from a nation which charged them with an impossible task and which wishes to thank them for not being disgraced. The trainer packs the bags.

West Germany won the 1974 World Cup two weeks later in the Olympic Stadium Munich, defeating Cruyff's Holland by two goals to one in an undistinguished final. They had timed their run nicely, becoming stronger as the tournament lasted and when Helmut Schoen, their kindly old manager, plodded out to hug his captain Beckenbauer at the end of the match, his country permitted themselves one long and unspontaneous roar of approval. The next morning it went back to work.

## AT THE GAME

Moving an orange ball
Through clogging snow
Can frustrate players:
The whirling flakes
Mirror their bemusement.
The elements are difficult to tame.

Elsewhere, huddled groups
Sporadically bray
Their regimented hymns
Of bias, bigotry and hate.

A twelve-year-old,
Safe from admonitory eye
Of parent, policemen, teacher,
Hurls down the terracing
A snowball
Random and viciously cemented,
His face masked with malice
For victim claimed;
Then gauchely gulps
The lumpen approbation
Of pals bedecked and raucous.

Later, a vulgar hail of
Toilet-rolls,
Filched from who knows where,
Arches its way towards a field
Rimmed with moving uniforms;
And hands are clapped in hatred of the ref.

Is this a place of skills displayed
And savoured?
Or rather a situation
Where failures are forgot

And new criteria offered
Of self-fulfilment?
Cheap wine and ale in cans
Serve potently –
And precociously –
To banish the self-loathing.

Too sour and cynical to conclude:
Too many of the wrong kidney
Are having too many children.

The elements are difficult to tame.

John Lewis

# The Thistle and the Grail

ROBIN JENKINS

Fernbank was a village in agricultural Lanarkshire, and its menfolk had travelled down in two special buses. Their faces were as red as the rosettes pinned to caps or jackets. Ploughmen, cowherds, carters, and blacksmiths, they had no right in society to show such vulgar condescending glee towards miners, steelmen, and paper-makers like Drumsagart men; nor was their crude dialect ever intended to convey swagger and arrogance. Yet there they gathered in a shaggy phalanx in the centre of the terracing opposite the pavilion, smelling of cowdung, barbarians from their sun-smacked faces to their tacketed shoes, yet assuming a superiority and certitude of victory that would have been intolerable even in the worshippers of the mighty Glasgow Rangers in their own shrine at Ibrox. Unfortunately the Drumsagart men were hampered in their retaliation; not by instincts of hospitality, but by the foreknowledge that soon on the sunny field might be displayed ample justification for this dung-nourished *hubris*.

No Drumsagart rosettes were to be seen, and only two scarves, worn by Mysie Dougary and her grandfather. They had been invited inside the pavilion barrier to protect them from the wrath to come if Elrigmuir failed. Tamas had been given a chair.

Tinto the prophet, licking at the handle of his stick, tasted both sweat and doubt. When someone mentioned to him the new minister was at the match, standing yonder in front of the pavilion, Tinto declared himself absolved of any responsibility. 'When I prophesied Elrigmuir would turn out to be a champion,' he muttered, 'when I said the Thistle would win, I was never told there'd be a minister here. Everybody kens a minister at a football match means bad luck.'

'It could be bad luck for Fernbank,' pointed out Crutch Brodie.

'He's our minister,' snapped Tinto, 'so it's our bad luck.'

'Bad luck for everybody,' growled a bystander. 'Take a look at history.'

'If that's so,' said another, keen to pursue theology even in those hallowed moments before the entry of the gladiators – 'if that's so, God pity Glasgow Celtic then, for every time they're playing at Parkhead yonder the grandstand's black wi' priests.'

Even if a touchy Catholic had heard no argument could have ensued, for a clamour of voices and ricketies and one bugle heralded the arrival upon the field of Fernbank United in their red jerseys.

Drumsagart was dismayed.

'Look at them,' they muttered. 'Every damned one six feet and thirteen stone. No wonder they're at the top of the League. They'll kick our chaps off the field. Fed on new-laid eggs and prime steak. Is that the Afton the papers hae been bumming about, him all the senior clubs are after? Looks fast, eh? God help old Turk peching after that one. And just look at that hairy-kneed monster that's centre half. That one will crush Mysie's Elrigmuir like one of Rutherford's mouldy bannocks. Boys, we're in for a worst slaughter than last week. Only a flood of rain or a storm of snow could save us now, and the sun's shining and the sky's blue.'

Nevertheless, despite this daunting muscularity of the enemy, Drumsagart eyes watched for their own team to appear. It began to be rumoured they were on strike in the pavilion, in protest against the size and weight of their opponents; they were banging their heads on the floor, howling for their mammies to come and save them. Though it was a Drumsagart man who started the rumour, the Fernbank contingent took it up, without subtley or pity, and turned it into brutal insult.

Soon, however, the Thistle trotted out, led by Lachie Houston, with his scalp as laundered as his white pants. Bellows of loyalty and encouragement were mingled with hoots of foreboding at the sight of Turk McCabe, seen now to be balder, fatter in the belly, and altogether uglier than in the past. Moreover his jersey was too short for him and his pants too long; and his boots too big apparently, for the first kick he took at the practice ball was a foozle, which caused him to go down anxiously on one knee and rub the offending toe-cap, as if with lucky spittle.

'Is that you, Turk,' shouted a wit, 'resting already?'

Affronted, Turk leapt a foot into the air and began to run in a vast earnest circle. As a demonstration of physical fitness it was not convincing, but even the gloomiest sceptics found it hard not to laugh.

Elrigmuir caused disquiet for the opposite reason: he looked so like a football player that everybody, except Mysie and Tinto Brown, was sure it must be some kind of deception. Tall, fair-haired, erect, he moved with speed and grace, and his first practice shot sent the ball whizzing into the net. That could easily be a fluke, but there was no gainsaying his legs were powerful and had that delicate degree of bandiness so essential to the complete footballer.

The referee appeared, received his meed of jeers, supervised the spinning of the penny, and thereupon blew his whistle to start the game.

Never was there such a start. The Thistle having lost the toss, Elrigmuir as centre forward kicked off. His inside left tapped it back to Turk, who banged it prodigiously far upfield, where Elrigmuir at full tilt met it as it fell, controlled it without losing any of its impetus, swung it and himself past the mountainous centre half, evaded the left back's desperate lunge, and smote the ball past the Fernbank goalkeeper, who threw up his hands as much in horror at this improper impetuosity as in an attempt to save. It was a goal, and the swiftest and cleverest and most splendid goal ever seen on that field. The archangel Gabriel, wings and all, could not have excelled it; no, nor Alan Morton himself. Even the chawbacons from Fernbank felt the fearful glory in their souls, though they uttered no sound at first and later, minutes later, only profane exhortations to their own team to waken up and avenge that blow, so inhospitable in its suddenness and so ominous in its hint of obliterative power.

In the midst of the Drumsagart hysteria of joy Mysie stood in silence, her hands clasped; while her grandfather was peevish,

for using his handkerchief to wipe the moisture from his eyes
he'd missed the marvellous goal.

The Fernbank players, nettled at thus being caught napping
by these incompetents at the foot of the League, charged down
on the Thistle goal. The dexterous Afton dodged this defender
and that, manoeuvred himself into position for a shot at goal,
raised his deadly right foot, and found only air to kick, Turk
having nipped in to steal the ball from him and thump it to a
far-off harmless place. Convinced, by a scrutiny of the aged ape
in the blue jersey, that the theft had been lucky, if not absolutely
unintentional, Afton was soon trying again, causing his partisans
to shriek in appreciation of his craft, bringing lumps of apprehension into Drumsagart throats, and making the Thistle defenders
bungle in panic, except one, Turk McCabe, who remained as
cool and as awkward to get round as an iceberg. Wherever
Afton's foot meant to be, Turk's was there the instant before;
similarly in the contest of heads. Afton was supple and sprang up
like a gazelle; Turk ascended as if with the hook of a crane in
his back; but he was always that half-inch higher or at that better
angle. When he headed the ball, too, it by no means dropped like
shot from weary putter's hand; it flew as if spat from cannon.

Twenty minutes passed, and the Drumsagart faithful began to
believe it possible that the Thistle might win by that single wonderful goal, provided only that Turk under the stress did not
disintegrate into a heap of sweat, fat, beer, fags, and rusty bones.

Then in the twenty-first minute the Thistle's outside left, a
long-haired much reviled man who normally pranced about like
an inefficient fakir on red-hot stones, found the ball at his feet
as a result of a ricochet from an opponent's jaw. He did not,
as usual, get rid of it as if it was a wasp's byke, but caressed it
with his left foot, went gambolling along the sawdust line, side-
stepping two furious adversaries, and at the crucial moment, as if
all was predestined, he kicked the ball across in a cunning parabola
so that it avoided the heads of all United players and found
Elrigmuir's, which flicked it neatly into the top corner of the goal,
where it struck the net and thence dropped to the ground to be
picked up by the goalkeeper in disgust as if it was a cow's turd.

It was a second goal, equal in beauty to the first, but dearer in that it built another thickness to the wall shutting out defeat. Like men long beleaguered and now hearing at last the Lucknow music, the Drumsagart supporters on the terracing howled hosannahs; while the Fernbank faithful, fed on fat wins for weeks past, spat out in nausea the thin wafer of defeat and contumely.

'Pick me oot ony prophet in the Bible,' yelled Tinto Brown, 'and I'll show you a better.'

Harry Lynn, who was still begging, found his cap showered with thanksgiving pennies and ha'pennies.

In the midst of the pandemonium of glee Rab Nuneaton dismally smiled and remembered how his daughter's eyes had filled with tears when he'd struck her with his cap.

On the field the Thistle players clawed at one another in ecstasy, so that the outside left emerged from their embraces blinded by his hair and by a blaze of self-esteem. Elrigmuir's shorter hair stood the rumpling well, and so, many noticed, did his modesty. He returned smartly to the centre of the field as if he would rather score more goals than be buffeted with praises for those he'd already scored.

The game became rough. Finding their skill thwarted, the United used their brawn. The Thistle were peremptorily commanded to retaliate; they obeyed. The referee, harming only the grass he trod on, became the most abused man on the field. If he awarded a foul-kick to Drumsagart, Fernbank abused him, while Drumsagart's praise was sarcastic; and vice-versa. Every tootle of his whistle brought vilification; to blow it soon needed much moral courage. His decisions, clear enough at first to himself if obscure to every partisan, became obscure to him too. When two men clashed murderously together and both fell, certainly it was a toss-up who was the greater culprit. The referee was not allowed by the rules to toss up, or hold an enquiry; he had to decide instantaneously, and latterly he could not have said by what principle he decided.

In this mood of confusion, aggravated by ricketies rattled and bugle blown, he awarded a penalty-kick.

Luckily he awarded it to the Thistle, whose adherents were,

of course, far more numerous, although it was a Fernbank man who had the bugle. Luckily, too, for his conscience later, it was a just award, as Elrigmuir, well inside the fatal area, had been charged in the back by one United defender while another was in the act of sweeping his legs from under him. Nevertheless Fernbank screeched in protest; the ricketies clattered; the bugle snorted and stuttered sonorously.

Sergeant Elvan had had enough of bugling. Although the taking of a penalty-kick is a crisis on a football field, inflaming all nerves, he ran up to that part of the terracing where the bugler was and roared to him to hand it over or be locked up.

There was an astonishing temporary alliance: both Fernbank and Drumsagart united in rejecting that arbitrary demand. A bugle was a legitimate instrument of encouragement. Did the sergeant think it'd alarm the local Territorials playing soldiers on Drumsagart Hill? Or was he just sensitive about music? If he wasn't careful he'd be hearing the Last Post sounded over him. Let him go to Germany or Russia if he wanted to be a tyrant. His job was to take his big feet so many times round the field; his big ears had nothing to do with it at all.

The sergeant paid no heed but climbed over the wire ropes and pushed up through the Fernbank men till he reached the bugler. This was a stalwart with a red muffler round his neck and slavers on his lips. He held on as the sergeant tugged. He explained the bugle was his, he'd owned it since his Boy's Brigade days, he'd paid for it by instalments, he'd been doing no harm, he was really a trained player, he could give the sergeant a demonstration if he liked. The sergeant said nothing to all that, but kept tugging till he'd wrested the bugle away. A tremendous ironical cheer greeted his success. With the trophy above his head he shoved his way down through the crowd again, climbed over the ropes, and marched haughtily along to his subordinate, Constable Dunsmore, to whom he handed the bugle, and who took it as gratefully as if it was a coiled cobra. Then the sergeant waved to the referee to resume the game.

To Turk had been given the honour and the onus of taking the penalty-kick. During the bugle incident he waited, arms

E

adangle, mouth agape, and head in tonsured dwam. An opponent
had slyly placed the ball on the penalty spot, in a tiny hollow,
which he hoped might cause the kick to be fluffed. Most men
would have gone to the ball, patted it, placed and replaced it,
and even prayed to it to fly straight and true, with no grotesque
deviations upwards or sideways. Not so Turk. He waited, sober
as convict or monk. As soon as the referee blew the whistle, and
while the air on the field sensibly thinned through the sucking in
of every breath, Turk, as if strolling towards the Lucky Sporran
a good hour before closing-time, approached the ball, kicked it,
and then blinked at it where it lay behind the sprawling goalkeeper. Thereafter he disappeared under his ardent colleagues,
who leapt on him, wielding felicitations like clubs. When he was
again seen he was as unperturbed as ever, with perhaps a little
sheepishness at the edges of his solemnity.

Half-time came, with the score three-nil for the Thistle. The
teams retired to the pavilion, and the spectators began to fight
the semi-conflict over again. Into the arena strutted the pipe
band, gigantic with moth-eaten busbies, playing 'Cock of the
North'. Their kilts were faded tigers and their sporrans were
like fistfuls plucked from long-dead sheep. But never had they
blown so imperiously. The whole British army might have been
behind them.

Mr Lockhart, reconnoitring from the pavilion steps, was forced
to admit that the band would be a difficult competitor to dis-
place. It did not perhaps play well, nor march with much military
precision, but it made an intimidating noise and brought forth
from the crowd volleys not only of compliment but also of pennies,
which were pecked off the grass and dropped into bags not unlike
kirk bags by two small men, asiduous as feeding ostriches, who
seemed to be well known and whose honesty seemed to be
seriously questioned, judging by the many imputations to the
effect that half at least of the tribute would find its way into
Mr Malarkin's pockets, in return for beer and whisky. Certainly
the two collectors, who made rude rejoinders, did not appear
abashed by those arraignments; but Mr Lockhart, to whom
scrupulous integrity in pecuniary matters was a virtue higher

than cleanliness, thought he had discovered the Achilles heel of the band, through which he should be able, for one afternoon at least, to keep them sulking in their practice shed while here on the battlefield he strove for God. He was about to compliment himself on this conclusion when he realized that, unaccountably, though his hopes were rising, his heart was sinking.

In the pavilion behind him, at the very heart of the jubiliation, had appeared the worm of a moral problem. Among the onlookers had been identified the scout of a first-division senior club. He had confessed to Sam Malarkin he was present to report on Afton, but was more taken with young Elrigmuir; in fact he was prepared there and then, on the strength of his intuition, to make an offer, which would leave the youth richer by as much as fifty pounds. The Thistle, he added, would be compensated for their loss. Malarkin as a publican had much experience of tongues too loose. With his own in splints of caution he had tepidly praised Elrigmuir and concealed the fact that the young man was not a Thistle player at all, being merely on trial.

The thing to do, as all the committee except one agreed, was to keep the poacher away and have a form ready for Elrigmuir to sign at half-time. The dissentient was the president. He considered the scheme unfair to the lad, who ought to be told the position and allowed to choose; otherwise they were cheating him. The conference was the quickest in the committee's history. Rutherford found no seconder; even Donald Lowther shook his head. Elrigmuir was a football goldmine, to keep him murder might pardonably be done.

Therefore when the team tramped into the dressing-room, bathed in sweat and triumph, Wattie Cleugh and Sam Malarkin, after going round patting the damp backs, with two pats for Turk, took young Elrigmuir into the committee room, laid a document in front of him, handed him a fountain-pen with Malarkin inscribed on it in fancy gold letters, and told him where to sign.

Other committee-men stayed with the rest of the team, while

two outside the pavilion locked the scout in conversation.

Elrigmuir was coy; indeed, he showed more interest in the pen than in the form.

'Maybe I shouldn't,' he said, grinning. 'What if I'm a haddie? You've only seen me play half a game.'

'We know that, boy,' agreed Wattie Cleugh, 'we know that. Granted you're a bit raw in patches. But we can recognize good stuff when we see it. Sign for us and you'll not regret it. I think Mr Malarkin will back me up when I say our terms are as generous as any junior club's in the land.'

'Some pen this,' commented Elrigmuir, with his mouth full of orange. 'It must hae cost a quid or two.'

'Sign for us, Alec,' whispered Malarkin, 'and I'll get you one the identical same, with your name on it.'

Sam had been trying to see beyond the sweat and glisten of the football genius to the human being, the tasty young fellow of nineteen, the collier, the sweetheart of Mysie Dougary. He saw smooth cheeks, a neck strangely free from extinct or active boils, a skin altogether caressable, lips exciting in spite of the orange juice, a nature unsuspicious and ingenuous, and a brain promisingly simple. Sam felt exhilarated, despite the odour of sweat so rank and masculine. He bent so close his whiskers tickled Elrigmuir's neck; he stroked the young man's back.

'Wattie's right, Alec,' he said. 'Sign for us, and we'll take care of you. We'll nurse you till you're ready for senior football. There's money here for the right kind, and you're the right kind all right. We'll have you out of the pits. We'll have you rising in the world. Sign that, and it's the first step in the making of your fortune.'

'Mind you,' confided Elrigmuir, 'I like playing football. My teachers used to say it was the only thing I was good at.'

'Just sign this,' murmured Cleugh, holding the form as if it was a mirror in which Elrigmuir could see his face crowned with Drumsagart laurels and cash. 'The rest is easy.'

'I don't think I've got any objections to signing,' said Elrigmuir. 'Will Alec do, or should I write Alexander?'

'Alexander's more legal,' said Cleugh.

Elrigmuir laughed. 'Some folk call me Sandy. I've a middle name as well: Moffat.'

'Alexander will do.'

'I'll let you gentlemen into a secret,' said the young man as, tongue out, he wrote painstakingly. 'I'm doing this for Mysie's sake.'

'Ah, sweet bonny Mysie!' Cleugh winked.

'I think the world of her, Mr Cleugh.'

'And so you should.'

Malarkin neither winked nor smiled. His hand flew off the youth's back and alighted on the point of his own moustache. His nose twitched.

Elrigmuir paused at g. 'But we're not what you would call sweethearts,' he said.

Cleugh poked him in the ribs.

On Elrigmuir's frank brow, amidst the smudges left by the ball, appeared a shadow. 'It's true,' he insisted.

'Whatever you say, Alec. That's your business and Mysie's. You'll settle it between you. Just you finish signing. There's the ref out on the field already.'

Elrigmuir signed. 'It's her,' he said. 'She's not in favour. I don't ken why. Sometimes I think it's because I'm a collier. She denies it. But if it's no that, what is it? I've asked her a hundred times. There's nothing wrong wi' me, is there?'

Cleugh waved the form about to dry it.

'Sure there's nothing wrong wi' you, Alec. There's a whole lot right wi' you. You keep on asking. Women are like that. You ask a hundred times – no good; you ask again and you've done it – you don't ken why, and you don't care. Is that not so, Sam?'

Malarkin's smirk had anguish in it, superciliousness, frustration, anxiety, and sadness. He said nothing, for there were no words to express that mixture.

Cleugh saw nothing peculiar. 'Off you go, Alec; and re-member, the sure way to win Mysie's favour is by scoring more and more goals for the Thistle.'

Elrigmuir rushed so as not to be last on the field. Last

would be conspicuous; conspicuous was boastful, and Mysie had said a thousand times she didn't like boasters. He glanced at her as he passed. Strangers threw invisible bouquets at him, but she pretended to be interested in some gulls high up in the sky.

'You know something, Sam?' said Wattie Cleugh, inside the pavilion. 'I envy that boy. He's got a wonderful future ahead of him. He's braw and he's young and he's a grand player and Mysie's a bonny lass. By God, I do envy him.'

'Sometimes, Wattie,' hissed Malarkin, 'you talk a lot of –' Then he dashed out, curiously, on his tiptoes.

'What's eating him?' asked Cleugh, of himself. Soon he was told the answer. 'Well, well,' he murmured. 'I'll have to keep an eye on you, Sam old girl.'


The second half began in catastrophe for Drumsagart. In two minutes the United scored a goal; Afton outwitted the whole defence, including Turk. It was Fernbank's turn to rejoice. Drumsagart blenched, though they also smiled: the poor bumpkins were entitled to this chip of consolation. Afton was good, but Elrigmuir was better. Then Turk stumbled, Afton sped past, the ball again was in the Thistle net. That chip by this addition became a feast, and the Fernbank manners, as they wolved into it, were revolting.

Pessimism spread like plague among the Drumsagart men. Nathaniel Stewart, who had not coughed once during that salubrious first half, now began, crying in the midst of it that Turk, damn him, was out of training, he was letting them down, he should have stayed in England, for though he'd given them all a glimpse of glory, true enough, it was only to strike them blind again.

Rab Nuneaton at last found his ideas flowing. Maybe it was a good thing, he said, that defeat was coming after all, for there would have been no enduring the conceit of Rutherford and the rest of the committee.

Archie Birkwood, arriving in uniform in time to see the United's goals, refused to believe the story of that ascendant first half, especially as it was related in downcast voices. He felt he had come from one graveside to another.

Tinto Brown was silent: so far his demi-god Elrigmuir had hardly touched the ball this half; it seemed to be a case of *ichabod* with him as with old Turk. If the United scored more goals, and this seemed very likely, for they were now furiously assaulting the Thistle goal, Tinto thought that, after a melancholy pint cadged in the Lucky Sporran, he'd creep home to die.

Turk muttered: 'Keep the heid.' One or two of his team-mates heard and felt it would be better advice for him to keep his feet, for twice his stumbles had betrayed them. They did not say so. Turk looked worried rather than villainous, but with a face like his transition could be quick. Really his advice was to himself: 'Keep the heid, Turk.'

He kept it too, and his feet. There were more stumbles. Aching with weariness, stiffness, and bruises, he toiled with the selflessness of a saint. Any spectator, such as Mr Lockhart, for instance, to whom football was not sacred could never have believed that Turk's payment was to be seven shillings and sixpence and perhaps the privilege of suffering again next week. Certainly his superhuman efforts in such a cause made Mr Lockhart ashamed of his own misgivings about the revival.

Thus the game ended, three goals to two for the Thistle – a harrowing but magnificent victory; and for the United their first defeat of the season. The yokels from Fernbank as they made for their buses still sported rosettes; their bugler on his restored instrument sounded no shamefaced retreat. They were disappointed but not despondent. Indeed, one of them stuck out of the bus window his great empurpled face like a prize turnip and bellowed to all Drumsagart the succinct truth: 'We was beaten by a freak.' He meant Turk McCabe, and everybody knew it.

The trouble about freaks, as the Drumsagart men confided to one another, was that they couldn't be depended on. That afternoon Turk had played a game that no man in Scotland could have bettered. Next Saturday, though, the magic might fail, and old Turk (for he was thirty-six if he was a day) left to his own natural resources would sag and fumble and miskick and maybe have to hang on to a goalpost to keep from collapse; and next Saturday was the first round of the Cup competition. Some even expressed the opinion that the old state of certain defeat was preferable: to be at the mercy of miracles would shrivel the nerves.

Jock Saunders was at the Cross when the forerunners approached.

'Well, what do you think of that, Jock?' he cried.

'Of what?'

'Of the match, dammit! We won, Jock; we won three-two.' The speaker, though he had been there and seen, had to force the words past his own incredulity.

'I heard five roars,' admitted Saunders. 'I thought the score was five-nothing: for Fernbank.'

'That's what we all thought it would be. The United are at the top of the League.'

'What happened to them?' asked Saunders. 'Did they all eat poisoned fish suppers last night? Did a steamroller run over their bus on their way from Fernbank?'

'Aye, a steamroller did run over them all right. Two steamrollers: Turk and young Alec Elrigmuir. What a game they played!'

'So it was a glorious victory?'

'Glorious is too tame a word, Jock.'

'Yet none of you,' he observed, 'seem to be in what I would call raptures.'

It was true. Looking at one another, they had to admit it. Yet to explain would be difficult, especially with dry throats and palpitating hearts. Later perhaps in the Lucky Sporran someone might hit on an explanation.

'All the same, Jock, you missed yourself. Yon was the sight of a lifetime.'

'I've enjoyed myself here,' he said, 'watching the leaves come doon.'

From *The Thistle and the Grail* by Robin Jenkins (Macdonald 1954).

# THE JAGGING OF HEARTS

As I was oot yae Setterday
Betwixt the darkenin' and the licht,
I heard yin to his neebour say:
'Oh, Thistle jagged the Herts the day!'

They'll no can hud their heids sae hee
Tynecastle is dang doun the nicht' –
'Ye mean the lads in cramassie?'
'Aye, Thistle jagged the Herts the day!

Sae sicker and deliverlie
And hooly did they pass the ba',
And busteous Herts! – But what say ye
Since Thistle jagged the Herts the day?'

'Still dearest and still *A per se*
The Herts is still aboon them a',
Christ, what is Partick anyway?
Let Thistle jag the Herts the day!'

James T R Ritchie

# 'Memories are made of this'

TREVOR ROYLE

It had been a bad evening. Hibs had played elegant football for 90 minutes, yet a dour Leeds defence had stubbornly resisted their efforts to put the ball in the back of the net. No score at full time and the crowd held its breath as the issue was decided by penalties. Stanton missed one and out went Hibs from the UEFA Cup. Out beaten 5-4 on penalties even though they'd shown the white-shirted hard men how to play skilfull football. There was simply no justice left in the world.

What a sad defeat for a Hibs team which had played a special brand of football typified by sweeping midfield play, long passes to the speedy wingers and ruthlessly taken goals. In a game dominated by static defences and cast-iron marking their play shone like a candle in a wicked world.

They attracted typical footballing metaphors too. They are the bonny fechters who refuse to bludgeon their opponents, always preferring the rapier to the claymore. 'Elegance' and 'intelligence' rather than brute force and hardness have been their hallmark. But they have a soft underbelly. They become mesmerized by the harmony of their play and let it dominate them. After chasing the ball all over the park they lose interest in the game and let the other side score. Somehow it just doesn't seem worthwhile to go to the bother of actually scoring goals, just to show their superiority. It was like that against Leeds.

So out we went from Easter Road on a misty evening to ruminate on what might have been. In the pub afterwards the talk turned to past glories. It always does in the hour of defeat and as we Scots have had more defeats than most our memories tend to be longer and more vivid.

'Dae ye mind the Famous Five? The £50,000 forward line?

'Aye thon Willie Ormond just used his right leg for staunin on, his left was that powerful.'

'Three broken legs too.'

'Ye couldna beat Nicker Johnston though . . .'

We listened to those older and wiser in the lore of the game and the talk drifted on until it seemed that those events belonged to a Golden Age whose glory had long departed from this world. The harsh reality of the recent defeat slowly disappeared in a background of fond remembrance and warm beer.

In the weeks following the Leeds game Hibs seemed to be as ordinary as everyone else in the league. The goals came but not the vital spark of genius. There was no respite in going across Edinburgh to watch the Hearts either.

They were going through a desperately bad patch when every team in Scotland was queuing up to take the points off them. A normally douce Edinburgh crowd was heard to be yelling for the manager's head after a stupid defeat. Other teams might set their watches or herald new seasons with a game of all-change at the top, but not the Hearts. Even their newfangled strips made them look ill at ease.

If the Hibs Golden Age began in the fifties and is still with them, then Hearts seem to have been constantly remembering their share of the same glory. Hearts supporters have long memories and the unkind among us will say that they need them. They talk not about what is happening now but about what might have been. In the supporters' club the talk constantly goes back, as it does in Easter Road pubs, to the great days of the fifties. Everyone it seems has his own memory of great goals and high-scoring victories . . .

It was the first hot day of summer and Pete and I, innocent nine-year-olds, were being let loose in the world for the first time by ourselves. The Bluebird bus rattled and jostled us over the hill through the quiet country roads to the bad lands of West Fife. Places with strange sounding names – Methil, Dysart, Buckhaven, Wemyss. Strange that the home team was called East Fife and their stadium with a name more suited to a south coast boarding house.

I can't remember much of the game. We hadn't come to watch
East Fife anyway. Our heroes wore maroon and were then the best
team in Scotland. Their names still roll off the tongue like a
litany – Duff, Kirk, Mackenzie, Mackay, Glidden, Cumming,
Young, Conn, Bauld, Wardhaugh and Crawford. They beat East
Fife easily and for weeks afterwards Pete and I basked in the glory
of having seen the Hearts. For we were in no doubt that we had
seen a great team, a team that had an inside forward trio whose
nickname had come straight out of 'Roy of the Rovers'. How
could the United and their sloping pitch at Recreation Park ever
again compete with what we had witnessed?

From that magical moment onwards I supported the Hearts
fervently even though my allegiance had once owed more to their
name than their performance. When I had first come to Scotland
the train bringing us north had crossed the bridge at Gorgie Road
on its way to Princes Street Station. It was a Saturday afternoon
and predictably it was wet and overcast. What were all those
men doing? What excitement had captured them as they streamed
along the damp streets?

'They're just off to see the Hearts get beat again.'

'Nonsense, this is Hearts' year.'

And so it was. The 1954 League Cup victory against Motherwell ended the years in the wilderness.

How could I have supported any other team than the Hearts?
I immersed myself in the lore and magic of the club. Willie Bauld
was the greatest hero. He was strong and brave. He was skilful
in the air and was one of the most cultured players ever to appear
on a Scottish park. He should have been a great centre-forward
for Scotland but he made one tragic mistake. Poor Bauld, the
polished artist, missed an open goal against England, and Scotland denied herself a place in the 1950 World Cup. He missed
History's call to fame and never played again for his country.
It was the law of the playground. You were out if you dropped
the ball playing 'Keepy Up'.

My love for Hearts reached its height in 1956 when they beat
Celtic 3-1 in the Cup Final. I collected every newspaper cutting
I could lay my hands on and kept them in a Sharpes toffee box.

In a state of divine hero worship I carefully cut around a photograph of the SFA cup vowing that it would be destroyed if Hearts lost. I still have the box, the cuttings and an intact spindly silhouette.

Nothing survived that excitement and although Hearts were to go on to win the championship twice in the same decade, they were also busy creating their own legend. Little did we know as we lived through those years that their victories were so soon to become the stuff of legend and long-lost glory.

Nostalgia takes me back occasionally but as the Wanderer puts it better than I can, the glory has departed, the goal-hoard emptied.

Tynecastle on a warm late summer's afternoon. The football season in full swing in the middle of the Edinburgh Festival. Rangers come out onto the park, neatly dressed, crisp shorts and stockings firmly pulled up. They look for all the world like a well-turned out rugby team. They play neat and methodical football too.

A group of spectators on the north terracing have just drawn their players in the weekly sweep.

'Hearts, number five. Aw no, I've got Anderson! That balloon couldn't score to save himself.'

Looking at the big fellow in maroon commanding his troops in midfield, it's not difficult to understand the punter's dismay. He's hardly a striker. Wave upon wave of Rangers shock troops pound the Hearts defence but somehow they hold out. Then in the first quarter tragedy strikes. A smart cross from the Rangers right is covered by Anderson and the big pivot rises majestically to clear the danger. But somehow, unexpectedly and unfairly, the ball goes the wrong way and floats past an astonished Cruikie.

'We arra people'. Joy, joy, the clarion call of the royal blues.
'Aw Alan, you're bonny, the fiver's mine.'

Minutes later Hearts oblige yet again with another own goal and the game as a contest is over. Even the referee starts making quaint decisions to the Edinburgh team's consternation.

We wait for the annihilation that never comes. It gets too much for some and sensing that that's it, Rangers fans start streaming from the park with a good twenty minutes still to play. Outside in Gorgie Road the throbbing buses wait to take them west.

The metallic voice of the Tynecastle loudspeaker directs them.

'Will the Shettleston Loyal Rangers Supporters Club meet outside at the Roxy Bingo Hall where their bus is waiting.'

'Hey ref, did ye hear that?' answers one wag. It's the only bit of humour on a warm and dispiriting summer's afternoon. Typical Hearts weather.

How fickle we are! As the star of Hearts slowly waned on the west side of Edinburgh the Hibernian cluster was still shining brightly over Leith. There they are still weaving their own story. It is a story of elegance and hard shining brilliance, but it can frequently be less than heroic.

How often have we had the unworthy thought that we have got it all wrong? Hibs, like any other team are after all only composed of eleven journeymen who are paid handsomely to score goals and to stop the other team from scoring. Throughout the winter we turn up looking for golden goals, breathtaking saves and masterly movements. More often than not we are treated to two sets of clowns booting the ball around the park. It's usually raining too, or will be before full time. The Bovril will be tepid and the pies soggy. Even the chanting and the songs will be muted. How can this possibly be the reality of our hopes and dreams?

But then from out of the gloom a goal will be scored, an unusual goal from 30 yards out or a well taken header from a corner. It may even be a scrambled unsatisfactory sort of a goal, but it will be the goal to make the afternoon worthwhile and raise the spirits. It will even improve afterwards with the telling.

'See Harper, he beat three men on his own before he cracked it in. What a man!'

And so new legends are born which are reinforced week by week until they in turn create their own Golden Age. Even Stanton's miss against Leeds has become a more important part of the myth than if he had scored that winter's night . . . can it only have been two years ago?

# Playing the Lead

JOHN FAIRGRIEVE

In a lounge bar just off Princes Street, an establishment much favoured by football folk after the game, and sometimes before the game, Willie Hamilton was talking about the best players he had ever known.

'There was Pele,' he said, 'well, you've got to include Pele. Yes, and there was Di Stefano, and Tom Finney.'

Somebody prompted him. 'Any more?'

'Sure,' he said, 'there was me, wasn't there?'

A few of us smiled, but respectfully. Nobody who ever watched Willie Hamilton in action, and who appreciated the supreme arts of football, would have argued with him, not even if they were looking for an argument.

Willie played for Hearts, Hibs and some nondescript English team at a time when English managers were looking for men who could and would run through doors. That was not his scene, because he did not interpret it as football.

He was not, is not, a modest man. Yet nor was he boastful. He spoke the truth, and saw no reason to adjust the truth for the sake of what would have been false modesty. He should have included Jim Baxter in his personal pantheon, but I can appreciate why he didn't. They were too much alike.

Neither believed in the virtues of a retiring nature. Both needed to think – nay, to *know* – that they were the best. In the course of comparatively short careers, neither found good grounds for self-doubt.

Like Baxter, Willie Hamilton did not believe in moving quickly. He left that to the labourers. I don't think he ever quite recognized that any other player had the right to be on the same park, although maybe, if in charitable mood, he would make an exception. He could have played football, wearing a monocle and smoking a cigarette through a long holder, and I'm not saying that such a thought didn't cross his mind.

He was languid, elegant, arrogant. He could beat a man gently. Shuffling around in the midst of a frenzied, humiliated defence, he was the eye of the hurricane. He always had time. He would pass a ball three yards or 30 yards, and watch its progress as a mother might watch a favourite child, fondly, confidently. He would seldom bother about such energetic exercises as being in position for the return, but there was no need. When Willie Hamilton passed a ball, it stayed passed, and there wasn't very much a defender could do about it.

Once he played for Hibs against Real Madrid. Jock Stein was manager of Hibs, and Willie was not taking the match too seriously. It is said that Stein informed Willie at half-time that, unless there was an improvement very soon, he, Stein, would personally come on to the park and carry him off. If the story is true, it may be assumed, I think, that Jock Stein was bluffing, but Willie wasn't taking any chances. He moved from neutral into first gear which, for him, was going some. Nothing more was required, and it was the first time I ever felt sorry for Real Madrid, a fine side but unaccustomed to tackling ghosts.

Baxter and Hamilton in the same side would have been like Olivier and Gielgud on the same stage, but I don't know who would have played the lead.

# TYNECASTLE

I never get doun tae Tynecastle thae days
It's a guid lang while nou sen I've been
I never get doun tae Tynecastle thae days
– tho they're sayin they hae a guid team
   But the team that I mind
   is the team o langsyne
when we swept aa the prizes awa
   an the boys in maroon
   were the pride o the toun
the best lads that e'er kicked a baw!
I'm thinking o Parker an Broun an Big Tam . . .
Aw, the thousands that cheered them aa on!
An my thochts haud them yet
   for I'll never forget
        My Bauld
           an My Wardhaugh
           an My Conn.

Donald Campbell

# 'A Surfeit of Bad Sex'

GORDON McGILL

The big American had wandered the London streets for an hour and was feeling in need of an explanation. He had watched the crowds coming back from Wembley and occasionally, as they passed, his brow would wrinkle and he would shake his head in bewilderment.

Someone had been sick too close to his shoes. Men had cursed him for no obvious reason. Others had joked with him. A few had roared incomprehensible slogans into his face. And three times he had been offered a 'nip', whatever that was.

At his suggestion, we hit the nearest bar. It was a small Snug with a juke box and five of The Lads were there draped in tartan and Lion Rampant flags, gulping from pint glasses and growling at each other from under their tammies.

One finger emerged, jabbed at the juke box and produced the voice of Frank Sinatra. They all joined in, and when Ol' Blue Eyes reached the line:

'And I will drink the wine . . .'

they fell about laughing: 'A right wino, that yin. Gaun Frankie get tore intae the veepee . . .'

So I'm explaining the joke and why the singer was undoubtedly not thinking of the red biddy as he crooned that particular line, when one of The Lads catches the American looking at him and then I'm having to translate 'yiz-wantin-a-photie-pal? eh–' as we head smartly for the door.

What puzzled the American was something he called 'the age factor.' He'd lived in London for sometime and had grown accustomed to seeing droves of Manchester United and Chelsea kids roaming the streets. He'd read all about Rangers and Celtic and he'd wondered at headlines which read: 'Only 30 arrests at

Old Firm game'. But he couldn't understand the obvious fact that so many of The Lads had long since left adolescence behind.

'I can figure the kids because they're still living at home and not getting laid. So they've got all that energy to use up. But what's with all these old Scotch guys?'

He couldn't understand. It's not as if he was an idiot or an ivory-tower-dweller. He was a street-smart New Yorker who had lived for years in Greenwich Village where strange things happen all the time. And he was a supporter of the New York Jets, an American football team of the helmet and pads variety, so he knew all about violence on the field because there's no game quite like American football as far as contact sports are concerned.

But he'd always watched the Jets sitting on his ass on a comfortable seat, sipping his beer from a paper cup. No one had ever been sick near his shoes and, as far as he knew, no one had ever been arrested.

So the inexplicable was explained to him: the tanner ba' was explained, the gemme, the religion, the weather, the poverty, the escape route. The traditional warmth of the Scots fan was described to him. The over-exuberant lads and the good guys. The grand sight of the Rangers stormtroopers at Barcelona and the Celtic men at Lisbon. The good humour, the good nature, the minority of animals, the well known and indisputable fact that our excesses were always tempered by our unique sense of the absurd.

And the jokes, the great classic jokes, like the supporters who collected a bunnetful of coins for the 'driver' of the Jumbo jet which was taking them home from a foreign match . . .

But he didny get it. The big mug. He didn't know the ground rules.

So he was told the story of the boy's trip to Denmark.

The boy expected things to be different in Denmark. It was foreign after all and the boy was no fool. In his twenty years, he'd been on his holidays to Arran and Scarborough. He'd done two Wembleys and a Newcastle. And there was that week in Black-

pool when he and his chinas had really shown the English what
wenching and drinking was all about.

Sure, he expected it to be different. His mates had nudged
him about the foreign women. Especially them Danes with their
free love and a' that. Dead dirty lot they were.

He'd be playing away from home but he knew he could handle
it. He was an arrogant wee man; ten stones of wiry little Scotsman. His hero was Billy Bremner who was the best there was
and forget all that nonsense about him being an Anglo. The boy's
big brother didn't rate any of the Anglos and called them traitors
but the boy reckoned that anyone who didn't make as much as he
could out of the game was plain daft.

So far, all was well. The farmer who was employing him for
the summer was straight enough. And the peasants – as the boy
called them – were an easy-going crowd, although the boy knew
from past experience to keep himself to himself for the first few
days and not give anything away.

Soon he was writing home. He wrote to the boys, to his
parents and to his girl and he warned her not to go shopping
around while he was gone: there would be a few jelly noses round
town if he ever found out she was making a fool of him.

The boy's first major surprise came on the fourth day when
the biggest of the peasants started talking football. The boy called
him Big Clogfoot, a cheery harmless character whose English had
been picked up from cowboy films so that he said 'swell' and 'sure
thing baby' in that daft sing-song accent they all had.

The two of them were lying on sun loungers during the dinner
break sipping Carlsberg straight from the fridge. The whole
family drank beer with their meals, even the kids who were under
age and no one seemed to think anything of it.

Anyway, Big C was going on about his favourite team called
B1902 or something – after the year it was formed – and the boy
made the point that Scotland would butcher them when the international came along. He wasn't expecting any argument. It was
obvious; like you don't get an argument from a Cowdenbeath
man when they've got the Rangers in the Cup; not a real argument at least, just a token few jokey lines of patter maybe. Of

course the Cowdenbeath man might come up with that dafty day at Berwick, the one-nothing game, but he wouldn't be silly enough to go on too long about that, not in front of The Lads.

Anyway, here's this clown saying that Denmark would probably beat Scotland. Just like that – PROBABLY BEAT SCOTLAND. He just said it quietly without passion; what the sports writers would call a realistic appraisal. The boy felt his knuckles go white.

Did the man not understand about Scotland? Who was the big banana anyway, supporting something called B1902? What had the Danes ever done except produce a lot of fairy tales and dirty pictures? Who'd ever heard of their Hansens and Petersens and Jorgensens? They just didn't compare with the wee man and all the rest of the boys in blue.

Yet still he went on, this big Dane, asking what had Scotland ever won. So the boy listed the great games: the World Cup, the time they had stuffed the English after Bobby Moore and his team had stolen the Cup after five games on their home patch; the European Cup; the Cup Winners' Cup.

And still the man wasn't convinced. He was saying that England was a world-rated side but that Scotland was a backward nation, soccer-wise.

Of course, if he'd been at home, it would have been all over by now. The heid woulda went in and it woulda been goodnight Vienna. But the boy was playing away from home. The sun was shining and he was lying on his back. It wasn't like standing in a pub or being jostled on a terracing by somebody who stood on your foot and didn't say sorry.

And the beer was nice and gentle. It was so cold you had to sip it. Not like the great bellyfuls you could whip down in a one-er in the pubs.

At home the brewers always went on about strength. Youngers' strong beer. The Preston kicker. All strength, strength, strength; get you on your back as fast as possible. Here they seemed to be more concerned with the taste. Fairies . . .

And still Big C was rambling on. He'd remembered the 9-3 game and it didn't do any good coming back with the line that the Danes had never done anything because the ignorant peasant just shrugged and said it wasn't important.

So, the hell with it. What did he know anyway? It wasn't worth having a go at him. He had a big daft grin on his face and it would have been a shame to spoil it. So the boy let it go with a quiet growl and a 'don't-ever-come-that-line-in-Scotland-or-ye'll-get-melted.' But the Dane, if he understood, didn't seem to care and when the whistle went, he clapped the boy on his shoulder and trotted off to the fields.

The second surprise came at the weekend when the boy accepted Big C's invitation for a weekend in Copenhagen.

They left early on Saturday morning and took the bus into the city. Big C lived up a close with his parents. It was a cheery building. Noisy, with painted window frames and doors. Blues and yellows, with flower pots on every sill and where you had to really work hard to spot a speck of muck.

The Dane's mother was a solemn fat woman and his Dad was a big railwayman who puffed at a pipe and guffawed a lot for no apparent reason. And the girlfriend was there. Not a bad wee thing, thought the boy. Maybe a bit fat and giggly. She spent most of the time chattering to the mother in that funny language.

The surprise came after the meal when the mother was sewing by the window and the father was reading his paper by the fire and chortling to himself.

The boy was half asleep and the girlfriend was sitting on the peasant's knee and, for a moment, the boy thought he was dreaming when he saw what she was doing to him. The boy looked up, startled, and blushed. Suppose the mother was to see. Worried he looked across to the window and the woman smiled at him. Then she turned to look at her son and smiled again.

'We call it the Copenhagen Press,' said Big C as the girl continued to massage his groin. And the whole family laughed.

Later that night, the boy, being a bright and impetuous youth, began to add two and two and made six. And for the first time in his life, he began to have doubts.

Back home, the boy's big brother was coming home from the game. It was the last of the season and it had been a dismal affair. Basically, there had been nothing at stake since January when they had gone out of the Cup. And way back in September they had lost any chance of the league, with one point from the first four games.

It was between the Big Two again, as always. They didn't even have the perverse delight of battling against relegation. There they were in no man's land, just under half way up the league and the whole team about as much use as a set of chocolate tea-cups. The only thing to look forward to was the Internationals and let's hope to Christ we take them English apart again.

At home, his wife put on the tea and waited. As she stirred the pots on the stove she found herself muttering the names of the team.

Wullie in goal; Billy and Johnny at full back; Bertie, Harry and Jockie at half back. And – please God – Jimmy and Willie or whoever, just score a few goals today into the stupid net so that he'll come back with a grin on his face and we'll be in for a nice evening.

And so she sang her favourite song to herself:
'Oh his wife she says she'll leave him
'If he disny keep
'Away fae fitba' kickin'
'At nighttimes in his sleep.
'For he calls him Charlie Tully
'And other names sae droll
'Last night he kicked her oot o' the bed
'And he shouted
'It's a GOAL.'

Sure, it was a joke that song. A great joke. Oh aye, so it was. Very funny, har-de-har, yuk yuk. Just once, she thought to herself. Just let that auld devil kick me oot o' the bed and it'll be down the jail with him and next stop the solicitors.

Still, she said, he wasn't a bad soul. A man's man, like most of them. He was sharp with the housekeeping and he was a good worker in the bed. Got it over quick. Wham bam thank you

Ma'am, like they say in America. He wasn't a bad soul like her neighbour's man who would come home after a game and take her right there in the scullery. What was it Maggie had said? Oh aye: 'it was a bit hard on the backside but at least it saved the sheets.'

The woman looked at the clock and thought that her husband must be in the pub again. She sighed as she pulled the pots off the stove.

Frustrated wife: 'Haw rerr Wullie. Sometimes I think you love the Rangers more than you love me.'

Husband (growling): 'Jeezuzz. I love the Celtic more than I love you.'

That was another great joke, she thought to herself. They all think that's a great one. Still, if there wasn't a bit of truth in it, they wouldn't know why they were laughing. No smoke without fire.

By the time he was into his second pint, the boy's brother was fed up. What a lousy season. He felt like whacking somebody.

She'd be waiting with the tea. The hell with it. He'd have another pint. Someone was talking about the 2-1 game at Wembley in 1963. Now that was a day. Must have been the greatest day of all, when Jim Baxter beat the English all on his own. It was the nearest thing to perfection he'd ever seen. The sun had shone, there was enough beer money in his hip for the weekend and then there was Baxter with those long thighs that the hairies used to scream about at Ibrox.

Wasn't he the man that day? First of all taking the ball off Jimmy Armfield cool as you like and leaving him stranded on his back like a turtle before slotting it in the pokie from an impossible angle.

And then the penalty; Baxter just standing there waiting in the sun. Arrogant. Oh Jesus was he not just arrogant? No hurry. He knew where that ball was going. He bends over, places it on the spot, looks towards the goal, walks back casually and just stands there while the whole world is holding its breath. A goal here would make it two-nothing and the ba' would be oan the slates for the English. And didn't he just stand there as if he knew this was going to be his greatest moment, when he had the whole of Scotland in the palm of his hand. Like a god he was at that moment. Tall erect, arrogant.

He scored, of course. He put the keeper one way and tucked the ball into the other corner. Nae bother. He could have taken us all with him that day. Just say the word and the 40,000 would have taken over London. The hell with Bonnie Prince Charlie and all them historical fairies with wigs on. Slim Jim could have been King that day if only he had said the word.

And what a night that was. No need to play the hard man in the West End because Jim had done it all for us.

Back home the wife didn't understand. He came home with no voice and a head full of bells and all she could go on about was new carpets or some such thing.

There had been an almighty rammy and it was the only time he had ever whacked her, right across the mouth when she said he was a great poof, the way he kept going on about Baxter. So he clocked her one.

And then she had said, from the floor, that she could never give him what Baxter had given him. Which, he supposed, wasn't a million miles away from the truth.


And so, amidst the tammies and the scarves, the American began to understand and we came to the conclusion, he and I, that the barmy behaviour of the tartan hordes was all to do with sex.

Take a sexually repressed society, give it a substitute and let the spectators sublimate their energies on to the terraces.

Each week there is the anticipation of a glorious climax during an hour and a half on a Saturday afternoon, but more often than not the orgasm is never achieved. Too many bad passes, too much rainfall, bad shooting, sloppy tackling, the ball rarely bursting the net from 30 yards. And so frustration sets in.

The Scottish erection, we decided, was the raising of the fist.

A wise wee man from the *Guardian* newspaper was to sum it up thus:

'. . . the theory is that Glasgow's violence and Scotland's shame is a surfeit of bad sex, and that if Scotland's football hooligans had it off before they reached the terraces they'd be less likely to reach for the nearest sharp object to stick in the opposition.'

Like the boy in Denmark, we added two and two and came up with a glorious over-simplified generalization, a theory which can't be enumerated, tabulated or made into a statistic and which got up the noses of a couple of academics who were asked to comment on it.

'Rubbish,' said John Mack, Senior Research Fellow at Glasgow University, when interviewed on the subject by the *Daily Record*. The theory, he said, couldn't be taken seriously without one hundred case histories.

How does he know that the sex life of the Scottish hooligan is of a low quality, asked consultant psychiatrist Dr Fergus Stallard. Does he go round and ask their girlfriends?

No, gentlemen. We'll leave that particular exercise to the imaginations of Billy Connolly or the Monty Python team.

But of course, they have a point. The Scot, has he not, has always been suspicious of such pompous, pretentious theorizing.

Just dip into the bumper fun book and you'll see . . .

There's this little sociologist with funny ideas. He's probably English with a hot tattie in his mouth and nae chin and he uses those daft sociological expressions which refer, for example, to going on the batter as 'indulging in beer-seeking activities.'

Let us suggest that this little skinny fellow wants to discover why, in his terms, there are so many punch-ups in and around the Scottish football grounds. He wonders why grown men should act in such a fashion. So he goes along to a Rangers-Celtic game, armed only with his notebook and his curiosity, and he finds the archetypal wee Glasgow bachle standing by a barrier and peeing into a McEwan's can.

In a stammering, stuttering voice he explains his business and describes his belief that there may be a positive correlation between the sexual inhibitions of the working-class Scot and his antisocial, aggressive behaviour manifested through soccer. And he asks the wee man why, in his opinion, these dreadful things happen every other Saturday.

The bachle thinks for a moment, sniffs and says: 'Cos we're a' animals, mister.'

It's guaranteed to raise a smile, that one. See, the wee man has shown the stumour up again as one of the daftest, most pretentious, mumbo-jumbo talking, pansy-blossom eedjits that walked. The wee man KNOWS, you see. He's been there, all the way and no clown from down South or up the University is going to put one over on him.

So there.

Now, try this other one for size.

This time your sociologist is a sweet young thing, all teeth and good intentions, and she's been going round the country surveying the male population on their sex lives and preparing a nation-wide graph of the nightly frequency ratio of sexual intercourse. Naturally the hotshots of Chelsea and Kensington claim five or six times a night. The little Welshmen claim four times and the big blunt Yorkshiremen average out at seven.

Finally she comes north and corners the same wee man in a pub and puts the question. How often?

Again he sniffs, takes a pull at his pint and replies:

'Wance.'

Astonished, the girl asks what on earth his poor wife says in the morning.

'She says: "get aff Jimmy."'

And so the wee man wins again.


It would of course be tantamount to treason to suggest that maybe the sociologists and the daft theorists might have got something and perhaps the Scots in question (the Minority, the Troublemakers) shouldn't be so goddam cocksure of themselves: that there must be a few good reasons why the Scots football fan is a unique animal.

But that day in London, with a bewildered American in tow, was no time to test out the argument on the five Lads round the juke box; not while they had bottles in their hands anyway . . .

### 'THERE WAS THAT TIME . . .'

there was that time charlie tully
took a corner kick
an' you know how he
wus always great at gettin thaem
tae curve in, well charlie takes the corner
and it curved in and fuck me did the wind
no cerry it right intae the net, but they
disputed it, and the linesman hud the
flag up and they goat away wae it and tully
hud tae take it again. an fuck me does he no get
it in the net again. you should've
seen it. it just seemed tae go roon
in a kind o' hauf curcle. above aw their
heids. fuckin keeper didnae know where tae look.
and there was that time john cassidy went into
the toilet and there was no
lightbulb and he just had to fix up with some
water he found in a bucket. and here it was piss.
he didnae discover it until it was actually in
him. he was very sick after that. he goat
very bad jaundice.

Tom McGrath

# From the Press Box

Fitba' has spawned a few million words in Scottish newspapers this century. The man on the terraces devours each sentence like a fish feeding on plankton. The fading files give some impression of what it all meant, as it happened.

These are extracts from the match reports of three of Scotland's most famous internationals – The Roseberry Game of 1900, the Wembley Wizards of 1928, and the comeuppance of World Champions in 1967.

The first is from an anonymous writer in the *Glasgow Herald*. The second is the work of the late Sandy Adamson of *The Evening News*, now sadly closed, and the third was written by John Rafferty of the *Scotsman*.


## SCOTLAND 4 ENGLAND 1
Celtic Park Glasgow – 7 April 1900

Prompt to time the referee had the men sent on their international mission and the match was opened in a most sensational manner. As soon as M'Coll sent the ball off it was taken in charge by Campbell and A Smith. They quickly had it in front of the English goal and before the Englishmen had time to realize the match had commenced, the ball was placed past Robinson and into the net. The credit of the goal was due to M'Coll and Campbell, M'Coll having the honour of putting it in the net.

Walker Bell and M'Coll each had the ball in succession flying into Robinson's hands. Robinson as frequently cleared till he ran out in his anxiety and Bell rushed between the posts with the ball at his feet.

More open play ensued. Each goal was in turn visited. As a

result of a passage of arms between Gibson and Plant, N Smith got the ball and placed finely to the left. Alec Smith and Campbell then broke through all position but Campbell spoiled the work by dallying with the ball. So far there was nothing brilliant on either side.

Raisbeck, getting the better of G O Smith and Bloomer, gave his forwards an open field and M'Coll took full advantage of the chance, placing the ball into the English net for the third time. Though badly handicapped, the Englishmen did not relax their efforts and the improved dash of the visitors led to a well deserved success, Bloomer, whilst close in on Rennie, having little difficulty getting England's first goal.

Just three minutes from time Bell, getting the ball from Walker, made a splendid run and when close to goal he coolly, to avoid Oakley, passed to M'Coll and the Queens Parker at once sent the ball spinning into the net. Time was then called, leaving the score: Scotland 4 England 1.

As soon as the game restarted, the Scotsmen were at the front of Robinson, and M'Coll repeated his brilliancy of the first half by driving the ball twice into the hands of the English custodian. Fifteen minutes from time the score was unaltered. It then seemed as if England were a beaten team. It was only occasionally that they got over the centre of the field, so admirably were they held in check by the combined and brilliant movements of Raisbeck, Gibson and Robertson and the strong bustling work of Smith and Drummond. They confined the Englishmen to their own quarters. The match ended in a brilliant and merited victory to Scotland by four goals to one. The gate money came to £2,569 17s 6d. Altogether, with the stand money and the drawings from the enclosure, the sum would amount to probably £4,000. This is a record.

At the close of the match Lord Roseberry, in reply to shouts for a speech, said – I am pleased to have been present to see Scotland win such a glorious victory over England today. We hope that no worse civil war will ever occur between us.

**Scotland:** Goal H Rennie (Hearts); backs N Smith (Rangers) and J Drummond (Rangers); half backs N Gibson (Rangers) W Raisbeck (Liverpool) and J Robertson (Rangers, captain); forwards J Bell (Celtic), R Walker (Hearts), R S M'Coll (Queens Park) J Campbell (Celtic) and A Smith (Rangers)

## ENGLAND 1 SCOTLAND 5
Wembley Stadium London 31 March 1928

Unexpectedness gives piquant flavour to a gift or triumph. Barren of a single success in the international arena this season, and still licking the wounds of a 6-2 League humiliation, Scotland could be pardoned for viewing the Wembley encounter with appropriate modesty. The somewhat timorous demeanour, however, did not possess the players. The reason: eight of the eleven were Anglo-Scots. I will explain. Following the Ibrox debacle, Scottish players in England were placed on the Saxon spit and roasted and basted. In every club drawing room they were teased unmercifully about what Hulme and Dixie Dean had done, and what they would do at Wembley.

The baiting served Scotland well. The eight Anglos knew what awaited them if defeat was their portion – a whole season's malicious chaffing than which nothing is more galling to a lone Scot or two placed among dozens of Englishmen. In order to save their own reputations and the reputations of every other footballer in exile in England, victory had to be won, if possible. Never again, after this English match, should the Anglo-Scot chosen to play for his country be regarded up home as a 'foreigner'. The more home Scots in an international team the better, other things being equal, but if an Anglo is picked because of superior ability, the 'interloper' idea must now be dropped completely. The Anglo has even more to fight for than the home player. The latter is not subjected to shafts of English wit which, if not very subtle to Scottish ears, can always elicit a loud 'Ha, Ha' at the expense of poor 'Scotty'.

Scotland scored in six moves without an English foot touching the leather . . . a zigzag advance which ought to go down to posterity as a classic of its kind. M'Mullan, Gibson, James and Gallacher placed Alan Morton in possession. The Ranger lofted the ball in beautifully and Jackson headed cutely down and into the net . . .

Exultant Scots indulged in cat and mouse cantrips. Full revenge was extracted for all the London press forecasts about Scotland's midgets being foredoomed to heavy defeat. From toe to toe the ball sped. The distracted enemy was bewildered, baffled and beaten. One bit of weaving embraced eleven passes and not an Englishman touched the sphere until Dunn closured the movement with a skyhigh shot over the bar . . .

Jackson is gifted with a sublime disposition for the great occasion. His close dribbling, now halting, now accelerating, all with the ball tied to his toe, put Jones in a state of stupor. Only with a lassoo could the Englishman have stopped this Scottish deerfoot. Morton marked his seventh 'go' at the old enemy with touches of his palmiest days. Scraping past Goodall with not the space of a tram ticket between the two men and plunking the ball into goal, the Ranger enjoyed a jubilant time . . .

Gallacher fearlessly rushed the English defence and suffered for his temerity. Dunn played well but with ordinary shooting 'Tim' could have made the score eight goals. Law may develop to the full international standard. Only nineteen years of age, he did not fail in a testing ordeal. Harkness proved himself a goalkeeper worthy of the day. His advances from goal were well timed . . .

Jack Harkness secured the ball at the finish. 'It's not April 1st yet and we've been made a damn fool of already,' remarked an Englishman. Scottish excursionists travelling north yesterday were a quiet company. Their voices had conked out after so much singing and shouting.

'It's been a day,' muttered a haggard looking Scot as he boarded the forenoon train at Euston Station yesterday. Of course, if you counted it from seven o'clock Friday night, it certainly was a day. Lyon's corner house was a favourite rallying point for the tartan tourists. They not only made the welkin ring with their choruses. They broke it into wee bits.

What a smashing ball Jackson drove into the roof of the net for his third goal. The whole netting structure shuddered as if an elephant had leaned against it. By accident one of the Scottish players was about to help himself to an interval refreshment of methylated spirits when someone stopped him in time. Alan Morton was half strangled by jubilant Scots at the close of the game. With attendants pulling him one way and his countrymen tugging the other, Alan thought he was going to be distributed as a souvenir.

**Scotland:** J D Harkness (Queens Park); Nelson (Cardiff City), Law (Chelsea); Gibson (Aston Villa), Bradshaw (Bury), M'Mullan (Manchester City); Jackson (Huddersfield Town), Dunn (Hibernian), Gallacher (Newcastle United), James (Preston North End), A Morton (Rangers)


## ENGLAND 2 SCOTLAND 3
Wembley Stadium London – 15 April 1967.

Call in the witches from the blasted heath; bring up *Cutty Sark* from the ruins of Kirk Alloway; commission them to conjure up a new set of Wembley Wizards – the need is urgent. A new set of Wembley Wizards will have to burst into football legend and we would not be too fussy from where they came. We have seen in London town this morning poor wan drawn faces, blanched by a hard night on the train south and seen them topped by bizarre tartans and we would not want further trial and woe to be heaped upon them.

The mood this morning is to search for comfort, to try and build up a bit of confidence to take us to Wembley, so that when the bands march and the singing starts and we approach that great moment when the voices swell to 'Scotland, Dear Old Scotland for Ever' and the final word is held until it shakes the twin towers, the waves of sound may rise from swelling chests and not from hangdog shoulders.

On the face of it, England's status as holders of the World Cup

F

is fearsome, but maybe Law or Baxter could become devils and without selling our souls we could have another set of Wembley Wizards – and the time is appropriate.

Now, as the sun comes down over London Town and starts to dry the pitch which has been soaked by heavy rain this week and which is bound to play soft, we watch the invasion grow and marvel that 30,000 staunch Scots should face the discomforts of travel and the wild pace of living on Wembley weekend and surely they are not gathering to watch a Roman holiday with their heroes the victims.

They swarm in Piccadilly, call for pints and sing boldly in Soho's pubs. Some we would want to disown, but so many we see are decent, friendly characters and, strangely, they have an obsession that England's title of World Cup winners is a false one. 'We are the people' they say and I am beginning to think that maybe we are. . . .

Victory was exciting. There were many who had not liked the footballing thesis of Sir Alf Ramsey with which England won the World Cup. They had deplored their willingness to concede the midfield and put their faith in a sound defence and hectic breakaway. That made for dull, tedious football of the sort that England played up to the World Cup Final and which they played again on Saturday. Bobby Brown is the new lion of those who want good ball players used throughout the length of the field . . .

It is still so near the frenzy of Saturday, so near the wild excitement, when the sliding feet of Law scored the first goal, when a solid sweep of Lennox's foot made the second, so near that instant when the new hero, McCalliog, planted the third in the English net. We would write off England's two as irritating freaks that distorted the picture.

Then there was the second Wembley victory, which we report without commending, elated Scottish supporters defeating the police and spilling on to Wembley's turf in their thousands and kissing it and howking out souvenir clods. They had been grievously annoyed by the arrogant writing in the London newspapers which had slashed contemptuously at the poor footballing cousins from North of the Border – so, too, had the Scottish players.

When little Billy Bremner told me 'That was a good one to win' he hissed the words and in the venom of them was the pent-up feeling of an exile who had been sorely tried. There was wild frolicking in the West End at night and the great Lion Rampant flags being paraded perilously in the swirl of traffic in Piccadilly Circus. The taxi driver said 'They're mad. They should play it in Scotland every year.' We saw his point.

We felt sorry for Bobby Moore, whose honours seemed to weigh heavily on him and he lumbered about like a Clydesdale among racehorses.

**Scotland:** Simpson (Celtic); Gemmell (Celtic) McCreadie (Chelsea); Greig (Rangers), McKinnon (Rangers), Baxter (Sunderland); Wallace (Celtic), Bremner (Leeds United), McCalliog (Sheffield Wednesday), Law (Manchester United), Lennox (Celtic).

# The Saints came marching in

WILLIAM HUNTER

Our Town lost its head on a wet Saturday night in April 1959. On that night, mums pushed their babies out into the rain. Paisley's eastern approaches were lined with glistening pram hoods. Douce burghers – lawyers, doctors, shopkeepers, the like – forgot themselves, hurrahing in the streets. Lesser lieges stood at tavern doors, roaring, getting wet outside instead. Strong men, who know better, wept that night when the Saints came marching in.

So St Mirren brought home the Cup. For accuracy's sweet sake, it should be said they brought it home again. Only – *only* – 33 years before had happened the first great victory. (St Mirren 2, Celtic 0, Peter Craigmyle refereeing.) Time had little erased the tablet of this poem:

> Bradford; Findlay and Newbiggin; Morrison,
> Summers, and McDonald; Morgan and Gebbie;
> McCrae; Howieson and Thomson.

Now the 1926 ode turned to the sonnet of 1959:

> Walker; Lapsley and Wilson; Neilson, McGugan,
> and Leishman; Rodger and Bryceland; Baker;
> Gemmell and Miller.

Willie Reid, the manager, yon bonnie half back with the legs of teak, coached them to beat Aberdeen 3-1 (Jack Mowat the referee) before a crowd of 108,000, which means, in terms of ordinary arithmetic, they were watched by every fit man and boy in the town and by a lot of the lassies, too. (Since ordinary arithmetic has intruded, it may need to be mentioned that St Mirren have attended three other Cup finals, all against the Old Firm, which – as history, that jade, keeps harping – produced against the Saints a total of a dozen goals to one, but who's counting?)

Nothing about that April day and night was ordinary. Local superstition had given assurances of victory. The win was noble in the double sense of being expensive: the Cup cost Paisley £400,000, but not of real football money – fairy gold. During the semi-final occurred one of the most arousing, and least recorded, emotional moments which the Scottish game has experienced . . . All of that in just a couple of minutes, as the football lads on the telly like to say.

Meanwhile, it should be recorded how on that night fizzed the busy chemistry which can sometimes happen between a football club and the folk around its gate. How big business and the big ball game sometimes score together has been kicked around often enough. Local factory productivity rises with the club's position in league table and Cup race. That night, however, the sociology was not workaday. It was climacteric. By replaying through the mind those Cup scenes, it becomes possible to see that, all in a wet April evening, much had started to change in the municipality of Paisley, some of it not for the better. (Because of the reorganization of local government, the town, officially, isn't even *there* any more.) At least, the Cup meant that the new epoch began to happen with a bang amid high excitement shared by a town and its team.

Everything about Paisley is wrong, but exactly. It is exactly the wrong size and in exactly the wrong place. It was Scotland's biggest burgh (population: 96,000): not big enough to be brawny in terms of civic muscle, too big to be braw. To look like a separate place on the map Paisley lies too near Glasgow, only seven miles east, with Ibrox just up the road.

To remain their own people, Paisley folk, the Buddies, had to fend off Glasgow. Big brother had to be kept at arm's length, fists clenched. Despite geography, Buddies retained their independence. (It is said we don't even talk the same as Glasgow: something to do with our bucolic 'a's'.) There has been a price to pay for staying separate. We are, yes, gritty, and, maybe, aggressive. Civic mateyness, town togetherness, has never lightly been expressed, or even admitted to. That is Buddy tradition.

History, which kept the town whole, was the work of the

weavers – independent (or cussed) men of toil, literate, philosophi-
cal, radical, diligent, vigilant. They had their own parliament.
They protested much and often. When they went out into the
streets at the sound of a big drum (still kept in the town museum)
is was to be *agin* something. Three times in this century for large
local reasons Buddies have unprotesting, filled the streets. Once
was to attend with deep pride the funeral of Willie Gallacher, the
Communist MP and a Buddy; twice to acclaim St Mirren.

Each time the town's women gave an extra texture to the
occasion. Buddy lassies are special. Under the skin they are sisters,
all mill girls – hard-working, high-earning. In Paisley the hand
that rocked the cradle also made cotton thread for the world.
The town's prosperity rested on their skill. When they took a hand,
we couldn't lose. In 1926 they found flowers to give to their men
when they returned from the match; they marshalled the victory
route with their prams in 1959. With many men too choked to
speak that night, the women were also left to articulate the occasion. They could even be cheeky about Tommy Gemmell.

Tommy Gemmell was the genius of the team, a small dark
man who carried his power compactly; massively reticent. As the
team bus inched its way through the delirious lieges, he sat shyly
grinning. He looked almost frightened, this lad who in his time
took on the field, without complaint, as much bruising attention
as anybody has ever taken. But one woman made fun of our Tam,
oh yes. 'That wee fella Gemmell isnae so shy,' she said archly,
'he smiled at me through the window.'

Two wimmen discussed Gerry Baker, the centre forward, who
was born in America.

'Gerry, an American? Has he got an accent?'

'Must have – my John says the big centre halves cannie make
him out.'

Two others discussed how the bus might, finally, be permitted
to crawl to the town chambers.

'What route will they take?'

'Down past Well Street to County Square – seeing they won.'

'What was the other route?'

'Down Well Street – into the gasworks.'

St Mirren's 1926 route to Hampden had been majestic and marble-inlaid. Taking out the Old Firm, they beat Mid-Annandale, Arbroath, Partick Thistle, Airdrie, then Rangers and Celtic. That adorned with purple a glorious reign. They had won the Victory Cup in 1919; in 1922, when top British clubs with missionary zeal took the game to Spain for a tournament, St Mirren captured the Barcelona Cup, which they still hold at Love Street. Wee Johnny Cochrane, a manager who had not been a player, led them to greatness. He later moved to Sunderland and did the same for them.

The 1959 road to Hampden was, comparatively, a low road – Peebles Rovers (10-0), Motherwell, Dunfermline. Then came Celtic and a most remarkable semi-final. The Celts were having, for them, a lean year. Even so, all conventional wisdom rooted for them. Celtic's tradition and experience of winning would carry the day, the soothsayers insisted. St Mirren were living beyond their dreams.

Only small local voices predicted that, one generation after 1926, it would be Paisley's turn again. Some daft mysticism was bound up in the fond forecast. It had come to be believed that St Mirren would never win the Cup until the tramcars had totally left town. And, lo, all the car lines had, at last, been lifted. At a cost of £400,000 the town treasurer, Neil McMillan, pointed out, forbearing to say, but only just, that Paisley expected back its money's worth.

By half-time St Mirren were three up. Into the second half, impossibly, they made it 4-0. Out of nowhere the Buddies started to sing.

*Sing!* St Mirren have always had the most hard-to-please – not to say grumpy – supporters of any team in Scotland, except, perhaps, Airdrie. We are not rough or boisterous or bad but, my, are we crabbit. Right from the start in 1877 Paisley boards of directors have received especially wondrous abuse. The modern practice of throwing things on to the pitch may have begun with an irascible butcher who used to sit, this side of apoplexy, in the stand at Love Street, throwing sweetie papers. Cairters' Corner, tucked under the east gable of the stand, was the most noisome stretch of terracing in Scotland, perhaps the world. Local carters, fresh from the stable, gathered there to make the air as blue as the thick plug tobacco they smoked between mouthfuls of advice to their heroes.

Four up, their spiritual descendants suddenly changed the tune. Hampden filled with a great, growing unrehearsed surge of, not song exactly, but happy sound. Before that semi-final afternoon the kids who lined the front of the terracing, whiles, had cheeped out the 'Saints.' Now everybody was giving them laldy. A group of dyers from the thread mills may have activated the choir.

The West of Scotland is a hard place which breeds hardy men – caulkers, cairters, riveters, the men from the foundries and yards. But the hardiest of all may have been the textiles dyers. Theirs was a damp hard darg. Yet some of them developed an apparent difficulty about controlling their face muscles and tear ducts while their lungs worked like bellows. Nobody knew the words, of course. The hell with the words, they got on with the singing:

> Oh, when the Saints go marchin' in,
> Oh, when the Saints go marchin' in.
> Dum, dum-dum, dum dum
> Dee dum-dum,
> When the Saints go marchin' in.

Long before the end, the Celtic lads had furled their banners and crept home. The choir had Hampden to themselves. It was all ours. After that, semi, even in this lousy, imperfect world, there was no way the Cup could get away. At the final whistle Davie Lapsley and Jackie Neilson hugged. It was unusual in those days for giants to embrace, like a couple of lions doing a wee waltz.

Aberdeen beat Third Lanark in the other semi-final. So be it. Wheel them on. But, first, some proper preparation was called for. The spontaneous choir had been great; a proper band would be greater. Frontline trumpets, clarinets, trombones were brought out to practise the 'Saints' for that day. In the *Paisley Daily Express* it was mildly suggested that we might be the better for learning some words – not *the* words, our own.

An effusion of verse engulfed the *Express*, for it remains the conceit of Buddies that we dwell on the higher slopes of Parnassus. We fancy our chances with the soul juice. That was aye the weavers' way. It is the basic Paisley joke that when a visiting speaker at a dinner proposed the toast to the Town's Poet (meaning Robert Tannahill), everybody else present rose to his feet to reply.

> Oh, when the Saints go marchin' in,
> The Buddies roar them on to win.
> It's the Lullaby of Love Street,
> When the Saints go marchin' in.

Every verse form was plundered and repainted by the black-and-white minstrels for the occasion:

> Tommy Gemmell, the quiet man,
> Is the favourite of every fan.
> He came to Saints from Irvine Meadow.
> There's no right half can stop the fellow.

A shopkeeper who found a heap of lum hats in his basement sold the lot in a couple of days – when he added white stripes to them. After the 1926 victory, when the players were given a bottle of whisky, David McCrae (who scored one of the goals) resolved not to touch a drop of his until Saints won the cup again. David appeared on the telly with his bottle to show he had been as good as his word. In the backroom of the Bull hostelry in New Street where the excited talk was all about deep strategy to dish the Dons, one of the group barely spoke for several nights. Suddenly he broke silence. 'I've made up my mind. I am going to take the dug,' he declared. Schoolboys built scrapbooks to their stars entitled THE GREATEST TEAM THAT EVER WAS. And there was Davie Lapsley to carry the ball.

Of all the great Saints – Willie Kelly, Willie Telfer, Johnny Deakin, Alex Linwood, Jimmy Drinkwater, Bobby Ancell, John Patrick, Johnny Cameron, Donald Greenless, Michael McAvoy, Dunky Walker – the greatest clubman was Davie Lapsley.

[Finlay Cunningham, that curly-headed lad, deserves a special footnote for how he once bounced the ball off his own goalie's post to jouk past Jimmy Smith of the Rangers.]

Davie Lapsley came from Tranmere Rovers in 1946 as a centre

forward, switched to right back. He was a gentle ox of a player, with a low centre of gravity (somewhere just above kneecap height, it sometimes seemed) and a high boiling point. He was aroused to anger seldom, but it could be spectacular. When once he banjoed an opponent who irked him it was right out on the track in full sight of the central stand.

The approach of Saturday kick-off times did not set clanging panic bells in Davie's psyche. Young fans used to take it in turns to pace him down Love Street to get him to the dressing-room on time. He missed a match because he missed his bus.

He didnae miss penalties, but. Davie and Jackie Neilson had a formidable formula and when the whistle went for a penalty kick, Jackie ran and grabbed the ball to place it on the spot, while Davie pawed the ground at the far end. He believed in using every inch of runway available. Sometimes it seemed he must have started his charge out of the west from Caledonia Street or, going the other way, from midway across the playground of the North School. Goalkeepers were beaten before he had roared over the centre line. Davie was a one-man thundering herd. That was our captain.

So we won, of course, rating one other line in the Wee Red Book. That is a lot but it may have been more. With hindsight, that year of 1959 now seems some sort of annus mirabilis, or no' a bad year. We won the Second Eleven Cup as well. Paisley Pirates ice hockey team became British champions. Part of old Paisley that year died, but gloriously.

There was an old-fashioned simple clarity about the geographical battle lines of the Final: St Mirren versus Aberdeen, thread against fish. Aberdeen has since become a much more complex place; Paisley textiles have precipitately declined. It has become a mixtie-maxtie town – whisky, mainly, in terms of money and, maybe, motor cars – compared with what it was and so far as it is, officially, permitted to be a town at all. And going down lonely Love Street these modern Saturday afternoons, you find it hard to tell whether the big team are at home or away.

That night we behaved badly *well*. Packed into Jail Square, steaming like cattle in our wet clothes, we were, in football parlance, robust. Rowdy, if you will. To get the Cup unscratched from the team bus into the town chambers they had to throw it over our heads. We made much noise, certainly. It was our crowded hour. Football had put our town together, happily, into the streets, which had only happened once before and that, too, was through football. Paisley again became the right size and in the right place, exactly.

George Carruth, the local football reporter, who travelled back from Hampden with the team, spoke for the town.

'I was kicked in the face by Jack McGugan as his legs dangled from the roof of the open bus – and I hope to bear the mark to my dying day. That's how proud I was,' George wrote in the *Paisley Daily Express*.

Next morning in the *Sunday Post* the back of my head appeared in a picture along with a street-full of other demented heads.

# Scotfree

PATSY THOMSON

Chucking-out time on an October Saturday afternoon and the Maryhill Road was stowed out with teenage parents shopping with the weans, old folks out for an airing, and the punters who oozed reluctantly from the Queen's Cross Vaults.

The young marrieds with their gleaming chrome push-chairs and sweetie-sucking offspring looked limply in the pawn-shop windows. Here, that stereo would go fine in the corner of the room, and that wasn't a bad-looking Zephyr over in the used car saleroom. Decent humane housing was irrevocably beyond their reach – littered streets, sodden reeking closes and outside lavvies made up their seventies habitat. But inside their own wee flat, media-induced fantasies ran free. Automatic washer, colour telly, deep-pile carpets, cocktail bar – fair enough, but no compensation for the constantly impinging rigours of tenement life. Sunday Supplement journalists on a self-sufficiency kick might be running skittishly away from the consumer society, rejecting their architect-designed au-pair-laden lifestyle, but they wouldn't get much comprehension from Maryhill marrieds.

The pensioners with their stout message-bags and empty purses tramped the length of Maryhill Road pricing two ounces of corned beef. Their rooms and kitchens were, by necessity, traditionally appointed – jaw-box and bed-recess, lino floors and shiny toilet paper.

It was the punters, though, who made the street tick. Some still hung about the shuttered pubs – asserting by their immobility their contempt for Scotland's licensing laws. They grouped and gabbed – working men, young, middle-aged and old. The young ones looked flash – preening in their Gatsby suits and glimmering violence. The old fellas, apprehensively nearing the pension, ambled off to the gushet and the game. It was the middle-aged men that were the centre of attraction. They were sturdy, slightly sloshed and sentimental. Just right for a lift over. Wee boys swarmed, sizing up their chances.

Fernie picked out a fit-looking man with two cans of export in his pockets and a Thistle scarf knotted buoyantly round his neck. Fernie trailed him as he sauntered over the zebra, past the church, and along to the ground. It's a fine art getting lifted over. Men's sensibilities are delicate after closing time. Make your move too soon and you're sworn at, rejected as being too heavy or too premature. But if you wait, like Fernie, till the man is just thinking of looking in his pockets, is just ready to stop by the turnstile, then chances are you're on a winner.

Fernie played his fish well. 'Hey mister, give us a lift over.' The man felt the tug at his jacket, and stopped to consider the wee boy.

'Aye, right enough. Up you come, son.' Fernie was hoisted by his armpits into the narrow gate and up over the turnstile. Thirty-five pence changed hands, the turnstile clicked once and he was landed safe inside Firhill.

Oh but it was a great feeling to be inside the ground at last. Dollyjags crying out the half-time draw, fans in their scarves, country music blaring over the Tannoy, and everywhere the smell of hot pies and urine.

Nearly kick-off time. The teams were announced laboriously over the loudspeaker and the ballboys erupted on to the pitch. Fernie despised and envied them – wee ponces in their red track-suits. But not a bad life, eh, shying the ball each week to Evan Williams, Cruickshank, Rough and the like. The visiting team emerged from the tunnel – Falkirk shiftily wearing their pseudo-Scotland strips. On seven points and a hiding to nothing before the whistle even blew.

Then the great moment – Partick Thistle jogged out on to the park, resplendent in gold and scarlet. Old-age pensioners clapped and wee boys squeaked in delirium while able-bodied males swore encouragingly.

'Get in to them. Get in to them.' The young neds chanted in

happy monotony. The weeny-bopper fans countered with a falsetto rendering –

> *For ever and ever,*
> *We'll follow the Jags.*
> *The Partick Thistle,*
> *The Harry Wraggs.*

The old fellas, husbanding their physical and nervous energy, contented themselves with muttered invective.

The referee and linesmen, black, dapper, alien, took up position and the game was on. Four thousand spectators, dappled along the terracings, were prepared for drama. Fernie had business on his mind. He could only allow himself ten minutes or so to give the men a chance to get in to their screwtops. Then after that it would be all go, scurrying up and down the passageways, weaseling out newly-abandoned beer or lemonade bottles.

The first skirmishing minutes of the game showed Thistle to be on form. Intricate mid-field sashaying was followed by shots crassly wide of goal. Fernie howled his frustration with the rest. 'Away, McQuade, you big dumpling.' He was standing right by the advertisement boarding edging the pitch ('Mackay's Pies, Satisfies') and even his nine-year-old voice was sure of reaching target. McQuade returned penitently to mid-field. Thank Christ for the Thistle defence. Not much wrong with Alan Rough these days. There wouldn't be many goals the day and Fernie set off philosophically on his rounds.

He'd a wee string message bag in his parka pocket and a couple of plastic carriers too, in case of a bonanza. It was thin pickings as he headed up the stone steps. Two bottles and a clip on the ear from an old fella intent on collecting the 2p on his screwtop himself. You had to look sharp, slipping the swag away before the man noticed you, or else you'd to gauge carefully how steaming he was – steaming enough not to mind losing two pence worth of glass, or else meanly drunk and ready to lash out at anyone, failing that wee fucker of a referee.

Higher up he went past the languishing queue to the stall where pies, hot Bovril and cash changed hands. Still not many screwtops to be had. A trendy conservationist without knowing it,

Fernie abhorred cans and non-returnable bottles. His income had dwindled as drink packaging became more ephemeral. Thank God for Barr's Irn Bru and the last bastions of bottled beer. Cans of export would be the death of him yet. There was a good find, but. A carryout bag with three deposit-worthy bottles. Its owner was up back having a slash. Fernie grabbed the bag and scuttled off past the line of urinating men facing the wall like a row of demented penguins.

Methodically Fernie worked his pitch, up and down the worn terracings. He wasn't the only operator in the ground. Other weans scrummaged about, picking their way under the barriers, squirming past adults' feet to whip away their booty. Fernie was sharp though, and collected as good a haul as any. By half time the bulk of the bevy was consumed and there were few fresh bottles to be lifted. He could rest now, tally his takings and watch the game again – always keeping a weather eye on his carrier bags. He'd not done badly the day. Twenty pence. He'd get a six of chips, a big bottle of Cola and a Bounty bar on the way home. All for free and whole second half to watch.

The match was dragging on as a dispiriting goalless draw. Fernie, again stationed by the touch-line, thumped his fists against the hoardings. 'Come away the Partick Thistle – get tore into these animals.' Falkirk foulling clumsily and pointlessly bore the brunt of the crowd's abuse. It was good-tempered abuse for the most part and as likely to hassle the home team as the visitors. 'Glavin, you're horrible. Fucking horrible,' wailed an exasperated Jags fancier.

Eventually even the referee was forced to take note of a particularly blatant foul inside the box. He made the time-honoured gesture towards the spot, and the crowd tensed. No Thistle supporter views a penalty for his side as an unmixed blessing. He knows his team too well. Jags marksmen fell over each other avoiding the captain's eye. McQuade was to be the scapegoat this time. Reluctantly he placed the ball on the spot, communed silently with himself and took a self-effacing run up. Instead of the usual ineffectual shot over the bar, foot connected magically with leather and sent the ball flirting past the keeper to home in safely to the back of the net. An unnerved McQuade feigned Leeds United nonchalance with team-mates and crowd. The fans knew better, saw through the act, sympathized, and loved their hero all the more. The goal was hanselled in with roars, scarf-waving and a delighted impromptu chant – 'Denis, Denis McQuade, everyone knows your name.' Fernie gave it laldy with the rest of them. McQuade, no longer a dumpling, was a super-star and would remain so at least till the next home game.

There was little more in the way of excitement that afternoon and the scoreline stayed at one-nil. Still, Fernie thought as he picked his way over the rattling beer cans and headed out of the ground just before full time, there were worse ways to spend your Saturday afternoon.

From *Scottish Short Stories 1975* (William Collins and Sons Ltd)

# Six years of the Famous Five

ALAN BOLD

When I think of what Hibernian Football Club meant to me as a working-class child in postwar Edinburgh my central image is of a magic carpet of green green grass on which five immortal mortals, dressed in green and white, bewitched their friends and astonished their foes by juggling a ball between them. Of course there were eleven players in the team but five of them, The Famous Five, were more than players. They were members of a charismatic athletic quintet who, while observing the rules of football, still managed to improvise fresh variations for each game. They combined grace with power and blinding technical expertise. They were the good guys and the amazing thing was that the good guys won. The era of The Famous Five, 1949-55, was the most successful in Hibernian's hundred-year history.

The facts speak for themselves. I was born in 1943 and so was six years old when the Hibs forward line first read, from right to left wing, Gordon Smith, Bobby Johnstone, Lawrie Reilly, Eddie Turnbull and Willie Ormond. In 1948-9 Hibs finished third in the league and the next year they were runners-up. In 1950-1 Hibs won the League Championship and also reached the semi-final of the Scottish Cup and the final of the Scottish League Cup. In 1951-2 they were, glory be, League Champions again. Only the law of goal average stopped them lifting the League title for a third successive year in 1952-3.

Significantly, too, for the supporters who identified fiercely with such a team, Hibs made a marvellous international exhibition of themselves. During those magical years 1949-55 each member of The Famous Five represented his country. Hibs became – in 1953 – the first Scottish side to play in Brazil. In 1954 they introduced a superb system of floodlights at Easter Road and the pitch and the players were bathed in a blaze of glory. In 1955 Hibs became the first British club to enter the European Cup (in which they reached the semi-final) but 1955 was also the year that Bobby Johnstone was sold to Manchester City for £22,000. More of that later.

Without the chance to live vicariously through Hibernian's Famous Five, those years 1949-55 – from my seventh to my thirteenth year – would hardly have been worthwhile. Hibs were the one massive crumb of comfort in an otherwise unspeakably dull world. Today when football supporters are widely execrated for their violent enthusiasm I condemn not them – but the appalling domestic, educational and social environment that makes football all there is to live for, the one bright light in a blank dark space. Because if there is nothing else then there is nothing like following a great team that is both exciting and successful. In such circumstances football becomes not so much a substitute for life as the quintessence of life itself.

I was born in Edinburgh and lived in a stair on the downward slope of Gayfield Square, the bit that passers-by didn't notice. That slope didn't bother us kids because, as we played football on it, it underwent a mental metamorphosis from cobbled gradient to the grassy slope at Easter Road where it all happened. But I anticipate. My first pre-Famous Five memories are of the area itself. A police station opposite meant that The Law was omnipresent to see there would be No Football in the Square gardens. At the top of the Square there was a view down Leith Walk and a trough for horses to drink from. Near the trough there was an iron toilet for men, an elongated Scottish version of a Parisian *pissoir*. The fumes from that combined with the horses' dung on the street and the result was nauseating. Across the road were two cinemas: the Salon, which was cheap; and the Playhouse, which was posh. We went to the Salon.

There was nothing in that area to stimulate a child. One could for amusement, place a copper (an old penny, not a policeman) in the tramlines so that the tram would, in running over it, give it a strange curved shape. Or one could join in the skirmishes with the Montgomery Street Gang – little confrontations in which the

participants were more verbally than physically violent. No, there
was nothing to inspire, simply the facts of cultural deprivation.
A fatherless house (because my old man had to work in Orkney
and when he came to see us he had too little time and too much
drink to bother about much) was 'home'. There was nothing to
read – except comics. There was no music except the rubbish that
was on the radio and the house was full of Woodbine smoke
puffed out by my mother and her brothers, because my uncles
lived with us. One uncle was a baker, one was a plumber, and
every Godless Sunday they would smoke and pontificate over
*The Sunday Post*.

Living three flats above the ground might sound as if there was
a room with a view. But from the front there was only the backside of another tenement and, at the back, the view of a wood-
yard. Money was short and so were tempers so that the whole
local climate was one of frustration. There was a sense of help-
lessness, a sense that life would never amount to anything more
than kicking one's heels on the cobble stones and making dams
in the gutters when the rain came down like a bucket of holy
water on the whole damned business.

But then something happened. When I was five I went to
London Street School and there I watched the older children
play football during playtime. Me and my pals were too wee to
join in with them so we started to play among ourselves. It was
vaguely interesting but also a bit pointless, an activity on a par
with throwing stones through someone's window or stealing apples
or tormenting the man up the road from the school by pulling his
bell and shouting 'Monkeyface' when his anthropoid features were
revealed. Thankfully 'Monkeyface' never caught us. What caught
our interest was the way the older boys spoke about Hibs. We
wanted to know who Hibs were. It appeared that that year, 1948,
when I started school was also the year Hibs became Scottish
Champions for the first time in 45 years.

At six I was too young and too innocent to go to a football
match on my own and neither of my uncles had any interest in
football. As luck, would have it – and I count myself exceedingly
lucky in this – the man who lived downstairs, underneath us, was

interested in football. Hibs daft, in fact. His name was Joe Valery and he had a son, Tommy, who was to become one of my best pals. 'Wee Joe', as he was known to his adult friends, said he would take Tommy and myself to see Hibs and so my introduction to football was in Year One of the Famous Five. They were worth getting up on someone's shoulders to watch.

I cannot remember now who Hibs beat – because they did win, I remember that – in that first game. It couldn't have been Celtic or Rangers or Hearts because that would have been un-forgettable. What I do remember is that the name Gordon Smith was bandied about as if it was the name of a God. And that during the match we were taken down close to the pitch so we could see Gordon take a corner at close range.

Going to Easter Road was a blessed release. It was the big world, the place to be. It represented an arena, away from home, where matters of moment were enacted. There was the warm sensation of walking along with Tommy and his dad as part of a big happy crowd. There was buying programmes (and remember that Hibs, at that time, offered the best programme in the country, a really professional job edited by Magnus Williamson). And there was the scarf. I remember having two scarves; an ordinary woollen one in green and white and a special one made of silk and decorated with a painting of a Hibs player heading a goal.

The silk scarf was for when Hibs played Hearts. Hibs and Hearts were, in our childish minds, symbols of good and evil, twin aspects of life. Apart from winning the League and all that, nothing tasted so sweet as a victory over the folk from Tynecastle. Hearts, with their dull maroon strip and their inferior stadium, seemed perpetually shabby. In Willie Bauld they had – we all knew it in our heart of hearts – a great player but we could not admit that. For me, in particular, Willie Bauld was a bugbear, a name that made me boil with moral indignation. And to make matters worse I was always teased about him. My father's name was Willie Bold so, of course, when that fact became known adults would laugh and say 'Willie Bauld – so yer faither plays fur Herts'. No, I would explain, his name was Bold not Bauld, but that just set me up for more ribbing. It did not cross my mind

that it would be a feather in one's cap to have a father like Willie
Bauld who had once played for Scotland and who was the idol
of half of Edinburgh. He might be a great player – but he played
greatly for Hearts. That was the rub.

I can remember that we Hibs fans used to delight in the colour¹
green. It was the first colour that symbolically entered my consciousness. Green was everything that was pure and, in contrast
to Hearts, Hibs players stood like knights in shining green-and-
white armour. The grass was green. The leaves on the trees were
green at the most glorious time of the year and when the leaves
threatened to take on a Hearts-like hue in Autumn – well, they
just fell to the ground. That seemed appropriate, as if the Gods
were on the side of Hibs.

One faintly comical memory remains vividly in my mind and
it illustrates to what extent Hibs players were, in the minds of the
kids who followed them, divine. One day I heard that Tommy
Valery, my pal downstairs, was ill. I rushed down to see him and
was admitted to his bedroom expecting to see him stricken. Far
from it. Tommy was excited and laughing and proud as a peacock in his green pyjamas. 'I've got pleurisy,' he beamed. At first
the significance of this escaped me. 'Pleurisy,' he repeated, 'just
like Lawrie Reilly.' To share any experience with one of The
Famous Five was to have some of their magic rub off on you.
So pleurisy for Tommy was not an illness, it was an illustrious
medical certificate that brought him closer to his idol.

To this day in Edinburgh The Famous Five are legends. Or
rather *a* legend because though Smith-Johnstone-Reilly-Turnbull-
Ormond was quite a mouthful it was invariably pronounced as if it
was the hyphenated name of one great player. The Famous Five
seemed to embody one multifarious footballing personality. So
much so that when, even now, Hibs fans lament the way the game
has changed and bemoan the loss of star players to England and
elsewhere, there will come a time when a gleam lights up their
eyes and they will say the magic words: Smith-Johnstone-Reilly-
Turnbull-Ormond. That cluster of names represents greatness.

The thing that still amazes me is that to watch Smith-Johnstone-Reilly-Turnbull-Ormond *was* to be aware of a unit for there

*was* something uncanny about the way they played together. Reilly would clip the ball to Smith who would take it forward, effortlessly, then slip an inch-perfect pass to Johnstone, that little box of tricks. Johnstone would ostentatiously play with the ball while the others ghosted into position. Then Johnstone would release the ball to Ormond way out on the left wing. Ormond would weigh up the situation with his darting little eyes and control the pace of the game with his clever footwork. Then he would turn the ball inside so that Turnbull could come thundering forward to unleash an almighty shot at goal. If the goalie was well positioned he might stop Turnbull's shot but he had to be a better man than Gunga Din to hold it. If the shot didn't go in it would rebound from the goalie and Last Minute Lawrie Reilly would be there to hit a low shot into goal.

In my memory's eye I can see The Famous Five going through just such a manoeuvre, but such a sequence of events was not in any way typical. The Famous Five, as opposing teams knew to their cost, were unpredictable and any permutation of five might result in a goal (*Rayyyyy!*) or a great shot at goal (*Ooohhhh!*). A Smith corner might curve beautifully into goal. Reilly, through on his own, might be blatantly fouled and Turnbull would line up for the penalty, would prepare for one of his 'specials'. If Turnbull's incredibly powerful shot didn't go into the net it would go so far above it that the ball threatened to go into orbit and the fans loved even these ballooning shots from Eddie. Or again, Johnstone might be about to pass when he would change his mind, turn and suddenly crash in a goal. Or Ormond would bamboozle defenders, tear over the grass, then let go with a murderous left-foot shot. They were always surprising defences, always delighting their fans.

Yes, The Famous Five were great and the greatest of these, for me as well as for thousands of others, was Gordon Smith. As every Hibs fan knows Hibs should never have let Gordon go after that ankle operation. For where did he go but to arch-rivals Hearts (Gordon playing for Hearts broke a good few Hibernian hearts) and then to Dundee? And what did those teams do with Gordon but become Scottish Champions? Gordon really was the complete footballer. In other words he had superb control, a wonderful temperament, a great visual appeal whether on or off the ball, and an unselfish regard for the goal hunger of his colleagues in The Famous Five. He is remembered as a great right winger (too bad that term now has unfortunate political connotations) but he started as a centre forward and never lost his goalscoring instinct – some 350 goals in some 700 games for Hibs is good going in anybody's books.

What we kids would have given to have been in Gordon's boots! When there was a game in the street everybody would want to go on the right wing. Gordon was special. Dark, handsome, elegant – even aloof and untouchable. He seemed to have time to consider every possibility and would never be hurried into making a clumsy move. The other members of The Famous Five had their first-names shortened by the fans. It was 'Bobby', 'Lawrie', 'Eddie', 'Willie' – familiar figures in a footballing fantasy. But Gordon was always Gordon. He was the supreme artist of the team, the man who never wasted a ball or put a foot wrong. If you were close enough to see his expression on the pitch – as he prepared for a corner or bedazzled a couple of opponents – you could see him acknowledging with a wry smile the song the fans were singing:

> A Gordon fur me,
> A Gordon fur me,
> If you're no a Gordon
> You're nae use to me.
> Lawrie Reilly is braw
> Eddie Turnbull an aa

But the cocky wee Gordon's the pride o them aa. Actually Gordon was neither 'cocky' nor 'wee'. He was earnest about his football and, in our eyes, walked taller than any other man in the game.

Bobby Johnstone, who joined Hibs in 1946 (five years after Gordon), was far more deserving of the epithets 'cocky' and 'wee'. He was a great dribbler and, like so many of Scotland's small players, had an indomitable spirit. Wee Bobby liked to parade his skills before the crowd, liked to mesmerize opponents with his footwork. He was a superb inside forward made even greater by the company he kept in the Hibs forward line. He, who filled the gap between Smith and Reilly, could push the ball to any point on the pitch. Gordon Smith and Bobby Johnstone were the Long and Short of a devastating right wing combination and if Bobby was a showy virtuoso then perhaps it was because he felt the long shadow of the right winger at his right shoulder. You had to be a star to shine in The Famous Five.

Lawrie Reilly was sixteen when he signed for Hibs in the year the war ended. He was to remain Hibs through and through, beginning and ending his magnificent twelve-year career at Easter Road. Reilly was a natural goalscorer and a joy to watch, a little wizard who flourished in the days before the tactical term 'striker' reduced the centre forward to the limited role of finishing off an attack. Although Reilly was top goalscorer in Scotland in Hibernian's two Championship years of 1950-1 and 1951-2, he was never content to just bang goals in, he had to be an integral part of the action that was The Famous Five. Although he played for Scotland 38 times the Caps did not go to his head. He was the plain man writ large, the ordinary bloke with extraordinary skills. He lacked the grace of Gordon Smith and the panache of Bobby Johnstone but he was, in every sense of the word, central to that great forward line. For all his achievements Lawrie Reilly remained plain Lawrie Reilly, the man who just did his job better than any other centre forward in the country.

On Lawrie's left Eddie Turnbull was the odd man out, in a way, of The Famous Five. He could not match his colleagues for sheer footballing brilliance, at footwork, or for expertise in passing the ball. But he more than made up for this by his relentless will to win, by the total commitment he brought to each match. The Famous Five needed Eddie's guts and drive. He was the human tank of the forward line, the muscle that moved at the service of The Famous Five's collective football brain. He had a wonderfully potent shot and was the man whose penalties you felt were going to smash through the netting. When Eddie hit a ball it was really going to go somewhere – into the net, over the bar and out of the stadium, off the post with such force that it ended up in the arms of his own goalie. He hit the ball like he meant to do it a serious injury.

Left winger Willie Ormond completed The Famous Five. Willie would have been a schoolboy hero, anyway, for the way he came back to the game after serious injuries. He sustained a broken leg three times and each time he returned to try, try and try again. He was small and wiry and as direct and persistent as Gordon Smith was elegant and elusive. When he was without the ball he looked awkward and almost comical with his piano-stool legs. But when he received the ball he blossomed. He would wrong-foot defenders, tear past them, then provide an immaculate service for Reilly. And he was, as they say, a great reader of the way a game was going. In short (and wee Willie *was* short) he was game for anything and gave everything in every game.

The Famous Five were football's perpetual motion machine. When they criss-crossed their way forward with a ball they were magical performers with a purpose. They were Edinburgh's (at least the part of Edinburgh I came from) five heroes and they could run rings round any other team. Today football is pre-packaged and safety-first. Such an approach would have been impossible for The Famous Five who dominated the game for these six years 1949-55. Of course they had, in Hugh Shaw, an outstanding manager – his coming coincided with the coming together of The Famous Five. What Hugh did was to get them going as a unit and leave the rest to them. They were intelligent players who did not need to be 'telt' how to play the ball. Their place was on the park where the ball was like the world at their feet. And what they couldn't do with a ball was nobody's business.

Alas, it was the business, not the art, of football that brought an end to their era. In March 1955 Bobby Johnstone went to Manchester City for a fee of £22,000 and that was the beginning of the end. Sure, Hibs had Bobby Combe – a fine player – but the spellbinding combination of Smith-Johnstone-Reilly-Turnbull-Ormond was broken. Individually the five were still marvellous players but that little bit of magic went out of the game when they began to break up. They had been together for six years and in

that time had produced a riot of colourful football. The elegance
of Smith, the zest of Johnstone, the precision of Reilly, the ten-
acity of Turnbull, the intensity of Ormond. It all added up to
something special. For me football would never be the same again
when they were no longer intact.

In a way Johnstone's departure was prophetic – for Hibs, since
1955, have seen several outstanding players nip over the Border.
Nobody can blame players who, with a short athletic career at
their disposal, go where the money is most abundant: financially
they have to make the most of their skills. By the same token
nobody can blame the fans either if they stay away when the spark
of genius has gone out of the game, when teams perform according to the wishes of an omnipotent manager and not for the
edification of the crowd. Hibs fans are reluctant to become bewitched again – there is always the fear that one of the stars will
shoot from the Easter Road firmament to land, on both feet, in
London or Liverpool. In 1950, that is the year after the formation
of the Famous Five, 65,850 fans turned up at Easter Road to see
Hibs play Hearts. Were Hibs to play Ajax or Barcelona or Bayern
Munchen next week would half that number turn up?

So in 1955 something precious was shattered. As for me, I had
to go to a 'senior' secondary school (Broughton) where, for the
sake of differentiating us from 'junior' secondary schoolboys, football was ignored and rugby was the official school game. Rugby
held no interest for me, for how could one empathize with Smith-
Johnstone-Reilly-Turnbull-Ormond with something that looked
like a squashed football, something that Eddie Turnbull's mighty
boot had deflated. The next year my father died in Orkney and
that was another end. As I have written elsewhere*:

> Nineteen fifty six was a momentous year,
> The year of Suez and Hungary and the death
> Of my father. I was thirteen. He was forty-nine.
> His body stiffened in the quarry for a day or so,
> His flesh submerged and became bloated
> While I sat at home full of premonitions of his death.

* 'A Memory of Death' in *A Perpetual Motion Machine*, London 1969.

The Famous Five was a thing of the past: ahead lay a totally uncertain future.

We know what happened to The Famous Five. After sterling service for Hearts (it still hurts) and Dundee, Gordon Smith became a publican. Johnstone went to England, had a second coming for Hibs, then went back over the Border. Reilly, after a cartilage operation, also went into pubs (on the sensible side of the counter naturally). Turnbull went on to manage Aberdeen and Hibs, and Ormond went on to manage St Johnstone and Scotland. And what happened to me, their fan? After doing this and that I somehow became a poet. And what has football to do with poetry?

Only this. At the emotional heart of almost all modern poetry there is a desire to recreate a moment of sheer happiness experienced in childhood. Eliot looked back to the rose garden, Edwin Muir wanted to repossess the insular Eden he had experienced in his Orkney boyhood, Dylan Thomas longed to relive his school summer holidays, on his aunt's farm, Fern Hill, in North Carmarthenshire. I had no Fern Hill farm to go to and no apple boughs to go under and no lilting house but I had something magical to watch so that when Dylan Thomas writes like this –

Now as I was young and easy under the apple boughs
 About the lilting house and happy as the grass was green,
   The night above the dingle starry,
     Time let me hail and climb
   Golden in the heydays of his eyes

– then I know what he means. In my case for Fern Hill read Easter Road . . . my escape from everyday dullness into timeless Saturdays. Famous Five of Smith-Johnstone-Reilly-Turnbull-Ormond: will ye no come back again?

# EASTER ROAD

Green leaf or blade ye'll hardly pass
By *Sweetie Lane* or *Smokey Brae*,
But here's the 'Colour of the Grass'
The Hybees in their Arcady.

A' tools are douned in Redpath Broun
Bliss beiks in every factory,
And here's that bomba'dierin' soun'
O' Hybees in their Arcady.

Above yon emerald gate they cling
And faces flicker, licht as confetti
As play rins tremblin', string to string,
Wi' Hybees in their Arcady.

A busker sings 'The harp that once . . .'
A sky-daft brimstane butterflee
Vaults the high wa' to see this dance
Green Hybees in their Arcady.

Frae Arthur's Seat to Restalrig
The blue's their roof eternally,
There's no a team as jimp and trig
As Hybees in their Arcady.

When racketies like crickets chirr,
The reeds in Lochend wave as bonny
And whisper words that must be myrrh
For Hybees in their Arcady.

*Long afore Parkheid saw the Cup*
*Or Rangers showed sae vauntily,*
*Never forget it was held up*
*By Hybees in their Arcady!*

Dusk fa's: the air is shrill wi' whistles
Directed at the referee,
Wee Bacchuses clink bags o' bottles
Roond Hybees in their Arcady.

And then like fireflies, matches spurt
Among blue zephyrs o' tobackie:
Triumphant yet owre glaur and durt
The Hybees in their Arcady.

James T R Ritchie

# Celtic in Europe

JOHN RAFFERTY

We were in a plane somewhere over Europe. Where was not important. All that mattered was that the nose was pointed towards Lisbon. The date was Tuesday May 23rd 1967 and neither was that very important, at the time. Indeed nothing mattered much and not even that Sir Francis Chichester, somewhere over on the right, was steering his little craft for home and a reception befitting one who had performed the near miraculous. It did not strike us then that on the Thursday afternoon Celtic were going to match his feat and win the club championship of Europe and be acclaimed as he was.

We should have guessed as much but the feelings that day were ridiculously subdued. That was strange for the mood throughout that season had been boisterously arrogant. We knew that in Celtic, the Scottish champions, we had the best team in Europe and in less sober moments we extended the territory to take in the whole world.

We knew that they would win the club championship of Europe, that they would break the Latin monopoly on the competition and be the first club in Britain to win the trophy. And so it had been but a matter of course that the tough Zurich should be eliminated and Nantes overwhelmed and then Vojvodina, although only by a goal headed dramatically by the captain Billy McNeill in the last minute of play.

The swaggering mood had held until the second leg of the semi-final in Prague against Dukla, and then, with a two-goal lead to defend, the terrifying truth dawned that all the talk of the previous few months was not braggadocio but instead something which was within a game of being shown as glorious truth.

It was not the dashing Celtic which played that second leg in

Prague but instead a bunch of apprehensive provincials who had cavorted through the forests but now had the city in sight and were shattered by its immensity. Gone was the gay spirit of adventure as they cringed back in defence with but one thought, to hold what they had. At times ten men defended and only the gallant Steve Chalmers was left in an attacking position to be available for the ball from defence and to hold it when it reached him, and take the cruel buffeting of desperate Czechs.

Every second he held the ball was precious, every wild clearance from defence was a masterpiece. That was not Celtic and the master himself, Jock Stein, knew it as he left Prague behind with the purpose of the exercise achieved. He swore that never again would Celtic be asked to play in that dull way.

And so Celtic were through to the final against the Italian masters of defence, Internazionale Milan, under their puppeteer, Helenio Herrer, the highest paid manager in the game. He had conned the football world into thinking that he was a football magician who could change a game with a snap of the fingers and dictate tactics from the dugout with mysterious signals.

Some sort of moment of truth was imminent. It was like the wee fellow who has been saying he will punch the big fellow on the nose, or the other one who has declared rashly, 'I'll bet you a hundred pounds.' It was time for action and the fear that words might have to be eaten. At such moments arrogance is subdued and small talk does not come easily.

And so we sat decorously in that plane headed for Lisbon and the final and read uneasily. Someone produced a notebook and started to do his homework. It would be as well to have the facts ready. 'When were Celtic established?' he asked and was quickly told that the year was 1888 and the reason was to provide soup kitchens for the poor of the East End of Glasgow.

A strange thought caught my mind as I remembered reading an old Celtic minute book. Said I, 'Celtic did not start till one night in 1893. Then it was agreed, "To allow the players the use of the ball on Tuesdays provided they do their usual training on Thursdays." The Celtic style of play depended on skill with the ball and it seemed that the acquiring of such skill was the object of that enlightened minute. In those days, and even after the First World War, there was a quaint theory throughout football that if the players were kept away from a ball during the week they would be all the more keen to get at one come Saturday.

As I was pondering on how proud those old gentlemen of the last century would have been to see each of Stein's players training with a ball and doing all his work with it. They would have seen that on that evening in 1893 they were right when they ruled that practice with the ball was essential for good football. And sitting up at the front of the plane was the Chairman Bob Kelly whose father had been chairman at that board meeting, and he had the same faith in ball play as had his father and his directors.

And the gremlins pushed another thought to the front of the mind and it concerned another minute on more practical matters. It read, 'That the players be given steak pie and toast after training on Tuesdays and Thursdays.' The present directors were just as practical, for down in the hold of the plane were parcels of steaks and good Glasgow bread and breakfast cereals. Upset tummies were not to be risked. The logistics of the trip have been carefully planned.

And then back to the homework as the well prepared one asks . . . 'How many clubs have won the European Cup for Champions?' We sort that out and find that in the eleven years of the competition but four clubs claim the honour, Real Madrid, Benfica, Inter Milan and AC Milan. All are Latins and from countries which can afford to scour the world for class.

Real Madrid used di Stefano from Argentine, Puskas from Hungary, Santamaria from Uruguay, Kopa from France and Didi from Brazil. Benfica were coached by Bela Guttman from Hungary. They brought in Eusebio from Mozambique and Coluna from Angola. AC Milan were strengthened by Hamrin from Sweden, Schiaffino from Uruguay, Schnellinger from Germany, and Inter were managed by Helenio Herrera who was brought up in the slums of Casablanca and became rich coaching in Spain and from there brought Suarez and Peiro.

No British club had ever survived the semi-final, and we were remembering an explanation for that advanced by a distinguished British manager, 'Our season is too long. It is impossible to keep up the pace, especially with the European ties in midweek. No British side will win this competition unless they are lucky enough to be safe in the middle of the league and lucky enough to be knocked out of the national cup in the first round. Then if they have a great team they have a chance.'

Awe-stricken we were noting that Celtic during that season played 63 competitive matches and had won the Glasgow Cup, the Scottish League, the Scottish League Championship and the Scottish Cup, and they were on their way to winning the European Cup. Surely they must be chasing the impossible.

And then we had landed and the guests and the press were disembarking while Stein kept the players behind and lined them up and inspected them to be sure that their uniforms were worn neatly and that their ties were straight. He always did this before they faced the international camera squad.

And so out to Estoril by bus with the mood changing by the kilometre until we reached the Palacio Hotel and marvelled at its pool. And there a shock for the players as Stein announced, 'You feel the heat of that sun. Stay out of it. If there's as much as one freckle on anybody's arm he goes home.' Professionalism had taken over and it held until that ecstatic moment two days later when the German referee, Tschencher, signalled the end of the final and Celtic were champions.

Celtic trained seriously in the quiet little world that was Estoril – until the supporters arrived. The players worked, then retired to the shade of the hotel reception room. Out at the pool-side Jock Stein held court with an all-pervading influence. He must have felt high tension but he hid it behind the bantering humour he used to keep the morale high.

The impact of the Celtic invasion on the nearby Catholic Church did not escape him. He told Monsignor Michael Ward who had travelled from Glasgow with the fine incentive that the Celtic Club was established at a meeting in a room in his church hall, 'They're getting some gates since we came. The nine o'clock and the ten o'clock masses tomorrow are all ticket. They've had to

G

send to Lisbon for extra plates. I think we should be into this 50-50.'

The tongue wagged continuously. I was with him in a little shop when he tried to buy a cap. The one he was offered was too small. He told the girl, 'That one would have fitted me last year.' And there were the serious moments, too, when he wondered if the mainspring of Inter, Suarez, would play. He poured forth his idealism in a select company.

His words were as memorable as any call to arms as he said, 'Inter will play defensively and that is their own business. We feel that we have a duty to play the game our way and our way is to attack. Win or lose we want to make this game worth remembering. Just to be involved in an occasion like this is a tremendous honour and we think it puts an obligation on us. We can be as hard and professional as anyone but I mean it when I say we don't just want to win this cup. We want to win it playing good football, to make neutrals glad we've done it, glad to remember how we did it.' How gloriously were his hopes fulfilled.

All the while the mass of supporters was building up but thankfully it was a fun festival. There were more laughs to the minute than in a Bob Hope Show. They reckoned that 7,000 had travelled from Scotland and every one had come to see the cup being won and were prepared to celebrate as soon as feet touched Portuguese soil.

It was strange that such a Scottish-Portuguese alliance should have developed, that there should have been so many swarthy faces above green and white scarves, but maybe the answer was in a remark of the giant Portuguese international centre forward, Torres. He said, 'I hope Celtic win. That Herrera talks too much.' The Portuguese preferred the Glasgow crowd to the Italians and some might say that there is no accounting for tastes.

Lisbon was taken over and Estoril was under siege and never did the invaded ones so willingly submit. And the invaders were a mixed lot, for partisanship had been forgotten for the big occasion and there were strange companions.

On Estoril beach sat two lads, both bookmakers. One supported Celtic and the other was a devoted follower of Rangers. Along the sand walked two other lads and they were not immediately recognized and then the Celtic supporter exclaimed, 'I'm sorry Father I did not recognize you without the collar.' They were two priests. There was some talk and then an enquiry about what the bookmakers were doing at night.

They were going to a club. There was food and a bit of music. The priests were told that they might not like it but the others were told that if they could stand it then so could the priests. They, all four of them, went.

They were having a good time when the Rangers' supporter took a fancy to a girl who was singing. He sent a note round to her asking her to join their table for a drink. The Celtic supporter was immediately incensed, saying, 'Behave yourself Willie. We've got two priests here.' 'That's what's worrying me' said Willie. 'I've a wife who's a good Orange Woman and if she found out that I had gone to a brothel she would be very angry but she'd forgive me. But if she knew I was having dinner with two Catholic priests and enjoying it she'd cut my bloody throat.'

And on the Thursday after a subdued morning there was the trek out to the National Stadium set in a picturesque hollow in the hills between Estoril and Lisbon and all was chaos. Of course the Portuguese were happy and carefree but they could not cope and the crowds swarmed in happy confusion and sweated in the sun and sang through the sweat and there were friends everywhere. One wondered what had happened to the Italians.

Somehow a path was made for the team bus. Stein sat pensive. As he left the bus he told me, 'It's caught up with us now. I've kept telling the team that the next one is the big one but now, indeed, the next one is the big one.' Two wee supporters called to him, 'Don't worry Jock. We will beat them with speed.' As he moved away he said, 'You know, they're right. We will beat them with speed.'

And there they were packed into the neat stadium and the 7,000 from Scotland seemed to be ten times as many and some had flown and some travelled by car and some hitch-hiked all of the 1,700 miles and in the seventh minute of the match came the first depressing incident of the trip. Inter had a penalty kick and the renowned Mazzola, son of a famous father, took the kick and beat Simpson with a fine low shot. Was the party to be spoiled?

But soon the fox, Bertie Auld, was cheekily taking over the midfield and the master, Murdoch, was striding mightily beside him and against Bedin and Bicicli these two fought the first stern battle. It was won and the centre field was Celtic's and from that advantage they hurled attacks at the formidable Italian defence with speed that was so sustained that Inter were confused. They waited for the break in pace, but Celtic were going to play no stop-start football. They were there to run and to incorporate in that running a wide array of skills.

From that seventh minute the dad of the team, Ronnie Simpson, was near to being a spectator in goal. He had a nodding acquaintance with the studious one, Jim Craig, but the flamboyant one, Tommy Gemmell, wandered far from him glorying in the overlap which was tearing the heart out of the Italian right defence. Gemmell thrived in the heady atmosphere of the big occasion and there could be no bigger one than this.

And Billy McNeill the captain moved warily, knowing full well the danger of these smooth Italians when they broke from defence. He dare not be caught a man short at the back. And beside him John Clark moved, with a splendid unadorned efficiency, a player's player dependable and composed. There was soon nearly a goal to tie the scores. Bertie Auld with an authorative wave of a hand took over the ball in midfield and weaved past three humbled opponents. He struck a precise shot and the ball had Sarti beaten, but it struck the crossbar and that was cruel luck for such a goal would have been fit to grace such an occasion.

But Auld and Murdoch had a firm grip on the play and personality enough to maintain it and stroke the willing forwards into aggression. They were taking Inter wide on the wings with Bobby Lennox and Jimmy Johnstone and strongly through the middle with Willie Wallace and the persistent Steve Chalmers.

The speed of Lennox was disconcerting but understandable to Inter, but the play of Jimmy Johnstone was beyond their comprehension. It would have taken a Glasgow man to explain to them that his was the intricate virtuosity of street football played with a tanner ba' and raised to the sublime. With Johnstone on one side and Lennox on the other Celtic had a balanced combination of wing play beyond their planning. And in the middle the cunning Willie Wallace matched them physically and tortured them with his close play and Steve Chalmers probed persistently.

And the hordes in green and white went into ecstasies that the Italian champions should be so outplayed, and then were quickly sobered when half time was blown and they discovered that, well as Celtic had played, they were a goal down. There was a general assurance, 'It's all right Jimmy. We'll score a bundle in the second half.'

In the dressing room Jock Stein allowed his players to settle and little knocks were attended to and they waited for him to speak. He kept them waiting and then when they were about to be called back to action he told them quietly. 'You're doing fine and you're going to win this one but you're just making one little mistake. You're taking the ball too far up the wings and sending it too close to their goal. Just take it as far as the eighteen yards line and roll it along that line.' That was maybe the most inspired advice given to any team.

Its worth was shown in the sixteenth minute of the second half, when Tommy Gemmell scored one of the greatest goals ever to embellish a great occasion. The film of the match shows clearly Jim Craig taking the ball up the right and beyond the penalty line and then seeming to remember Stein's instruction and turning and bringing it back. He rolled it precisely along the line and Tommy Gemmell in flamboyant stride was charging on to it.

No ball has been more truly struck and it streaked to the net. Gemmell's shot had been measured as the heaviest in Britain that season and the full power was in that one. And then Celtic were chasing the winner and the crowd were behind them, one second rising in elation and the next sinking into despair as yet another attack was smothered in the crowded penalty area. Gemmell struck the crossbar, a shot from Murdoch struck Picchi on the face, there was a blatant penalty kick denied when Wallace's leg was taken from under him, and then with but five minutes to play the cup was won.

Murdoch, obeying yet another of Stein's instructions, drove the ball hard into the crush in front of the Inter goal. Steve Chalmers stuck out a foot and the ball was turned into the net and as the terracing erupted in a cascade of Celtic colour the Italians knew there was no coming back. They played out time, accepting the second prize.

But with a couple of minutes to go Stein could stand no more and left for the quietness of the dressing room, and when I found him there and carnival was breaking out all over the field he filled up with emotion. He grabbed my shoulders and said, 'What a result! What a performance!' He had said it all.

And then the players were fighting their way to shelter beside him, and a motley crowd they were after the manhandling of their supporters. There was Bertie Auld naked to the waist, except for an Inter shirt round his shoulders, showing the flashing white teeth in a fanatical grin and shouting to the exhausted Ronnie Simpson, 'What are we son? What are we? Don't answer I'll tell you. We're the greatest, that's what we are, The Greatest.' There may have been some slight exaggeration.

Bill Shankly, the only manager from an English club to attend the final, meant no hyperbole when he strode into the dressing room where Jock Stein in shirt sleeves stood beside the cup which had been belatedly presented to Billy McNeill after he had been rescued from the supporters. With impressive sincerity he found the right words, 'John, you're immortal.'

And as the carnival became ever more boisterous the journalists who had travelled to record for history were in trouble. In the press stand, which stretched along one side of the field, 32 telephones had been installed. Not one of them was in working order. Each when lifted gave a screeching 'whee' sound and the boys became anxious as they realized that they had the greatest Scottish football story of all time but were cut off from their office.

Suddenly the festivities on the field and the celebrations in the Celtic dressing room were forgotten in the struggle for the few telephones in the concrete cabins down below. They were controlled from a small switchboard. The action was completely selfish. James Sanderson, a resourceful little man, commandeered a telex machine. The Union would not have approved but at any rate he served his organization.

Others of us switched between violent lovemaking and stern threats as we harassed the poor girls to put through our calls. And then there was the problem of thinking and talking through such a cacophony of languages such as had not been heard even around the Tower of Babel. Maybe it was flattering that from every country in Europe had come reporters to marvel at Celtic, but down where the work was being done we did not appreciate such points. I have loved for ever a colleague who brought me a drink when I was struggling sitting on the floor of the cabin with no shirt and trying to make literature from some sweat-splattered notes spread on the seat.

Yet it was astonishing how quickly everybody recovered afterwards, and that night in the Old Town in Lisbon among the black clad fado singers there was not one of us players or the following army who looked as if he had shed a drop of perspiration. Football's a great game when you're winning.

And the deep red wine served from the old wooden carafes brought on the philosophizing. Stein was deified and they searched for a place between the deity and archangel for Murdoch and Auld. And what about Big Caesar, the captain, himself, Billy McNeill? How could there ever have been a better? And Big Tam Gemmell, everybody's pal. Surely European Cups were made for his enjoyment.

And as arms leaned on shoulders and heads nodded in a mockery of sageness somebody made a shattering discovery, 'You know, there's a bit of the big man in them all.' Of course the preparation for and the winning of that final had been impregnated with Stein's personality. His was the brain which alone plotted the whole operation. There was cunning in the tactics, understanding and great humanity in his handling of the players. The big man had indeed been big.

There was a point about Jock Stein which was overlooked and probably because of its simplicity. He just knew more about football than the others. It is strange but your ordinary fellow will admit that somebody can know more about horse-racing or even medicine or music but he finds it hard to understand that such as Stein could know so much more about football and to a decisive degree. But that was the way it was. Such as Herrera had the publicist's knack of making a mickle seem a muckle. They were great talking managers. Stein knew and Stein put his knowledge to proper use. And so Celtic won the European Cup for Champions, the club championship of Europe.

That night new happy chapters were written into Scottish folk lore and before Saturday when it was reported that Lisbon had been handed back to the Portuguese, except for isolated pockets of resistance, there was a mountain of memorable stories.

Strangely most were true. The lad who wakened suddenly in Lisbon Airport then rushed outside and boarded a taxi and asked the driver to take him to Johnstone was a friend of mine. The several who were bundled into planes in Lisbon Airport and then, when they awakened at Glasgow, – remembered that they had travelled by car and that the car was still in Lisbon, have been authenticated. We have not been able to build up any proof of the hitch-hiker stopping a car on the road outside Lisbon and asking the driver where he was going and on being told 'Edinburgh' turned away saying 'That's nae use, I'm going to Glasgow.' That is not to say that it did not happen. Anything could have happened.

Indeed as startling an incident as any concerned that great club man, Robert Kelly, later Sir Robert. His was the brain that had fashioned the organization with Stein at its head. If he had a weakness it was in his obsession with the players of the past and especially the great Celtic team of before the First World War. The accolade was put on the trip when he declared solemnly and it seemed with some pain, 'This was the greatest Celtic team of all time.' He might have expanded the adjective to Scottish or even British and nobody would have questioned his judgement.

# We arra People

JOHN FAIRGRIEVE

They were singing Derry's Walls, hundreds of them, and they woke me up. Disbelieving, wondering indeed if this was the final hallucinating for punishment for a long and arduous period of conviviality, I padded, bleary-eyed, scratching, to the window of the hotel and looked out fearfully.

At least, it wasn't my imagination. But it was half-past six in the morning, and it wasn't Glasgow but Nuremberg. That particular street in which stands the Kaiserhof Hotel is not constructed for marching men – though doubtless the disadvantage had been made light of, on previous occasions – and the few locals unlucky enough to be up and about were pressed up against the walls, some ingratiating, some irritated, some awestruck.

A colleague, who had forgotten to put his false teeth in, stuck his head out of an adjoining window and mumbled something I know not what, but I could make a guess. He withdrew, returned a moment later, and said, simply, 'Bastards!'

He was, as I knew for a fact, a dedicated supporter of the Rangers Football Club, and his comment was obviously inspired by the sudden headache that comes with shattered sleep rather than any lack of sympathy with the ideals being expressed in song, four floors below.

Of course, we should not have been surprised. This was 1967, and the occasion was the European Cup Winners Cup Final between Rangers and Bayern Munchen. It was inconceivable that Rangers fans should not have followed their team to Nuremberg. A few, a very few, just might have been discouraged had the game been planned for somewhere in the middle of the Gobi, but I would not care to bet heavily on that.

Anyway, here was the advance guard, stepping and pirouetting daintily as the chanting switched to 'The Sash', and I don't suppose there was a raincoat, a suitcase or a traveller's cheque among the lot of them. The only visible items of luggage, so far as I can remember, were duty-free carrier-bags, and the contents of these had had a caning already. They carried on up the street to the railway station buffet, where a concession would be made to solid nourishment. I went back to bed, and put a coin in the slot that makes the bed vibrate – for some reason, they go in strongly for that sort of thing in Germany – but, far from inducing sleep, a hammering hang-over crept up, and it was keeping time to the beat of 'The Sash'.

Later that day, I took a taxi out to the stadium, the original one, the one that had given Nuremberg a bad name. It wasn't easy to hire a taxi, because the first two or three drivers deliberately misunderstood. I could see their point. They resented me as an intrusive tourist who wouldn't let them forget.

The sky was suitably grey, weeds dotted the vast square that had once been kept like the kitchen of a proud housewife. On the massive balcony and towers where the Leader had urged a nation to enslave a world, the stone was chipped and crumbling. Why had I come to this place? What was I looking for? Who knows? Maybe I was expected to feel something, a hint of evil from a previous age, a bristling of the hair at the back of the neck, as I stood where the torches had flared, where the storm-troopers had shrieked.

Nothing.

And nobody about, nobody . . . except, over there, hunched on one of the giant steps, an old man. I walked across, and he stared. My German is no use, but it didn't matter then.

'English?' he asked.

I nodded. The traditional denial – 'No, Schottische' – suddenly seemed inappropriate.

He waved his arms, in an all-encompassing gesture. 'I am here every morning. Soon, boom, boom, you know?'

I said I didn't know. He said they were going to blow the pillars up, to take all the stone away. I must have looked sympathetic. He spoke German for the first time.

'Ich bin Jude,' he said, and he began to cry.

'It's them,' he said then, jerking his thumb, 'them in the town. They shout like the Nazis . . . they could be shouting "Juden Raus"!'

Walking away, I glanced back at him once, and he was staring again. Then I felt the shiver.

The Rangers fans were reinforced in the afternoon, and, in the narrow streets of Nuremberg, there was more singing and dancing and chanting and swaggering. 'Look at them,' said another colleague who was not a Rangers supporter. 'Bloody animals.'

'Well,' I said, 'they're enjoying themselves. They're not too bad.'

He thought I was joking.

# The Centenary Scottish Cup Final—Saturday, May 5 1973

IAN ARCHER

Rangers 3 Celtic 2

The text must be taken from the book of Genesis, Chapter 41, verses 2-38, that part of the Bible which describes Joseph and the seven lean years.

On Saturday night, the Scottish Cup lay in the boardroom at Ibrox, taken there from Hampden Park by a Rangers team who knew that history demanded heroics and tradition some tangible evidence of their glories. It was their first triumph since 1966. In their centenary year the club brought Scotland's most famous trophy back to their own impressive building and there the champagne flowed. Moses McNeill, that Victorian oarsman from the Gairloch who stopped rowing long enough to found this Glasgow institution, would have loved and understood every minute of it all.

On Sunday morning, the only sign of celebration was an empty Coca-Cola bottle in the marble foyer. Jock Wallace knocked on a locked door and waited to be let into The Stadium. He brought with him people who wanted just to walk through this same door and sample the atmosphere. A telegram awaited, from the supporters club in Canberra Australia who had heard of the happenings against Celtic and who wished to send their Antipodean congratulations. A telephone call from Sweden followed.

The Cup, it is true, was won on Hampden's field by a Rangers team every bit as famous as those which had gone before it. It had been gained in front of an audience of 122,000, just as harshly committed as their grandparents had been in other times. The men who made it possible were John Greig, who stood in tears at the end, Derek Johnstone, so cool he might have been re-

frigerated, and Alfie Conn, that oddly arrogant successor to men
of previous generations who understood that football can enable
anyone to strike poetic attitudes. Tom Forsyth and Derek Parlane
played notable parts and no others should be forgotten.

But these people yesterday we did not see. Wallace, we did
see. And soon the Cup Final of the SFA's 100th year was put in
perspective. What follows will embarrass the man for he wants
credit to go elsewhere, but it needs to be said at a weekend that
was a landmark for the Scottish game.

The Rangers team manager talked reluctantly – 'I've said too
much . . . I've said too much,' he kept repeating. 'Give praise to
the players. No one knows how hard they have worked. They were
down, they picked themselves up, they're the men.' He agreed,
however, to fill in some details.

At the end of a torrent of a match, played in the middle of the
kind of pandemonium that would have made a Concorde landing
seem almost silent, the players of both sides had collapsed into
embraces that showed the bitterest rivals in sport knew the limits
of that antagonism, the basic truth that football elevates all of
them. Wallace went first to Bobby Murdoch of Celtic. 'When we
won the League Cup final, I walked past him when he wanted
to shake my hand. I didn't mean to, I was just carried away. That
night I got a row from my mother who saw it on television. I remembered it. Afterwards Jock Stein came up to me. He said
"Well done, you deserve it" I think a lot of Jock Stein. And then
John Greig arrived with the Cup, thrust it towards me and
shouted: "You asked for the Cup – here it is." '

These things Wallace told us and then we asked what it all
meant to him. For the first time a man who believes that three
words constitute a lengthy speech started stringing together his
thoughts. 'When I was eight or nine I would hang about at Wally-
ford with no money, waiting for the Rangers supporters' bus,
going up to the people and saying: "Mister, will you give us a
lift." Sometimes they took me, sometimes they didn't. I knew all
about the Rangers side – Brown, Young and Shaw, McColl,
Woodburn and Cox, Waddell and Gillick, Thornton, Duncanson
and Caskie. One week I went to Tynecastle and couldn't resist

buying a rosette for a shilling. That was my bus fare home. So I had to walk 14 miles.' Then, like a professional manager, he remembered 'Waddell didn't play that day. Rutherford was on the wing.'

Such talk made one recall that story he had told a few months before. 'When I was a boy, I had this friend and together we had a ball. He stood on the wing, crossing it. He was Waddell. I stood in the middle and headed it into the net. I was Thornton.' These anecdotes rather prove this game is never played in this country by higly paid and cynical men, rather it is inhabited by people who understand about the glory of it all. It is part of the culture of the country, a kind of national consciousness, possessed in club boardroom, manager's office and most of all, on the terraces.

These vast themes seem appropriate following the final, one of the greatest of the century. It was graced by Princess Alexandra, and, in turn, she was honoured by a vast concourse of spectators who shouted themselves hoarse. At five o'clock on Cathcart Road, sober middle-aged men were crying after a game that carried us all to new peaks of emotions.

So, at last, to the match. Celtic, eight successive Championships behind them, against a team beaten this season on their own Ibrox turf by St Mirren and Stenhousemuir of the Second Division, but who in recent months had persuaded their fans that they were worthy again of huge support. A contest between Scotland's finest teams. Celtic, attacking first, took the lead in 24 minutes. Dalglish, scampering on to a Deans pass, struck a shot past McCloy and turned in celebration.

Then, a curious thing happened. A wind that slanted down Hampden Park seemed to carry the shouting from one end of the ground up into the air and away over the back of the terraces. The ball had hardly been replaced in the centre of the field before we heard a defiant chorus rise from the Rangers end and cascade around the ground. They were not to be denied and the rest of the match belonged to them.

After 35 minutes Mathieson pushed a shrewd ball forward and MacDonald beat Connelly, drawn wide. His chipped centre to the near post brought Parlane away from his defender for the header which tied the match and bruised our eardrums with the noise that followed. Half time was not long enough for our pulse rates to drop and suddenly, seventeen seconds later, Rangers took the lead. Young passed forward, Parlane flicked on and Conn was left with a clear run on goal. McNeill looked tired and could not catch him. As in Budapest earlier this season when Celtic were knocked out of the European Cup, a certain lack of pace in defence betrayed them. Conn shot past the advancing Hunter.

But it was still the Parkhead team who made sure that this would be a great final rather than a very good one, by equalizing after Greig, in a grand impersonation of a goalkeeper, fisted a Deans shot off the line. Connelly, as icy as ever, ignored 65,000 whistlers and struck the penalty home with authority. Thus, an hour had proved nothing. The tension had partly abated and the 1973 Final was there to be won by the team with the most skill. That was Rangers.

MacDonald hit a post with a header, an overture to the vital goal which gave Rangers the Cup. McLean slanted over a free kick, Johnstone headed against a post and as the ball crept across the line and on to the other upright, Forsyth pushed it into the net. 'I was so excited I nearly missed it,' he said afterwards.

For the last half hour, Rangers cut holes in Celtic's style and morale. Conn and Young should have scored and such was their confidence that extra attacking players seemed to swarm about Hunter, who became a goalkeeper under siege. And at last it was over. Greig and Parlane wept and seven fat years seemed round the corner. Referee John Gordon left the field, a good day's work done. The Rangers fans were a lot slower departing, reluctant as they were to desert the battlefield.

'I knew that Celtic with their present team would have three plans. They tried two of them and we countered both,' Wallace said afterwards and declined to elaborate. Technically the match was won by MacDonald's surveillance of Murdoch, Parlane's selfless running which kept McNeill and Connelly at full stretch, as well as Forsyth's and Johnstone's strength and skill against Deans and Dalglish. But this is no time to remember tactics.

Celtic were forced in the end, through an injury to Brogan, to play Callaghan at full back, push Connelly forward and ask Johnstone to sprint through the middle. They looked confused but this was not their day. They will find their feet again and be a better side for knowing their greatest rivals are reawakened. This is a great side beaten, not an ordinary team destroyed. They share the glow that radiated from the match even if their medals are only losers.

The victors were Rangers in particular and football in general. People will still want to know about this sport in the aftermath of a fine afternoon and that is some legacy to bequeath to our children, among them the son of Jock Wallace. 'Dad,' he said at Ibrox yesterday: 'Can I have a ball to play with?' Moses McNeill would have approved and so Rangers entered their second 100 years.

Celtic. Hunter, McGrain and Brogan, Murdoch, McNeill and Connelly, Johnstone and Dalglish, Deans, Hay and Callaghan. Substitute, Lennox.

Rangers. McCloy, Jardine and Mathieson, Greig, Johnstone and MacDonald. McLean and Forsyth, Parlane, Conn and Young. Substitute, Smith.

Referee J R P Gordon (Newport-on-Tay).


From the *Glasgow Herald*

# A Dream of Perfection

ALAN SHARP

I suppose I'm here to testify that it doesn't work. If I had any remaining doubts they were dispelled about a week ago. I was sitting outside my house in Los Angeles wearing a Scottish International jersey with '14' on the back and watching a tall bearded man called Hal Moseley from Texas go in to sleep with my wife. I was stoned and in the midst of my considerable pain and confusion I had the desire to laugh at the cloudy but potent irony of the situation. Hal had, somewhat awkwardly, stopped to talk to me on the way in, and lost for the precise exchange demanded by the meeting, asked me if in the light of my attire, I was planning to play soccer.

So there we were in California, one day after the summer solstice, a fact that I add out of defence to verisimilitude rather than any profound conviction that it is significant; some weeks after the 5-1 game at Wembley this slow-speaking civil big soul who'd been trampling around in my life for almost a year (my wife met him while I was cheering the Boys on at Hampden before the World Cup) and me, farflung fragment of the Scottish provincial passion for escape ('run on boys, the polis have lassooed me'), and I wanted to explain to him how it came to be that we found ourselves at this synapse of time and circumstance. But I know that unless I told him about Cappielow and Charlie Morton's horse and Tommy McGarrity and Jimmy Cowan, and beyond such specifics, of Calvin and 'geegs' and 'the lonely prisoner who was in hisel', then nothing would be understood.

As I said I was stoned, but I wasn't that stoned, so I just said, 'no, I'm waiting for Charlie Cooke' which would have been a great title for the Scottish version of Godot, but which happened to be true, and so Hal went on in to the only too imaginable

delights of my bed and I sat outside, the camera moving in tight
for the slow dissolve that precedes all self-respecting flashbacks
and I reviewed how it was that in over 400 years of going at it
I found myself in such a plight.

Henry Thomas Buckle in his 'On Scotland and the Scotch
Intellect' gives a view of how it is that I and Scottish football,
and from what I can detect the Scottish psyche itself, find themselves foundered. He believes that the Scottish reasoning process
is deductive rather than inductive, that the characteristic Scottish
mental effort is from an assumption to something that will serve
as proof of that assumption, a buttressing of an innate conviction,
rather than the examination of facts to discover a possible conclusion. We make up our minds and then we work backwards.

This would not be the place nor I the person to defend that
theory against its detractors. I only know, in true deductive style,
that it is true of my race and of myself. It is so completely the
hallmark of the way I think and the way a roaring multitude of
my fellow Scots think that to those who would dismiss it I can
only offer the hallowed advice, 'away and work'. Buckle is des-
cribing in his book the manifestations of the psychic knot that I
call the Dream of Perfection.

It is this dream, as it relates specifically to my life and to
Scottish football, that I wish to call in question, because enough
evidence has become available to me, in the last decade, to suggest
that it is a false premise, that there has to be another way. Lest I
raise anybody's hopes that I am going to produce the blueprint
for success in the Argentine, I must say that for Scottish football
there probably isn't any other way to do it, and that for me,
skewered on my forty-first year, change will be more difficult than
anything that has preceded it.

You see, in my way, at the level of simple success and ego
achievement, I've done all right. Left school at fourteen, worked
in the yards, went to the Army, left Greenock, wrote novels, lived
in London, made money, went to Hollywood, worked in movies,
got to call Burt Lancaster big yin, the whole trip. Is known in
limited circles as a self-indulgent professional Scotsman who
must mean it a bit because he actually turns up from LA to

stand on the terracings at Hampden and Hamburg and Liege and Lisbon and kid on he's a punter. And that costs a few bob. Right.

And what's he been selling on those green savannahs of the heart's desiring (this phrase goes into everything I write about Scottish football, it's a kind of literary tic) that reflects anything of himself? Has the metaphor been apt? Has it no gist? That's the scary thing. I've seen, over and over again, the psyche drama of my life ritually enacted. I've seen my failings paraded before me and my virtues made lyric. I've stood in those bowls and looked down into my emotional landscape and been chilled and thrilled by what was revealed.

Let's be a little less abstract. I suppose if a poll were to be conducted among them I consider my general contemporaries as to who was the greatest Scottish player they ever saw, the outcome would be Jim Baxter. Maybe the question would have to be framed to dissuade some of them from being rational or objective, to exclude comparable talents like Charlie Cooke, or superior commitments like Bremner, or more utter instinctivism like Wee Johnstone. But if it were put right the answer would be Baxter. Now if one considers Baxter's game, and if folklore is your thing, then it will be clear that Scotsmen value things in this world far above success, or integrity or intelligence. What they value most is what Baxter had, they value the completely held conviction of their own superiority.

Baxter's game was the consummation of that fallacy. There was in him, consciously, sub-consciously and unconsciously, the belief in his singular genius. It was never more clear to me than when he was in decline. I saw him playing for Notts Forest against Chelsea one dreich Stamford Bridge afternoon. A rather portly figure, lamentably short of pace, being chivvied and hustled throughout a deeply unmemorable match. It wasn't that at moments there was a hush as his magic returned, I think he may only have made about three passes that reached anybody. No, it was that he just didn't seem to notice. He didn't struggle and he didn't give in. He just walked about as though encased in the interior certainty that he was better than the whole lot of them. Not had been better, was. Even though that betterness wasn't being demonstrated on the field in play, he still knew it.

Now you can judge that analysis for what it is, deeply, deductively, subjective. Maybe Baxter was swamped with chagrin at his performance. I don't know. What I do know is that I saw somebody enact the mental attitude I have described above and enact it with inordinate persuasiveness. The reason I could buy it from him, and not from Jim Smith of Newcastle for instance, is that I have seen Baxter when I would willingly have acquiesced in his own assessment of himself, when his whole game worked, at the highest level, when the sadism and narcissism of the man were at one with his accomplishment. Everybody who saw him has his own memories, mine is Wembley '67, and Scotland with their provincialism, fed by the grandeur of England's World Champion status, were putting it on. McCreadie went down the left (maybe giving the Scottish selectors one of those overlaps they asked for) and Baxter, in midfield, called for the ball. In some infection of Baxteritis, McCreadie, normally not given to flights of megalomania as a player, stopped the ball about fifteen yards from the half-way line, turned round and 'walked' away from it. Baxter strolled across, can you see that slightly hen-toed saunter, the socks crumpled, the florid, gallus expression?, and as he prompted his team mates into more advantageous positions, he played keepie up.

'My heart in hiding stirred for the bird.' I could feel myself gasp at him, at his sense of theatre, his exact awareness of how we Scots felt about winning and the English and about ourselves and life. Sure five goals is nice, but standing in Wembley, beating them bastards 3-2 and tanner ba'ing it, that's perfection. The trouble about it is, that despite its flamboyance, its compressed drama, it is deeply and destructively neurotic and indulging it is neither a coherent way of playing football nor of living your life.

When I went to the World Cup in '74 it was with a sense of things finally, obscurely, coming together for me, into a kind of focus. I'd been maimed three times, had a number of other protracted and expansive relationships, many at the expense of my present marriage. I had six children, of whom three lived with me, which I suppose is some kind of terrible pass mark. I'd been married to Liz for ten years and it seemed that after an incessant buffeting from my inability to recognize that I needed it more than the affairs to which I subjected it, our marriage was going to last and work. There had been a number of factors: one, I'd tried a lot of other people and found them wanting, two, I wanted my wife in bed more than I had ten years earlier and more than anybody else I'd known in that time, three and four and five were my children, six was that I was forty and beginning to think about who was going to bury me, the whole issue of conserving energy far the second half in order to press home those advantages won earlier. But most important was the Jim Baxter in me. In my own armoured, egotistical way I had decided that it was time for me to settle down and win the game. Well just about then Liz was falling at last, for the first time in our marriage, in love with someone else.

'Devil mend ye' my mother was wont to say. True enough. True product of the matriarchy that is Scottish I acquiesced almost gratefully to my punishment. I had gone to Frankfurt in fear and trembling. Scotland being there was some kind of harbinger of this personal sense of getting things together, of beginning to utilize one's remaining, vital energy. I swing a terrible, exhilarating pendulum between triumph 'four minutes left now and Scotland playing in the middle of the park with complete authority, Germany trying to come forward but held by the relentless tackling of Bremner and Hay . . .' to ignominy, that spectacle to which all Scotsmen have been treated on all too many occasions, eleven young men apparently unconvinced by the similarity of their jerseys that they're on the same side.

I always experience a profound identity crisis about Scotland's games. Profound is maybe too profound a word. Extreme is nearer the mark. For a time before, throughout and after I have the feeling that my personal worth is bound up with Scotland's success or failure. I know this to be true of all people who support, have the passion, for any football team, or doubtless baseball team or volleyball team. In that respect it is one of the most important ways in which I return from my statistically exceptional lifestyle and share a larger, broader area of experience. While I'm watching Scotland it's not Alan Sharp, novelist, screenwriter, lover extraordinary and general elitist who's panicking and pleading. It's some infinitely less protected and secure creature. I'm not saying the feelings it inspires are superior to the *agape* of early Christianity, but I know that at Scotland-England games I've kissed people I wouldn't normally shake hands with.

Frankfurt proved to be a harrowing experience. We managed to put ourselves in jeopardy with Zaire. In the light of the game itself I have no complaints. It was exactly the kind of confrontation we are not good at. Our mentality needs the prompting of imagined insult, we have to be able to turn it into an emotional threat. There we were, clear favourites, superior in all departments. Zaire needed merely to stay on the park to keep their side of the contract. Do you have any idea of just how dreadful a plight that is for a Scottish team who are then left to demonstrate their superiority to those who do not dispute it? This is a crucial thing because in my experience of them, collectively and singularly, Scots are not bullies. I know that's a kind of jejune thing to say but it's true in my experience. They are quarrelsome, braggart, nasty and narrow but the peculiar kind of mindlessness, the essential imperceptiveness of the bully is not theirs. Perhaps it's the lessons of having been bullied for most of their national life, perhaps the awareness of the precariousness of their own superiority, but whatever it is Scotland as a football team don't have the inflexible killer instinct which somebody like Mohammed Ali possesses. If they had then they would have taken Zaire apart rather like the Slavs did.

They couldn't and didn't and that terrible, instantly recognizable disintegration began to run through them. The Scottish game is a highly aesthetic one which demands severe stress as its chemical base. There is an ingrained tendency in Scottish players to the ornate, to embellishment. A way of cushioning the pass that imparts a kind of 'drag' to the ball, a pirouetting way with the body, a consciousness of elegance, of doing the simple thing with style and flair. Left to play at their own pace a Scottish team will apply these grace notes self-consciously, there will be a lily-gilding trickery about the straightforward which leads to the innumerable tiny disasters that set the game against you. As they find their passes intercepted, their jinking runs blocked, their dummies unbought, the terror seeps into each and every mind, 'maybe we're not the greatest'. Deductive thinking is prone to such dreads. The steps reaching up to the pinnacling assumption have not been worked out. The belief is unsupported no matter how passionately held. With the Scottish mentality there is no middle ground. Either you are of the Elect or you're bombed out.

The difference is clear when from the outset it is hard going. Then a whole different range of Scottish virtues comes into play. That fierce physical antagonism, their commitment to the tackle, to the challenge, to the confrontation; in short the infantry syndrome. It's when out of the base the little touches begin to show, the reverse pass executed not simply because it was the most efficient ball but because it was also the most beautiful. This is when the Scottish game begins to flow and it is this ingrained sense of aesthetics that makes it so wonderfully exciting at its best, when they go through the fire to forge, not chainmail but filigree. I remember still in Hamburg in '69 Bremner, Gray and Cormack playing wonderfully in midfield against a German side who, although they won, were mesmerized for about twenty minutes in the second half by exactly this kind of steely delicacy. When someone has matched you in the grim, entrail-destroying business of covering ground and recovering it in order to repeat the process two minutes later, and can then summon up the interior resources to start being elegant, that is scary.

Scotland in Germany in '74 never got quite to that place. Against Zaire the shrewd Bremner recognized a potential disaster as the rhythm started to go in the second half and retired into ball-owning containment. It was *real politik* and it ensured that we didn't lose a goal, which if we had would have made us awful susceptible to losing two. Which would have been 'aw daddy mammy'. In the next two games we played with splendid courage and commitment. The challenge in each case was high enough to bring out the determination to go down fighting. When it dawned on the team in each game that they weren't going to go down then they began to reach out for the prize. It is not my intent to be critical in any tactical sense, but the reason that drive never achieved specific fruition against Brazil or Yugoslavia is because Ormond didn't play Hutchison and/or Johnstone for a whole game and because Kenny Dalglish was exhibiting a singular disinclination to pay the real price of his exceptional skills, which is pain, physical, leg-killing, eviscerating pain. He employed those lovely floating accelerations in midfield rather than in and around the box, to gain which would have called for twenty earlier heart emptying strides, but where his touch and exquisite balance might have made Jordan's bravery something more than a personal attribute.

But against Brazil it was possible to believe that we had taken that step forward, beyond our intense infantilism, our terror of being found out, 'Foundout'. There's an epitaph for you. I have lived all my life waiting for that dread moment. I don't think I've ever been able to answer an accusation, about anything, without guilt. If I wasn't guilty I could have been, or had been in the past, or would be in the future. It means simply they'll see what I'm really like, not what I claim I'm like. We're all Calvinist, even the Papes among us, throttled by the horror of pre-election, doomed forever to pretend elitism while endlessly dreading discovery of the pretence.

Between Brazil and Yugoslavia fell the shadow. Liz arrived from LA, my life coming into my life. She brought with her an aura of wellbeing and brown skin and a record by a black singer called Dobie Gray which she was self-evidently in love with. I asked her, my nerve ends tingling at something, was she having a thing with him. Much laughter. It's funny how you know, even when you don't know. I could tell of a kind of privacy in her, a set of responses attuned to some source in which I wasn't included. She wasn't having an affair with Dobie Gray (just in case Mrs Dobie Gray has rushed out and bought a copy of this book) but the record was one she associated with Hal. She looked lovely and she felt lovely and I accepted these qualities as being somehow reflective of she and I and embraced her and her record and tried to make it mine also, to the extent of playing it while we made love. Hello there, how did ye get on.

Yugoslavia was a fucking agony. Peter McDougall and I wandered about Frankfurt before the game in a state of near nausea. Doogs tends to disguise fear with bellicosity. At intervals he'd mutter or shout, 'ach, we'll murder these bastards', to which I'd respond something like 'oh jesus christ'. It has a comic side I admit but it was, this dread, such an accurate forerunner of the condition I was shortly to inhabit for much of the next year that I have to examine it more solemnly.

I had a sense of implosion, an apprehension that I might cave in. I ascribed this feeling to the fact that I was hollow, that my interior identity was so insecure as to constitute an absence. I could not comfort myself with the fact that if Scotland lost it would not be the end or even a suspension of my life. Had I not just made a movie with Arthur Penn, did I not live this great life in California, wasn't I going to write shortly the great Scottish novel, etc etc. As far as all of that was concerned the world might well come to a close right after the game. In fact if we lost it might be preferable to endlessly re-running the event, seeking the irrevocable moment of calamity. I know now that my *angst* was completely genuine and completely neurotic. It just seems absurd to connect such a condition to a football game. When the same state engulfed me after Liz told me about Hal it was a much more acceptable, if unbearable, anxiety.

Well we all know that the Slavs were nothing great. They had a bigger toad sitting on their spring than we did. But we lost to them, or got beat or didn't win, something. Why we didn't win in particular terms I have already suggested, but why we didn't win in the wider sense I have to ascribe, wearily, to our being Scottish. There's no proof, I know, but it's too much like our pattern. We went at them and they put a bit of stick about but I honestly believe it was good for us, put us in a better place psychologically, gave us the thin smell of their fear in our nostrils, and we held the middle of the park and tried to make something go our way up front. Morgan kept getting boxed on the wing. Lorimer was a greater threat than an actuality and Jordan paid his dues in the box. Where was Wee Johnstone with his ankle-high vision of the world, undoing the conditioning of the modern defender by making him tackle, making him against his better judgement because the issue has been reduced to 'me against you', to tanner ba', to Baxter? Or Hutchison scything through with those long direct strides, raising another bogey that no amount of sophistication can match, 'maybe he can run faster than me'? There is still some atavistic shame in that. In school it didn't bother me that Johnny Swanson was a better player than me, but that Barclay Shearer could run faster I took as personal affront.

Well we should have had them and long before Hutchison came on. But we didn't, and rather than blame the apple in the barrel, Ormond, I'd rather conform, deductively, to my theory and say that in our coiled, self-destructive way we're trying to find a good way to lose and not some means of winning. The Slavs scored, a goal of unmemorable neatness and it was over. I remember sinking down in a kind of relieved grief. Of course it was over. Found out. Caught. I saw Billy Bremner on his knees and I wondered if inside all of his pain and disappointment there might not be a little voice saying 'Thank Christ'. If that's a churlish, would-be clever thing to say I apologize. God knows if anybody out there that afternoon had set his skills and qualities on winning it was Bremner.

And of course he got up and drove them forward, and of course Big Tom galloped through and we scored and it was gallant and at the time, any solace being preferable to none. I believed it was real, that we were undeterrably set on victory. But I don't believe that any more. Peter Swan told me the archetypal story of this theme, of running at the Greenock High School sports and being up against a little, awkward, completely unstylish runner in the 440 and of how coming round into the straight, while still leading, he, Peter Swan, for whom appearance was more important than reality, tripped himself up, recovered and came in a desperately close second.

That afternoon in Frankfurt, Scotland found a dignified, even uplifting, formula of solving once more the dilemma of not knowing if indeed you are of God's chosen. I hung around and watched in desultory fashion the rest of the games and convalesced from my trauma. I took pitiful comfort from such mantra as 'Scotland was the only team in the competition who didn't get beaten', and from the relieved enthusiasm of my countrymen at home at the team's return. And I drifted steadily towards the edge of my personal vortex and I still didn't know a thing. Not really. I still believed in doing it the way I'd been doing it. Oh to be sure I'd never be as blatantly arrogant about what I wanted, my resolve to be in the one place with my wife and myself was genuine. But I didn't know, could not guess the extent to which I was suspended over the abyss by the frail cord of my ego and of exactly how much that convoluted organism depended on external reassurance for its ability to function.

It will have dawned on the reader by this time that I am intent on wresting an encompassing metaphor out of my life, Scottish football and the history of the race. The pretentiousness of such an undertaking is openly admitted. It is also completely believed. I think the person I am is Scottish in a way that constitutes a king of subspecies. I now believe that encouraging that Scottishness in myself would be an act of wilful self destruction. I think Scottish football is in the same position. I think the more I try to open my mind, to escape the provincialism that is a universal predicament, the less Scottish I will feel and the less my identity will feel supported by that particular and powerful buttress. To allow that to happen, to admit to not being from Greenock, to say 'I'm lost' is one of the most demoralizing experiences I have encountered.

If I am to make that point with any cogency I must needs regale you with my interpretation of two complex processes. My life and the Scottish national psyche. Bearing in mind that I am working backwards from a hypothesis, which would be untrue for me even if it were unfactual, try to supply the subtext from your own experience that space and the fear of tedium forbid me to attempt.

Scotland, from what I can make out, was a real midden. Social histories place it a conservative 100 years behind the rest of Europe and light years away from the awarenesses of Renaissance

Italy or Elizabethan England. Mary of Scotland must have suffered extreme culture shock at coming from the putrescent subtleties of the French courts to the rabid dungheap of Knox's kingdom. She could not see the imperative that Knox embodied, could only observe a race at the mercy of faction and the English, surviving just above the subsistence level, racked by Regents and famine and barely able to recall the adrenalin of national unity that Robert Bruce and Bannockburn epitomize. A race living on neaps and scragend, sharing their existences with animals and the inclemencies of a dreadful climate, a lumpish hodden people without focus or vision.

And then 'Knox Knox. Who's there?', and among them came a visionary, a myopic, God-seeing demonically charismatic, history-changing human, bearing with him the ultimate in deductive dreams which the Scottish people, dreamless for so long, swallowed wholly and holy. They dreamed, in their narrow idiosyncratic way, the noblest of human dreams, on which all hopes must perish yet which we are so reluctant to give up, the dream of the Kingdom of Heaven on Earth, of Utopia, New Worlds, Promised Lands, Chosen Races, Manifest Destinies: the Dream of Perfection.

In Knox's terms, bequeathed him from Calvin, it was the ferocious Sectarian Concept of the Elect and the Non-Elect, of In or Out and with a weariness which only the comprehension of how hideous life was for people then can explain, they swallowed the biggest hook of them all. Pre-Election. Because God's gift of Grace is unilateral it draws the believer into the most enveloping of deductive fallacies. When Salvation is by Grace alone then it is absurd to imagine God in the infinite remotenesses of time dickering over the team selection, omitting players out of doubt. No Willie Ormond or Bobby Brown he. He knew who to include in the pool.

Your jersey was waiting from all eternity (I tell you something trivial, when I pulled on that Scottish jersey with the 14 on the back that Cookie brought me over, and looked at that badge riding high above my heart and that wonderful colour, I could still feel it, the echo of something, some singling out of me, this poor craven soul. It's not nothing, I'll tell you). So you're chosen, all you have to do is want badly enough to be chosen, and if you'd been swallowing the shit that the Scottish race had been swallowing for donkey's years you would want to believe so badly.

So they did. In a great, galvanic leap of faith, they joined, they climbed out of the bogs of their real life into the Scottish soul, elitism and the cry rose from the terracings of the Scottish soul, 'We Are The People'. Then for 400-odd years they strove to sustain that notion, battling its built-in contradictions. For instance, if you are chosen then your behaviour will have no effect on your status. God could not have been mistaken and you are as free to fornicate as you are to flagellate. But since proof of Election was in the final instance an arcane process, there grew up the whole attendant notion of appearances. 'Cleanliness is next to Godliness' my mother used to say, and she hadn't made it up. She meant appearances are next, and dare it be whispered, maybe prior to reality. Calvinism evolved a constricting network of social clues to the identity of the truly Chosen, the fetishes of a people who were discovering that that most desired of conditions, Salvation, was placed most exquisitely beyond their grasp.

They could not confess their sins for they had none, they could not advance the cause of their soul by good works because in the apple of God's eye they were already soul-certain. All they could do, poor bastards, was act like they were saved, thus persuading others and finally themselves because in the last analysis it is never social hypocrisy but always religious.

I was brought up in the very twilight of that dream. When I was a boy you didn't whistle on a Sunday, food was cooked on a Saturday to minimize disturbance of the Sabbath, you didn't break sticks or play football (the fact that Catholics did after twelve o'clock Mass seemed to my father the clearest indication of the Satanic nature of the Church of Rome) and you went endlessly to Kirk, or the mission or the Salvation Army or whatever your variant was. To this day I need only hear the dank euphonies of the Glasgow Orpheus Choir to be swallowed by that world and its grave terrors. There was a text in the kitchen which seems like a parody now, but wasn't: 'Christ is the Head of this House, the Unseen Guest at Every Meal, the Silent Listener to every conversation.' No chance.

When I was nine I went in fear and trembling, after three Sundays of resistance (out of embarrassment, not heresy, I should note), to the Mercy Seat to make public admission of my belonging to the Elect. I can still simulate the stifled horror I felt when nothing happened, when I wasn't made as new, when 'the burden of my heart' didn't roll away. For months I enacted the quintessential Scottish neurosis, I behaved as though I were saved, paying exquisite attention to every manifestation of God's eye upon me, because, absurdity of absurdities, I knew He knew I wasn't saved, but I acted it out for my parents, an endless appeasement of the guilt of having been found wanting. If I bumped into the fucking table I used to say 'sorry God'. Like I say, I was nine.

My father, God rest him, told me such vivid apocrypha as, 'when you die you go to Heaven and God opens up the big book and looks for your name.' (I used to dream about that book, troubled by how large it would have to be and terrified of having such a heretical reservation.) 'If it's there he says, enter in ye good and faithful servant. If it's not . . . (oh dread, oh agony), he says, depart from me, for I know thee not'. More final than that it's hard to get. That story terrified me and sowed rich and abundant the harvest of certainty that one day I'd hear those words or some paraphrase of them.

This manure was being spread on soil already well prepared to blossom with neurosis. I should state my capsuled conviction that there is no human upbringing capable of avoiding the implanting in the child of fear and reflection. I believe the act of being born places a palpitating membrane at the mercy of a series of shocks and traumas which to a markedly similar degree scars each and every one of us. I'm talking about infancy, about fears we'll never catch but the moon cast shadows of in our minds, memories and memories. The terrors of that far-off time, stemming as they do from birth and its abattoir, from the whole swaddling process of being a helpless, mucus-filled organism I call the 'geegs'. In that our plight is universal, but to that universal predicament comes the uniqueness of our environment.

I caught, full blast, the Scottish version. My mother, in herself a dear, demented, psychiatry-needful woman of limited intelligence and persistent headaches, could only coerce me into being good (by which she meant coming straight home from school, not giving up cheek, and going the messages willingly) by threatening to kill herself. She favoured throwing herself out of the third-storey window or gassing. I know I finally twigged the emptiness of these terrible chastizements enough to offer to open the window or get a pillow to put in the oven but on half a hundred previous occasions I shrieked and begged for forgiveness.

Maybe you say 'ah well, his old lady was obviously off her skull.' But she wasn't, not any more than most everybody else's mother, and father. Against such anecdotes I have to recount that my father and mother loved each other and me, that I grew up secure in the atmosphere of our warm, communal, non-violent (my father didn't drink) household, a happy, lacerated, active, introspective child. In short, the standard paradox. And at the appropriate age I received the gift of football.

We lived just behind Cappielow, Morton's home ground, in fact the area gave its name to the West end of the ground, Wee Dublin, and I grew up to support them with a passion that is among the purest things in my life. I formally date the end of my childhood from the Wednesday night Sailor Williamson scored in the replay of the 47-48 Scottish Cup Final. I left a littered Hampden tearful and exhausted, but with the sense, expanding within me, worse than my grief (and it was grief, bloody true it was), that it had never been on, that we, and me, had been bound to get found out. That fear, anticipated and survived a hundred times previously against Ayr and Falkirk and Queens Park and Airdrie and Celtic, finally stood upon its hind legs and crushed me. Since then I have never been at a Scottish game where I thought we would win.

The game and Morton were the pivotal experience of my life for about five years. Its mythology was woven into the fabric of my life. There used to be a rag and bone man who had his shed round our back whose name was Charlie Morton. His horse used to graze in Cappielow. The wonder of this was vast indeed. My mother, substantially disinterested in the national game as are most of the Scottish women I know, said she wouldn't be surprised if Charlie Morton had a fortune (another myth about the rag and bone men), and owned the Morton and that was why his horse got grazing there. Completely untrue it proved to be but it was magic. I'd slip into Cappielow to watch the endless track-lapping that passed for training in those days and stay to watch the horse browse gently where my heroes trod. Magic. Even the word Cappielow yielded its nugget of esoteric knowledge. I spoke it as though it were as commonplace as 'McDougall' or 'East Hamilton Street'. Later it thrilled me in a manner I cannot explain, to discover that it's an old Scandinavian word meaning 'a race between mowers' and conjured a Breughel-ian vision of a field being cleared by massive thewed men in Morton strips in order to play the great game. And the Lord said, 'verily shall ye clear this field and it shall be called Cappielow, and ye will pit doon yir jaikets and twelve will be half time and twinty four the winner. And lo, as it was commanded so was it done.'

I stood on the Wee Dublin end week in and week out and I learned the grammar of the Scottish game. The emphasis on close control, the preoccupation with dribbling and the ornamentation of the short passing game, not like today's, to retain possession, but out of a belief in embroidery as an essential element of expression. I was taught by the masters of the time, the Gillicks and Masons and Linwoods and Thomsons and Campbells, names that have risen above the tides of now forgotten players whose skills or commitments or healths were that little less. Tommy McGaritty who sold dummies at walking pace in knee-length shorts, Jimmy Whyte who combined a refinement of passing with murderous inclination to abuse opponents. I saw Woodburn, great benighted player that he was, and I revered Jimmy Cowan to whom some perverse deity proffered glory and ignominy in the same gift.

So what's new. I was daft about football. Big deal. What's all that got to do with where I am now, and existential dread or whatever it's called. Well it has everything to do with it, I'm afraid. Whatever I've omitted in this sermon, what I've included is what made me, formed me. There is in this constricted exegesis the danger of caricature but that can't be helped. Scotland and Joe and Meg Sharp and Morton shaped me, with help from John Knox and the Blitz and American movies, and produced a creature of a peculiar doomed Romanticism, guilty before the commission of the crime, obsessed with escape yet aware that like Alexander Selkirk it would all end in the final solitude of knowing he was trapped on his desert island.

I thrashed about through my years in the shipyards, in the Army, in, God help me, IBM, through my marriage, and its dissolution, through my 'freedom' in London and my other marriage and my affairs and my writing and my success, carrying with me the canker which would in the end infect everything. I'm talking about a condition of the ego to which I appoint Jim Baxter as Patron Saint. It is the soul in search of its humbling, defiant to that last moment when with a clarity that cannot be disregarded it is made evident that one has been wrong, that we must be borne again.

It has been told me, and if it's untrue it really doesn't matter because it is true, that some local pub team, short of a man, asked Baxter in his present days to make up the side for them. It's a bit like Veronica Lake when working as a waitress being called in to see herself and Alan Ladd in 'The Blue Dahlia'. There must be a moment when you see, I think it's called metanoia, and you are changed. You may not proceed to put your life to rights because it may be too late or too hard or too something, but you have seen and you know. Well I think I saw and I think I know.

In the months that followed my discovery that my wife loved somebody else I experienced an overwhelming dread of being nobody, of being an unloved child, an unworthy lover, a 'depart from me for I know thee not-er'. And worst of all I could not let myself heal, just as a child I had made myself walk up to the Throne of God each night knowing he would not find my name in the book because I knew I was guilty, knew I had never been picked in the first place, so would I enter my wife's bedroom in

H

order to confront the most specific of all proofs of my unworthiness, her joy at another man's body. You don't see much out of the eye of your cock, it being the apotheosis of tunnel vision, but what you see is awful clear.

The trouble with wounds in your head is that you think with them. The wounds themselves have a vested interest in remaining alive and in our efforts to perceive ourselves and our fate we must deal with their astigmatism. The healing process means letting go, letting go the comfort of the known pain for the discomfort of one less familiar. I am trying to give up much that has been the mainspring of my existence, a belief in a particular way of looking at the world, a belief in a certain kind of egotism, in a certain kind of arrogance. All of these things I find in Scottish football and I am bound to advise that fabulous beast that it should mend its ways. Should it be suggested to me that then it would not be Scottish football I would have to reply exactly.

So Charlie came up the stairs and got into the car and I said, sitting there like a right idjit in my Scottish ganzie, 'heh Charlie, you've got to laugh', which I want to tell you gentle reader was by no means a foregone conclusion. And Charlie said 'never mind, you can always put it in a book'. So here it is. I ask your indulgence for my indulgencies and your forgiveness for my apostasy. And I advise you all to leave, in some way, that prison that is the Scottish mentality. It's not that you're going to be free, but at least there's different writing on the walls.

SCOTLAND V. IRELAND

1884, Belfast, Scotland 5, Ireland 0; 85, Glasgow, Scotland 8, Ireland 2; 86, Belfast, Scotland 7, Ireland 2; 87, Glasgow, Scotland 4, Ireland 1; 88, Belfast, Scotland 10, Ireland 2; 89, Glasgow, Scotland 7, Ireland 0; 90, Belfast, Scotland 4, Ireland 1; 91, Glasgow, Scotland 2, Ireland 1; 92, Belfast, Scotland 3, Ireland 2; 93, Glasgow, Scotland 6, Ireland 1; 94, Belfast, Scotland 2, Ireland 1; 95, Glasgow, Scotland 3, Ireland 1; 96, Belfast, Ireland 3, Scotland 3; 97, Glasgow, Scotland 5, Ireland 1; 98, Belfast, Scotland 3, Ireland 0, 99, Glasgow, Scotland 9, Ireland 1; 1900, Belfast, Scotland 3, Ireland 0; 01, Glasgow, Scotland 11, Ireland 0; 02, Belfast, Scotland 5, Ireland 1; 03, Glasgow, Ireland 2, Scotland 0; 04, Dublin, Ireland 1, Scotland 1; 05, Glasgow, Scotland 4, Ireland 0; 06, Dublin, Scotland 1, Ireland 0; 07, Glasgow, Scotland 3, Ireland 0; 08, Dublin, Scotland 5, Ireland 0; 09, Glasgow, Scotland 5, Ireland 0; 10, Belfast, Ireland 1, Scotland 0; 11, Glasgow, Scotland 2, Ireland 0; 12, Belfast, Scotland 4, Ireland 1; 13, Dublin, Scotland 2, Ireland 1; 14, Belfast, Ireland 1, Scotland 1; 20, Glasgow, Scotland 3, Ireland 0; 21, Belfast, Scotland 2, Ireland 0; 22, Glasgow, Scotland 2, Ireland 1; 23, Belfast, Scotland 1, Ireland 0; 24, Glasgow, Scotland 2, Ireland 0; 25, Belfast, Scotland 3, Ireland 0; 26, Glasgow, Scotland 4, Ireland 0; 27, Belfast, Scotland 2, Ireland 0; 28, Glasgow, Ireland 1, Scotland 0; 29, Belfast, Scotland 7, Ireland 3; 30, Glasgow, Scotland 3, Ireland 1; 31, Belfast, Ireland 0, Scotland 0; 32, Glasgow, Scotland 3, Ireland 1; 33, Belfast, Scotland 4, Ireland 0; 34, Glasgow, Ireland 2, Scotland 1; 35, Belfast, Ireland 2, Scotland 1; 36, Edinburgh, Scotland 2, Ireland 1; 37, Belfast, Scotland 3, Ireland 1; 38, Aberdeen, Scotland 1, Ireland 1; 39, Belfast, Scotland 2, Ireland 0; 47, Glasgow, Scotland 0, Ireland 0; 48, Belfast, Ireland 2, Scotland 0; 49, Glasgow, Scotland 3, Ireland 2; 50, Belfast, Scotland 8, Ireland 2; 51, Glasgow, Scotland 6, Ireland 1; 52, Belfast, Scotland 3, Ireland 0; 53, Glasgow, Scotland 1, Ireland 1; 54, Belfast, Scotland 3, Ireland 1; 55, Glasgow, Scotland 2, Ireland 2; 56, Belfast,

Ireland 2, Scotland 1; 57, Glasgow, Scotland 1, Ireland 0; 58, Belfast, Ireland 1, Scotland 1; 59, Glasgow, Scotland 2, Ireland 2; 60, Belfast, Ireland 0, Scotland 4; 61, Glasgow, Scotland 5, Ireland 2; 62, Belfast, Ireland 1, Scotland 6; 63, Glasgow, Scotland 5, Ireland 1; 64, Belfast, Ireland 2, Scotland 1; 65, Glasgow, Scotland 3, Ireland 2; 66, Belfast, Ireland 3, Scotland 2; 67, Glasgow, Scotland 2, Ireland 1; 68, Belfast, Ireland 1, Scotland 0; 69, Glasgow, Scotland 1, Ireland 1; 70, Belfast, Ireland 0, Scotland 1; 71, Glasgow, Scotland 0, Ireland 1; 72, Glasgow, Ireland 0, Scotland 2; 73, Glasgow, Scotland 1, Ireland 2; 74, Glasgow, Ireland 1, Scotland 0; 75, Glasgow, Scotland 3, Ireland 0. Scotland won 56, Ireland 13, drawn 11.

## SCOTLAND V. WALES

1882, Glasgow, Scotland 5, Wales 0; 83, Wrexham, Scotland 3, Wales 0; 84, Glasgow, Scotland 4, Wales 1; 85, Wrexham, Scotland 8, Wales 1; 86, Glasgow, Scotland 4, Wales 1; 87, Wrexham, Scotland 2, Wales 0; 88, Edinburgh, Scotland 5, Wales 1; 89, Wrexham, Wales 0, Scotland 0; 90, Paisley, Scotland 5, Wales 0; 91, Wrexham, Scotland 4, Wales 3; 92, Edinburgh, Scotland 6, Wales 1; 93, Wrexham, Scotland 8, Wales 0; 94, Kilmarnock, Scotland 5, Wales 2; 95, Wrexham, Wales 2, Scotland 2; 96, Dundee, Scotland 4, Wales 0; 97, Wrexham, Wales 2, Scotland 2; 98, Motherwell, Scotland 5, Wales 2; 99, Wrexham, Scotland 6, Wales 0; 1900, Aberdeen, Scotland 5, Wales 2; 01, Wrexham, Wales 1, Scotland 1; 02, Greenock, Scotland 5, Wales 1; 03, Cardiff, Scotland 1, Wales 0; 04, Dundee, Scotland 1, Wales 1; 05, Wrexham, Wales 3, Scotland 1; 06, Edinburgh, Wales 2, Scotland 0; 07, Wrexham, Wales 1, Scotland 0; 08, Dundee, Scotland 2, Wales 1; 09, Wrexham, Wales 3, Scotland 2; 10, Kilmarnock, Scotland 1 Wales 0; 11, Cardiff, Wales 2, Scotland 2; 12, Edinburgh, Scotland 1, Wales 0; 13, Wrexham, Wales 0, Scotland 0; 14, Glasgow, Scotland 0, Wales 0; 20, Cardiff, Wales 1, Scotland 1; 21, Aberdeen, Scotland 2, Wales 1; 22, Wrexham, Wales 2, Scotland 1; 23, Paisley, Scotland 2, Wales 0; 24, Cardiff, Wales 2, Scotland 0; 25, Edinburgh, Scotland 3, Wales 1; 26, Cardiff, Scotland 3, Wales 0; 27, Glasgow, Scotland 3, Wales 0; 28, Wrexham, Wales 2, Scotland 2; 29, Glasgow, Scotland 4, Wales 2; 30, Cardiff, Scotland 4, Wales 2; 31, Glasgow, Scotland 1, Wales 1; 32, Wrexham, Scotland 3, Wales 2; 33, Edinburgh, Wales 5, Scotland 2; 34, Cardiff, Wales 3, Scotland 2; 35, Aberdeen, Scotland 3, Wales 2; 36, Cardiff, Wales 1, Scotland 1; 37, Dundee, Wales 2, Scotland 1; 38, Cardiff, Wales 2,

Scotland 1; 39, Edinburgh, Scotland 3, Wales 2; 39-46, No official games during war; 47, Wrexham, Wales 3, Scotland 1; 48, Hampden, Wales 2, Scotland 1; 49, Cardiff, Scotland 3, Wales 1; 50, Hampden, Scotland 2, Wales 0; 51, Cardiff, Scotland 3, Wales 1; 52, Hampden, Wales 1, Scotland 0; 53, Cardiff, Scotland 2, Wales 1; 54, Hampden, Scotland 3, Wales 3; 55, Cardiff, Scotland 1, Wales 0; 56, Hampden, Scotland 2, Wales 0; 57, Cardiff, Wales 2, Scotland 2; 58, Hampden, Scotland 1, Wales 1; 59, Cardiff, Wales 0, Scotland 3; 60, Hampden, Scotland 1, Wales 1; 61, Cardiff, Wales 2, Scotland 0; 62, Hampden, Scotland 2, Wales 0; 63, Cardiff, Wales 2, Scotland 3; 64, Hampden, Scotland 2, Wales 1; 65, Cardiff, Wales 3, Scotland 2; 66, Hampden, Scotland 4, Wales 1; 67, Cardiff, Wales 1, Scotland 1; 68, Hampden, Scotland 3, Wales 2; 69, Wrexham, Wales 3, Scotland 5; 70, Hampden, Scotland 0, Wales 0; 71, Cardiff, Wales 0, Scotland 0; 72, Hampden, Scotland 1, Wales 0; 73, Wrexham, Wales 0, Scotland 2; 74, Hampden, Scotland 2, Wales 0; 75, Cardiff, Wales 2, Scotland 2. Scotland won 49, Wales 15, drawn 20.

## SCOTLAND V. ENGLAND

1872, Partick, England 0, Scotland 0; 73, The Oval, England 4, Scotland 2; 74, Partick, Scotland 2, England 1; 75, The Oval, England 2, Scotland 2; 76, Partick, Scotland 3, England 0; 77, The Oval, Scotland 3, England 1; 78, Hampden, Scotland 7, England 2; 79, The Oval, England 5, Scotland 4; 80, Hampden, Scotland 5, England 4; 81, The Oval, Scotland 6, England 1; 82, Hampden, Scotland 5, England 1; 83, Sheffield, Scotland 3, England 2; 84, Cathkin, Scotland 1, England 0; 85, The Oval, England 1, Scotland 1; 86, Hampden, England 1, Scotland 1; 87, Blackburn, Scotland 3, England 2; 88, Hampden, England 5, Scotland 0; 89, The Oval, Scotland 3, England 2; 90, Hampden, England 1, Scotland 1; 91, Blackburn, England 2, Scotland 1; 92, Ibrox, England 4, Scotland 1; 93, Richmond, England 5, Scotland 2; 94, Celtic, England 2, Scotland 2; 95, Everton, England 3, Scotland 0; 96, Celtic, Scotland 2 England 1; 97, Crystal Palace, Scotland 2, England 1; 98, Celtic, England 3, Scotland 1; 99, Birmingham, England 2, Scotland 1; 1900, Celtic, Scotland 4, England 1; 01, Crystal Palace, England 2, Scotland 2; 02, Ibrox, England 1, Scotland 1; 02, Birmingham, England 2, Scotland 2; 03, Sheffield, Scotland 2, England 1; 04, Celtic, England 1, Scotland 0; 05, Crystal Palace, England 1, Scotland 0; 06, Hampden, Scotland 2, England 1; 07, Newcastle, England 1, Scotland 1; 08,

Hampden, Scotland 1, England 1; 09, Crystal Palace, England 2, Scotland 0; 10, Hampden, Scotland 2, England 0; 11, Liverpool, England 1, Scotland 1; 12, Hampden, Scotland 1, England 1; 13, Stamford Br., England 1, Scotland 0; 14, Hampden, Scotland 3, England 1; 20, Sheffield, England 5, Scotland 4; 21, Hampden, Scotland 3, England 0; 22, Birmingham, Scotland 1, England 0; 23, Hampden, Scotland 2, England 2; 24, Wembley, England 1, Scotland 1; 25, Hampden, Scotland 2, England 0; 26, Manchester, Scotland 1, England 0; 27, Hampden, England 2, Scotland 1; 28, Wembley, Scotland 5, England 1; 29, Hampden, Scotland 1, England 0; 30, Wembley, England 5, Scotland 2; 31, Hampden, Scotland 2, England 0; 32, Wembley, England 3, Scotland 0; 33, Hampden, Scotland 2, England 1; 34, Wembley, England 3, Scotland 0; 35, Hampden, Scotland 2, England 0; 36, Wembley, England 1, Scotland 1; 37, Hampden, Scotland 3, England 1; 38, Wembley, Scotland 1, England 0; 39, Hampden, England 2, Scotland 1; 47, Wembley, England 1, Scotland 1; 48, Hampden, England 2, Scotland 0; 49, Wembley, Scotland 3, England 1; 50, Hampden, England 1, Scotland 0; 51, Wembley, Scotland 3, England 2; 52, Hampden, England 2, Scotland 1; 53, Wembley, England 2, Scotland 2; 54, Hampden, England 4, Scotland 2; 55, Wembley, England 7, Scotland 2; 56, Hampden, Scotland 1, England 1; 57, Wembley, England 2, Scotland 1; 58, Hampden, Scotland 0, England 4; 59, Wembley, England 1, Scotland 0; 60, Hampden, Scotland 1, England 1; 61, Wembley, England 9, Scotland 3; 62, Hampden, Scotland 2, England 0; 63, Wembley, England 1, Scotland 2; 64, Hampden, Scotland 1, England 0; 65, Wembley, England 2, Scotland 2; 66, Hampden, Scotland 3, England 4; 67, Wembley, England 2, Scotland 3; 68, Hampden, Scotland 1, England 1; 69, Wembley, England 4, Scotland 1; 70, Hampden, Scotland 0, England 0; 71, Wembley, England 3, Scotland 1; 72, Hampden, Scotland 0, England 1; 73, Wembley, England 1, Scotland 0; 74, Hampden, Scotland 2, England 0; 75, Wembley, England 5, Scotland 1.

Scotland won 36; England 34; drawn 23

# SCOTTISH LEAGUE CHAMPIONSHIP

| Season | Winners | Pts | Season | Winners | Pts |
|--------|---------|-----|--------|---------|-----|
| 1890–91 | Dumbarton | 29 | 1920–21 | Rangers | 76 |
| | Rangers | 29 | 1921–22 | Celtic | 67 |
| 1891–92 | Dumbarton | 37 | 1922–23 | Rangers | 55 |
| 1892–93 | Celtic | 29 | 1923–24 | Rangers | 59 |
| First Division | | | 1924–25 | Rangers | 60 |
| 1893–94 | Celtic | 29 | 1925–26 | Celtic | 58 |
| 1894–95 | Hearts | 31 | 1926–27 | Rangers | 56 |
| 1895–96 | Celtic | 30 | 1927–28 | Rangers | 60 |
| 1896–97 | Hearts | 28 | 1928–29 | Rangers | 67 |
| 1897–98 | Celtic | 33 | 1929–30 | Rangers | 60 |
| 1898–99 | Rangers | 36 | 1930–31 | Rangers | 60 |
| 1899–1900 | Rangers | 32 | 1931–32 | Motherwell | 66 |
| 1900–01 | Rangers | 35 | 1932–33 | Rangers | 62 |
| 1901–02 | Rangers | 28 | 1933–34 | Rangers | 66 |
| 1902–03 | Hibernian | 37 | 1934–35 | Rangers | 55 |
| 1903–04 | Third Lanark | 43 | 1935–36 | Celtic | 66 |
| 1904–05 | Celtic | 41 | 1936–37 | Rangers | 61 |
| 1905–06 | Celtic | 49 | 1937–38 | Celtic | 61 |
| 1906–07 | Celtic | 55 | 1938–39 | Rangers | 59 |
| 1907–08 | Celtic | 55 | 1939–46 | No competition | |
| 1908–09 | Celtic | 51 | 1946–47 | Rangers | 46 |
| 1909–10 | Celtic | 54 | 1947–48 | Hibernian | 48 |
| 1910–11 | Rangers | 52 | 1948–49 | Rangers | 46 |
| 1911–12 | Rangers | 51 | 1949–50 | Rangers | 50 |
| 1912–13 | Rangers | 53 | 1950–51 | Hibernian | 48 |
| 1913–14 | Celtic | 65 | 1951–52 | Hibernian | 45 |
| 1914–15 | Celtic | 65 | 1952–53 | Rangers | 43 |
| 1915–16 | Celtic | 67 | 1953–54 | Celtic | 43 |
| 1916–17 | Celtic | 64 | 1954–55 | Aberdeen | 49 |
| 1917–18 | Rangers | 56 | 1955–56 | Rangers | 52 |
| 1918–19 | Celtic | 58 | 1956–57 | Rangers | 55 |
| 1919–20 | Rangers | 71 | 1957–58 | Hearts | 62 |

| Season | Winners | Pts | Season | Winners | Pts |
|--------|---------|-----|--------|---------|-----|
| 1958–59 | Rangers | 50 | 1967–68 | Celtic | 63 |
| 1959–60 | Hearts | 54 | 1968–69 | Celtic | 54 |
| 1960–61 | Rangers | 51 | 1969–70 | Celtic | 57 |
| 1961–62 | Dundee | 54 | 1970–71 | Celtic | 56 |
| 1962–63 | Rangers | 57 | 1971–72 | Celtic | 60 |
| 1963–64 | Rangers | 55 | 1972–73 | Celtic | 57 |
| 1964–65 | Kilmarnock | 50 | 1973–74 | Celtic | 53 |
| 1965–66 | Celtic | 57 | 1974-75 | Rangers | 56 |
| 1966–67 | Celtic | 58 | | | |

## SCOTTISH FA CUP FINALS

| Year | Venue | Winners | | Runners-up | |
|------|-------|---------|---|-----------|---|
| 1874 | Hampden | Queen's P | 2 | Clydesdale | 0 |
| 1875 | Hampden | Queen's P | 3 | Renton | 0 |
| 1876 | Hampden | Queen's P | 1:2 | Th Lanark | 1:0 |
| 1877 | Hampden | V of Leven | 0:1:3 | Rangers | 0:1:2 |
| 1878 | Hampden | V of Leven | 1 | Th Lanark | 0 |
| 1879 | Hampden | V of Leven | 1 | Rangers | 1 |
| 1880 | Cathkin Park | Queen's P | 3 | Thornlibank | 0 |
| 1881 | Kinning Park | Queen's P | 3 | Dumbarton | 1 |
| 1882 | Cathkin Park | Queen's P | 2:4 | Dumbarton | 2:1 |
| 1883 | Hampden | Dumbarton | 2:2 | V of Leven | 2:1 |
| 1884 | Hampden | Queen's P | | V of Leven | |
| 1885 | Hampden | Renton | 0:3 | V of Leven | 0:1 |
| 1886 | Cathkin Park | Queen's P | 3 | Renton | 1 |
| 1887 | Hampden | Hibernian | 2 | Dumbarton | 1 |
| 1888 | Hampden | Renton | 6 | Cambuslang | 1 |
| 1889 | Hampden | Th Lanark | 2 | Celtic | 1 |
| 1890 | Ibrox Park | Queen's P | 1:2 | V of Leven | 1:1 |
| 1891 | Hampden | Hearts | 1 | Dumbarton | 0 |
| 1892 | Ibrox Park | Celtic | 5 | Queen's P | 1 |
| 1893 | Ibrox Park | Queen's Park | 2 | Celtic | 1 |
| 1894 | Hampden | Rangers | 3 | Celtic | 1 |
| 1895 | Ibrox Park | St Bernard's | 2 | Renton | 1 |
| 1896 | Logie Green | Hearts | 3 | Hibernian | 1 |
| 1897 | Hampden | Rangers | 5 | Dumbarton | 1 |
| 1898 | Hampden | Rangers | 2 | Kilmarnock | 0 |

| Year | Venue | Winners | | Runners-up | |
|------|-------|---------|---|------------|---|
| 1899 | Hampden | Celtic | 2 | Rangers | 0 |
| 1900 | Ibrox Park | Celtic | 4 | Queen's P | 3 |
| 1901 | Ibrox Park | Hearts | 4 | Celtic | 3 |
| 1902 | Celtic Park | Hibernian | 1 | Celtic | 0 |
| 1903 | Celtic Park | Rangers | 1:0:2 | Hearts | 1:0:0 |
| 1904 | Hampden | Celtic | 3 | Rangers | 2 |
| 1905 | Hampden | Hearts | 1 | Rangers | 0:1 |
| 1906 | Ibrox Park | Th Lanark | 0:3 | Th Lanark | 0 |
| 1907 | Hampden | Celtic | 3 | Hearts | 0 |
| 1908 | Hampden | Celtic | 5 | St Mirren | 1 |
| 1909 | | | | | |
| 1910 | Ibrox Park | Dundee | 2:0:2 | Clyde | 2:0:1 |
| 1911 | Ibrox Park | Celtic | 0:2 | Hamilton A | 0:0 |
| 1912 | Ibrox Park | Celtic | 2 | Clyde | 0 |
| 1913 | Celtic Park | Falkirk | 2 | Raith Rovers | 0 |
| 1914 | Ibrox Park | Celtic | 0:4 | Hibernian | 0:1 |
| 1915–19 | *No competition* | | | | |
| 1920 | Hampden | Kilmarnock | 3 | Albion Rovers | 2 |
| 1921 | Celtic Park | Partick Th | 1 | Rangers | 0 |
| 1922 | Hampden | Morton | 1 | Rangers | 0 |
| 1923 | Hampden | Celtic | 1 | Hibernian | 0 |
| 1924 | Ibrox Park | Airdrieonians | 2 | Hibernian | 0 |
| 1925 | Hampden | Celtic | 2 | Dundee | 1 |
| 1926 | Hampden | St Mirren | 2 | Celtic | 0 |
| 1927 | Hampden | Celtic | 3 | East Fife | 1 |
| 1928 | Hampden | Rangers | 4 | Celtic | 0 |
| 1929 | Hampden | Kilmarnock | 2 | Rangers | 0 |
| 1930 | Hampden | Rangers | 0:2 | Partick Th | 0:1 |
| 1931 | Hampden | Celtic | 2:4 | Motherwell | 2:2 |
| 1932 | Hampden | Rangers | 1:3 | Kilmarnock | 1:0 |
| 1933 | Hampden | Celtic | 1 | Motherwell | 0 |
| 1934 | Hampden | Rangers | 5 | St Mirren | 0 |
| 1935 | Hampden | Rangers | 2 | Hamilton A | 1 |
| 1936 | Hampden | Rangers | 1 | Th Lanark | 0 |
| 1937 | Hampden | Celtic | 2 | Aberdeen | 1 |
| 1938 | Hampden | East Fife | 1:4 | Kilmarnock | 1:2 |
| 1939 | Hampden | Clyde | 4 | Motherwell | 0 |
| 1940–46 | *No competition* | | | | |
| 1947 | Hampden | Aberdeen | 2 | Hibernian | 1 |

| Year | Venue | Winners | | Runners-up | |
| --- | --- | --- | --- | --- | --- |
| 1948 | Hampden | Rangers | 1:1 | Morton | 1:0 |
| 1949 | Hampden | Rangers | 4 | Clyde | 1 |
| 1950 | Hampden | Rangers | 3 | East Fife | 0 |
| 1951 | Hampden | Celtic | 1 | Motherwell | 0 |
| 1952 | Hampden | Motherwell | 4 | Dundee | 0 |
| 1953 | Hampden | Rangers | 1:1 | Aberdeen | 1:0 |
| 1954 | Hampden | Celtic | 2 | Aberdeen | 1 |
| 1955 | Hampden | Clyde | 1:1 | Celtic | 1:0 |
| 1956 | Hampden | Hearts | 3 | Celtic | 1 |
| 1957 | Hampden | Falkirk | 1:2 | Kilmarnock | 1:1 |
| 1958 | Hampden | Clyde | 1 | Hibernian | 0 |
| 1959 | Hampden | St Mirren | 3 | Aberdeen | 1 |
| 1960 | Hampden | Rangers | 2 | Kilmarnock | 0 |
| 1961 | Hampden | Dunfermline | 0:2 | Celtic | 0:0 |
| 1962 | Hampden | Rangers | 2 | St Mirren | 0 |
| 1963 | Hampden | Rangers | 1:3 | Celtic | 1:0 |
| 1964 | Hampden | Rangers | 3 | Dundee | 1 |
| 1965 | Hampden | Celtic | 3 | Dunfermline | 2 |
| 1966 | Hampden | Rangers | 0:1 | Celtic | 0:0 |
| 1967 | Hampden | Celtic | 2 | Aberdeen | 0 |
| 1968 | Hampden | Dunfermline | 3 | Hearts | 1 |
| 1969 | Hampden | Celtic | 4 | Rangers | 0 |
| 1970 | Hampden | Aberdeen | 3 | Celtic | 1 |
| 1971 | Hampden | Celtic | 1:2 | Rangers | 1:1 |
| 1972 | Hampden | Celtic | 6 | Hibernian | 1 |
| 1973 | Hampden | Rangers | 3 | Celtic | 2 |
| 1974 | Hampden | Celtic | 3 | Dundee United | 0 |
| 1975 | Hampden | Celtic | 3 | Airdrie | 1 |

# Index